SEMEIA 21

ANTHROPOLOGICAL PERSPECTIVES ON OLD TESTAMENT PROPHECY

Editors of this Issue:
Robert C. Culley
Thomas W. Overholt

© 1982
by the Society of Biblical Literature

SEMEIA 21

Copyright © 1981 by the Society of Biblical Literature

All rights reserved. No part of this work may be reproduced or transmitted in any form or by any means, electronic or mechanical, including photocopying and recording, or by means of any information storage or retrieval system, except as may be expressly permitted by the 1976 Copyright Act or in writing from the publisher. Requests for permission should be addressed in writing to the Rights and Permissions Office, Society of Biblical Literature, 825 Houston Mill Road, Atlanta, GA 30329, USA.

ISSN 0095-571X
ISBN 1-58983-224-8

Printed in the United States of America
on acid-free paper

CONTENTS

Contributors to this Issue iv

Preface v
Anthropology and Old Testament Studies: An Introductory Comment
    Robert C. Culley 1

ARTICLES

An Anthropological Perspective Upon Prophetic
Call Narratives
    Martin J. Buss.. 9
Social Dimensions of Prophetic Conflict
    Burke O. Long 31
Prophecy: The Problem of Cross-Cultural Comparison
    Thomas W. Overholt... 55
From Prophecy to Apocalyptic: Reflections on the Shape of
Israelite Religion
    Robert R. Wilson 79

RESPONSES TO ARTICLES

Reflections on Prophecy and Prophetic Groups
    Kenelm O. L. Burridge 99
Problems and Promises in the Comparative Analysis
of Religious Phenomena
    Norman K. Gottwald 103
Prophets and their Publics
    Ioan M. Lewis... 113

REPLIES TO THE COMMENTATORS

On Social and Individual Aspects of Prophecy
    Martin J. Buss.. 121
Perils General and Particular
    Burke O. Long 125
Model, Meaning, and Necessity
    Thomas W. Overholt... 129
The Problems of Describing and Defining Apocalyptic Discourse
    Robert R. Wilson 133

CONTRIBUTORS TO THIS ISSUE

Kenelm O. L. Burridge
    Department of Anthropology and Sociology
    University of British Columbia
    Vancouver, B.C., Canada V6T 2B2

Martin J. Buss
    Department of Religion
    Emory University
    Atlanta, GA 30322

Robert C. Culley
    Faculty of Religious Studies
    McGill University
    3520 University Street
    Montreal, P.Q., Canada H3A 2A7

Norman K. Gottwald
    New York Theological Seminary
    5 West 29th Street
    New York, NY 10001

Ioan M. Lewis
    London School of Economics and Political Science
    Houghton Street, Aldwych
    London, England WC2A 2AE

Burke O. Long
    Department of Religion
    Bowdoin College
    Brunswick, ME 04011

Thomas W. Overholt
    Department of Philosophy
    University of Wisconsin-Stevens Point
    Stevens Point, WI 54481

Robert R. Wilson
    The Divinity School
    Yale University
    New Haven, CT 06510

PREFACE

The inside cover of *Semeia* has stated from the beginning that a primary role of the journal was to publish articles employing the methods, models, and findings of a number of different disciplines in the study of the Bible, among them social anthropology. The editors have always had anthropological and sociological approaches to the Bible in mind but for one reason or another were not successful in producing a volume directly in either of these areas. Several articles have kept sociological and anthropological issues alive, and there was one issue on oral tradition. The editors were quite pleased when a suggestion came from Thomas W. Overholt that the nucleus of a volume on anthropology and Old Testament prophecy was available. As a result, Overholt was invited to join with me in producing such a volume. Overholt was responsible for arranging for the main articles and inviting two distinguished anthropologists to write responses along with Norman Gottwald, a biblical scholar who is well-known for his interest in sociology. My own contribution was largely consultation with Overholt and preparation of the manuscripts for publication.

Robert C. Culley

ANTHROPOLOGY AND OLD TESTAMENT STUDIES:
AN INTRODUCTORY COMMENT

Robert C. Culley
McGill University

One of the areas which is attracting the attention of biblical scholars these days is anthropology. It is likely that this interest will grow. Thus, we need to begin to take stock of what is happening and to consider how recent publications apply anthropology, as well as related disciplines like sociology, folklore, and social psychology, to the Old Testament.

Anthropological perspectives have long played a role in the study of the Hebrew Bible. One need only think of William Robertson Smith, a name not unknown to anthropologists. The remarkable William Foxwell Albright, who influenced so many North American biblical scholars, ranged far and wide among the disciplines of the humanities and social sciences, not the least of which was anthropology. The nature and extent of the impact of anthropology, along with folklore and sociology, on past Old Testament studies may be seen in the survey of Herbert Hahn, as well as the more recent studies of J. W. Rogerson for anthropology and N. K. Gottwald and F. Frick for sociology.

The research of the past few years on anthropology and the Old Testament differs from earlier work in two noticeable ways. In the first place, anthropologists themselves, a small but distinguished number, have used the Old Testament as the basis for anthropological investigation. Perhaps the best known, and certainly the most controversial, of these studies is the application of structural analysis of the Lévi-Strauss variety to biblical texts by Edmund Leach (1969). More recently he has also used sacrifices described in Exodus and Leviticus as the basis for an examination designed to illustrate the usefulness of structural analysis for uncovering the cultural meaning of ritual (1976). A related approach to the Old Testament may be seen in the work of Mary Douglas. Her interest in the question of purity led her to a study of the purity laws in the book of Leviticus (1970). This investigation was broadened in later studies (1975). Uneasy about Leach's analysis of biblical texts, Julian Pitt-Rivers offered a substantial critique and then presented his own view of what an anthropological approach to biblical texts might be by examining the story of Dinah (Gen 34) in terms of marriage customs. The contribution of Peter Berger, a sociologist, to the discussion of the nature of Old Testament prophecy might also be mentioned here.

The second way in which recent work is different consists in a more substantial, systematic, and careful exploitation of anthropology, as well as sociology, folklore, and social psychology, than has been usual in the past. In my own work, field studies were used to gain a picture of the nature of oral tradition in order that a sounder basis might be created for the discussion of the role oral tradition might have played in the formation of the Hebrew Bible (see also Long, 1976a). Robert Wilson's book on Old Testament genealogies drew extensively on field studies by anthropologists but beyond this raised the important question of method. What sort of care is required when a scholar reaches out to another discipline in which he or she is not a specialist? Wilson thinks that considerable care must be taken and sets out six guidelines which he seeks to follow in his own use of the writings of anthropologists. On the whole, he wants to extract data from field studies carefully executed by trained scholars and leave behind the interpretive framework of the anthropological investigators. This is to ensure that the biblical text and biblical scholars will remain in control.

As far as sociology is concerned, Norman Gottwald's book on premonarchical Israel would have to be mentioned. In this book, he uses a sociological approach as an important ingredient in a historical reconstruction of early Israel. Following George Mendenhall, he interprets the conquest as a peasant revolt. In addition to the use of data from the studies of anthropologists and sociologists, he seeks to make deliberate use of sociological theory, employing a structural-functional model at one level of his analysis and a historical cultural-materialistic model at another. Sociology also plays a significant part in the studies of ancient cities by James Flanagan and Frank Frick.

It is within this wider discussion that the study of prophecy has emerged as an important topic. Once again, Robert Wilson has produced an important book which exploits field studies of anthropologists for information to help reconstruct the social settings of the Old Testament prophets.

Another recent book, *When Prophecy Failed* by Robert Carroll, is cross-disciplinary in the sense that the author makes use of a particular theory developed and employed by some social psychologists, namely cognitive dissonance. This approach is different from Wilson's in that Carroll is attempting to apply a theory rather than data from field studies. However, since Carroll is well aware of problems with the theory of cognitive dissonance, he is content to use it as a heuristic device to highlight features of the text which might otherwise go unnoticed. A way of reading the text is thereby opened up.

Apart from these two books, a number of articles have been written on the phenomenon of prophecy or some aspect of it in which use has been made of the writings of anthropologists, sociologists, and social psychologists. Herbert Huffmon has written on the origins of prophecy. Thomas Overholt has discussed the prophetic process. Simon Parker has dealt with the question of possession trance. The social psychology of prophecy has been investigated by Martin Buss. Burke Long has treated prophetic authority. The contributions to this present volume constitute a valuable addition to this material with discussions of the prophetic call, prophetic conflict, a model for the prophetic process, and the nature of apocalyptic religion.

Recent use of anthropology and other related disciplines in a more thorough and systematic way than heretofore has produced substantial results, even though this sort of work has only just begun. For example, the studies on prophecy which have appeared so far, including those in this volume, have clarified significantly the nature of Old Testament prophecy by setting it in the context of other similar figures described in field studies of anthropologists. One can think of many other features of the life of ancient Israel which could be examined usefully by biblical scholars with the aid of carefully selected data from field studies or through the use of models developed by anthropologists or sociologists. Beyond this, it is to be hoped that anthropologists and sociologists will continue to show an interest in analyzing biblical texts and commenting on the work of biblical scholars.

Already a number of issues are emerging which will bear further examination. Three may be briefly noted where, it is to be hoped, some lively discussion will develop.

One issue is the problem of method, that is, the question of how to do cross-disciplinary study. How should biblical scholars in a responsible way make use of work done in another discipline such that not only biblical scholars but also scholars in the other discipline in question, say anthropology, will take seriously what is being done? Wilson is very sensitive to this problem as may be seen in his establishment of guidelines in his own investigations. He inclines toward a prudent approach, and this makes good sense. Others, however, may feel more adventurous and less restricted in their use of data, models, and theory from other disciplines. Since most biblical scholars are not trained specialists in other disciplines as well, the problem of responsible use of material from another discipline is real.

Another issue has to do with the nature of the social sciences and what kind of perspectives they bring. In other words, how may they be used in biblical studies? So far, anthropology and sociology have been used on the whole by Old Testament scholars to reconstruct the social settings of phenomena like prophecy or the social system of a specific period in ancient Israel. This continues and expands the task of historical reconstruction which was one of the important aims of historical criticism. But, since the social sciences by their very nature deal with many cultures, and therefore repeated patterns and types, one might be just as easily led in a phenomenological direction rather than historical. The study of patterns repeated in several cultures and societies or the examination of social worlds constructed by varying factors in a common grid, poses the question of explanation and meaning differently than a historical approach usually has. It would be useful to have some fuller discussion of this.

Finally, there is the issue of the relationship between the study of society and the study of text. Along with a growing interest among biblical scholars in social sciences like anthropology and sociology, has gone an increased fascination in the implications flowing from the fact that the Bible is language and literature. The pages of *Semeia* have long reflected many different attempts to work out these implications. Many are inclined to see texts as structures of language in which literary patterns and features deserve primary attention. The tendency has been to compare literature with literature, within the Bible or outside it, before relating texts to social settings. The way in which a text may be said to reflect its social setting is seen as more indirect and the task of reconstructing social background from texts as more problematic than has usually been assumed. Furthermore, since many texts survive original social settings and are valued in subsequent societies and cultures, one may well seek the explanation for the power of these texts to survive in the text itself rather than a given social setting. On the other hand, language and literature are social. They do not exist in a vacuum. There is good reason to examine how texts are related to social settings, original and otherwise. We may look forward to a new kind of discussion of an old problem. (For an attempt to relate social sciences and hermeneutics, see Kovacs.)

WORKS CONSULTED

Buss, Martin J.
1980   "The Social Psychology of Prophecy." Pp. 1–11 in *Prophecy*. Ed. J. A. Emerton. BZAW 150. Berlin: de Gruyter.

Carroll, Robert P.
1979   *When Prophecy Failed: Cognitive Dissonance in the Prophetic Traditions of the Old Testament*. New York: Seabury.

Culley, Robert C.
1976   "Oral Tradition and the OT: Some Recent Discussion." *Semeia* 5:1–33.

Douglas, Mary
1970   *Purity and Danger: An Analysis of Pollution and Taboo*. Harmondsworth: Penguin Books.
1975   *Implicit Meanings*. Boston: Routledge and Kegan Paul.

Flanagan, James W.
1978   "The Relocation of the Davidic Capital." *JAAR* 46:224–244.

Frick, Frank S.
1977   *The City in Ancient Israel*. Missoula: Scholars Press.

Gottwald, Norman K.
1979 *The Tribes of Yahweh: A Sociology of the Religion of Liberated Israel, 1250–1050 B.C.E.* Maryknoll: Orbis Books.

Gottwald, Norman K. and Frank S. Frick
1976 "The Social World of Ancient Israel." Pp. 110–119 in *The Bible and Liberation.* Berkeley: Radical Religion.

Hahn, Herbert F.
1966 *The Old Testament in Modern Research.* With a Survey of Recent Literature by Horace D. Hummel. Philadelphia: Fortress.

Huffmon, Herbert B.
1976 "Orgins of Prophecy." Pp. 171–186 in *Magnalia Dei, The Mighty Acts of God.* Eds. Frank Moore Cross, Werner E. Lemke and Patrick D. Miller, Jr. New York: Doubleday.

Kovacs, Brian Watson
1979 "Philosophical Issues in Sociological Structuralism: A Bridge from the Social Sciences to Hermeneutics." USQR 34:149–157.

Leach, Edmund
1969 *Genesis as Myth and Other Essays.* London: Jonathon Cape.
1976 *Culture and Communication: The Logic by Which Symbols are Connected.* Themes in the Social Sciences. Cambridge: Cambridge University.

Long, Burke O.
1976a "Recent Field Studies in Oral Literature and their Bearing on OT Criticism." *VT* 26:187–198.
1976b "Recent Field Studies in Oral Literature and the Question of *Sitz im Leben.*" *Semeia* 5: 35–49.

Overholt, Thomas W.
1974 "The Ghost Dance of 1890 and the Nature of the Prophetic Process." *Ethnohistory* 21: 37–63.

Parker, Simon B.
1978 "Possession Trance and Prophecy in Pre-Exilic Israel." *VT* 28: 271–285.

Pitt-Rivers, Julian
1977 "The Fate of Shechem or the Politics of Sex." Pp. 126–171 in *The Fate of Shechem or the Politics of Sex: Essays in the Anthropology of the Mediterranean.* Cambridge: Cambridge University.

Rogerson, J.W.
1978 *Anthropology and the Old Testament.* Oxford: Blackwell.

Wilson, Robert R.
1977 *Genealogy and History in the Biblical World.* Yale Near Eastern Researches. New Haven: Yale University.
1980 *Prophecy and Society in Ancient Israel.* Philadelphia: Fortress.

ARTICLES

AN ANTHROPOLOGICAL PERSPECTIVE UPON PROPHETIC CALL NARRATIVES

Martin J. Buss
Emory University

ABSTRACT

Reports of a prophetic call in Israel are comparable to call accounts found throughout the world. These phenomena reflect common human structures and are in part connected historically. Theoretical analysis indicates that they can be understood in terms of basic sociopsychological categories.

A call summons the recipient to a specialized role, which becomes increasingly differentiated as a society grows in size and complexity. Persons with a revelatory task are normally believed to receive a call directly from the spirit world. Not infrequently, reluctance is expressed in the face of a challenging assignment.

A prophetic call selects persons who can communicate insight beyond what is already known, for the guiding of decisions. In varying ways such individuals transcend the established structures of their group.

The idea of a call attributes the ground of a diviner's activity to a spiritual reality. This eases the burden of personal responsibility and at the same time supports a perspective wider than that of private interests.

Questions of Method

0.0   Comparison is an inevitable aspect of any investigation, since all concepts by which a phenomenon can be understood involve a degree of generality. Comparison, furthermore, includes the making of contrasts (cf. Wright). Thus a meaningful question is not whether, but how, one should engage in comparative study.

0.1   It is possible to recognize three kinds of comparative procedures. One, that of detailed description, draws attention to specific characteristics which may appear within a limited range of space and time. This procedure is useful primarily for a recognition of historical connection, or diffusion. Another, that of typology, outlines forms of expression and behavior, which may be observed quite widely. This approach introduces order into the perception of multiform data and has been applied extensively during the twentieth century. A third, that of theory, seeks to account for observable similarities and differences by placing phenomena into a framework which can give a reason for their appearance. It requires much more attention than it has received so far in the study of religion.

0.2   A theoretical procedure makes explicit the ideas that are otherwise implicit in an investigation. Every study stands under the influence of a more or less coherent set of conceptions which guide the selection, organization, and presentation of data. An important issue, therefore, is the appropriateness and validity of concepts employed. For human phenomena, both psychological and sociological considerations are relevant, as is recognized by many anthropologists (e.g., Lewis: 25; Beidelman: 406); indeed, one of the strengths of the discipline of anthropology lies in its relative comprehensiveness in supplying perspectives on human life.

0.3   The development of theories is, then, to be actively sought. It should be recognized that conceptions are always subject to improvement /1/. A theoretical approach does not yield greater finality or safety than does one oriented to historical chronology; rather, it asks different kinds of questions–questions designed to produce an understanding of phenomena. If there are differences of opinion, that fact does not undermine the significance of the endeavor, but points to the need for further research.

0.4   For biblical scholarship there is pronounced value in examining comparative data beyond the borders of the Near East, for both historical and structural reasons. With regard to history, it is necessary to consider that Near Eastern data may be incomplete. The phenomenon of a prophetic call is an excellent example of such a situation. Initiatory experiences occur in many parts of the world, yet few appear in the literature of the ancient world surrounding Palestine. (Perhaps such events were not normally included in a written account; in fact, in some societies the narrating of call dreams is discouraged [Wissler: 71; Underhill: 266]). An erroneous impression of Israel's antecedents and early history can arise if one's vision is limited to the records of its immediate neighbors /2/.

In regard to functional-structural concerns, it is often useful to compare phenomena that are not closely connected historically, in order to determine whether they fit a certain kind of psychological or sociological context. For instance, one can give attention to the level of social complexity of a society and to the age group for which a given literary form is intended. Quite a few of the observable similarities and differences between phenomena can be explained through reference to such factors.

0.5   It is true that the historical and structural dimensions sometimes cannot be distinguished easily. For instance (as is well known in anthropological circles), many parallels obtain between Israelite and African life. Are these due to the fact that ancient Israel and tribal Africa exhibit similar levels of social complexity, based to a large extent on a comparable agricultural economy? Or has there been extensive historical interchange between Africa and the Near East? Probably both of these questions need to be answered in the affirmative. Certain similarities are undoubtedly a result of "convergence," the independent appearance of similar phenomena under similar conditions. Others may be due to diffusion, even apart from social appropriateness. Most African-Israelite parallels, however, quite likely reflect the operation of both historical connection and sociological conditioning; after all, a cultural trait does not spread readily if it does not fit well the receiving society.

The relative importance of the different dimensions can frequently be estimated through a survey of the geographical spread of certain features and through statistical analysis of their covariance with social conditions. That requires a wide sampling—and eventually a reasonably complete account—of phenomena of a given type. For divination, prophecy, and possession, notable steps toward such an overview have been taken in anthropological discussions, by focusing either on specific types or on certain geographical regions; yet more integrative work is needed.

0.6 An anthropological study of Israelite call narratives, then, appropriately focuses on two basic issues: a theoretical understanding of the nature of a call and an assessment of the place of Israelite prophecy in the history of humanity. The following analysis will seek to deal especially with the former, in the hope that future scholarship will continue to advance with fuller data and better concepts. Specifically, the call to prophesy will be viewed with the aid of notions drawn from social psychology concerning role, communication, and the attribution of cause and responsibility. These concepts are employed since they appear to fit the data of ancient literature as well as of field observations in various groups.

Induction into a Social Role

1.0 A call summons a person to a specialized role /3/. In a simple, usually small, community relatively little differentiation occurs. Thus, for instance, some groups have neither religious nor political specialists (Turnbull: 181). As a society grows, normally the first emerging specialty (the practitioner of which can be called a shaman) is one that combines the performance of curing and other rituals with the giving of advice on the basis of a special relationship with normally unseen realities/4/. This differentiation apparently emerges gradually, since only a mildly specialized shamanic role, for which a member of a family is designated informally, appears in moderately-sized communities /5/. Such data indicates that the task of a religious specialist does not stand in sharp contrast to general human existence, but that it represents in acute form one aspect of human life. (Indeed, universal participation in prophecy is portrayed as an ideal in Num 11:29 and Joel 3:20.)

1.1   Frequently, the role of a comprehensive religious specialist is believed to be assigned by one or more spirits through dreams, protracted illness, or special experiences of some kind /6/. At the same time family connections are important, in that a new shaman is quite commonly chosen from among the relatives of an older one (see, e.g., Eliade: 13-20; Métraux, 1949:589; Knuttson: 190). As a society increases in membership, the religious duties are divided among several specialists, differing in task and procedure of selection. Ritual becomes the responsibility of the priest, while supernatural communication is the sphere of the diviner and curing the job of the doctor. A diviner who receives insight primarily in a personal, non-mechanical manner (for instance, through visions) can be termed a medium or prophet. Such personal diviners, who may also act as curers by spiritual means, are typically inducted into their work through a call from the spirit world. If they function as one kind of religious specialist among others, their selection is usually carried out with little attention to heredity /7/. The other roles—which do not require direct revelation—are acquired largely through inheritance (this is true especially for the priest) or voluntary training (especially for mechanical divination); partly specialized roles are sometimes designated by a medium /8/. In practice, a personal call received by a shaman or a medium often also needs to be recognized as such by an established diviner, and a period of apprenticeship commonly follows /9/. In any case, processes of selection become on the whole differentiated in conjunction with a divergence in tasks.

1.2   Political roles, too, emerge with a sharper focus in a larger society, although they may continue a close connection with the more strictly religious ones. For instance, a chief or royal person can act as shaman, as in early China and Japan (Weber, 1951:26-31; Eichhorn: 16-17; Hori: 187, 196) or can be viewed as possessed by a spirit from the moment of installation on, as in parts of Africa (Butt, 1952:63; Chadwick: 40). Depending largely on their presumed relation to the spiritual realm, such leaders have often been believed to be selected directly or indirectly by deity. Thus the Basuto prophet-chief Mohlomi reported a call to rule his people (Ellenberger and McGregor: 90). More frequently, divination has played a part in the selection of a political figure—at least in Africa, including Egypt and Ethiopia (Tanner: 285; Schenke: 70-71). In ancient Mesopotamia, kings could be termed "the called one" and described as the object of divine choice /10/.

1.3   According to Israelite tradition, God personally called the early leaders, whose task was quite comprehensive in character (Abraham, Gen 12:1-3; Moses, Exod 3:7-4:17; 6:2-13; 6:26-7:5 /11/). Thereafter, persons with primarily military and political duties were summoned by deity—particularly Joshua (through Moses, Num 27:18-23 and Deut 31:7-8; directly, Deut 31:23 and Josh 1:1-9), Gideon (through an angel, Judg 6:11-24), and Samson (through an angelic appearance to the parents, Judg 13:2–23). Such leaders are described as being possessed with the spirit of God (Moses: Num 11:17; Joshua: Num 27:18; Othniel: Judg 3:10; Gideon: Judg 6:34; Jephthah: Judg 11:29; Samson, a holy person as a "Nazirite": Judg 13:25; 14:6, 19; 15:14). An immediate divine call is reported for Samuel, who was prophet, judge, and ritualist (1 Sam 3:2–18—like Deborah, Judge 4:4–5:31). In subsequent centuries, prophets were believed to be commissioned directly by God (Amos 7:15; Isa 6:1–13; Jer 1:4–19; Ezek 1:1–3:15) or to receive the task and spirit from an older prophet according to the divine will (Elisha: 1 Kgs 19:16, 19–21; 2 Kgs 2:9–15 /12/). Kings were designated by prophetic revelation (especially the first of a royal line) and were viewed as possessed by God's spirit, at least in early times (Saul and David: 1 Sam 10:6, 10; 16:13, 14; 2 Sam 23:2) and in the ideal future (Isa 11:2). The notion of a call became quite important for Second Isaiah, who applied it to the general prophetic-royal figure of the "Servant of Yahweh" (42:1, 6; 49:1–9) and in particular to Abraham (51:2), Israel (41:9; 43:1; 48:12), and the Persian king Cyrus (45:1; 46:11; 48:15) /13/. Biblical accounts of a call, then, like those in other societies, are closely adjusted to the role to which a person is assigned. Comprehensive leaders or specifically revelatory intermediaries receive a direct assignment by deity. Other important personages, especially kings, are designated indirectly through prophets.

1.4   A call by a deity or spirit commonly summons the recipient to a lifetime of special service; that is true especially if selection occurs already at, or before, birth /14/. Stories of more limited commissions, however, are also told. They follow, on the whole, a pattern similar to that of long-term assignments, so that it is not easy to draw a dividing line between them /15/. Indeed, mediumistic activity occurs in temporary, non-professional forms (e.g., de Groot: 1214; Eder: 372; Gouldsbury and Sheane: 83, with warnings described by the group as the roar of a lion). Amos appears to have declared that he is one who prophesies without being a professional prophet (7:14–15 /16/). Even a life-long activity as shaman or medium very frequently does not constitute a full-time occupation /17/. Thus the professional quite regularly pursues an ordinary career. It is possible, then, that a number of the Israelite prophets earned their living by means of a priestly or secular occupation.

1.5   In the Bible and elsewhere, stories of a summons repeatedly include an element of hesitation, ranging from mild caution to stubborn rejection. Reluctance is reported for non-Israelite shamans and mediums /18/ and for such general religious leaders as Moses (Exod 3:11; 4:10, 13; 6:12) and Christian popes (Mühlbacher: 2). Diffidence is expressed in accounts of early political figures /19/ and to some extent of Israelite prophets /20/. One can wonder whether hesitation is a matter of politeness or pretended humility or whether it is genuine, based on awe or on a wish to escape an unpleasant involvement. Undoubtedly the various possibilities enter into play at different times, even in combination. In any case, it is to be noted that all of these possible motivations have a common logical ground, namely the assumption that the task is an important and demanding one /21/.

A good description of reasons for reluctance is the following given by Kuper: "It is considered best to be normal, not to be limited all one's life by special taboos on sex, food, and general behaviour; not to be exhausted by the demands of someone stronger than oneself; not to have to shoulder responsibility for the life and death of others" (164) /22/. A narrative of a hill tribe in India relates that the first shaman, chosen by the sky god to protect and heal men when no one volunteered, declares: "But how can I do such a thing? I am a poor man and ignorant" (Elwin, 1955:131). Many recipients, however, accept a call without conscious (or reported) remonstration, acknowledging the power of spirits and perhaps welcoming the task /23/.

Communication

2.0   One can now raise the question why a call from the spirit world is viewed as appropriate for a personal diviner. A major part of the reason lies in the belief that such a person is in contact with a reality which in some sense stands higher than the human, for a summons implies that the one who extends it is superior to the recipient. An especially significant advantage of a spirit over an ordinary human being is believed to lie in the realm of knowledge. Access to such special knowledge is important for the communicative function of a diviner, aiding human beings in making large or small decisions. Decisions require, in theory, a very large amount of information for assessment of the over-all consequence of an act; since such information is not readily available, they are, to some extent, always made in the dark. To pierce this darkness, guidance is sought from those who are thought to be able to furnish relevant insight. (Cf., further, Buss, 1980:nn. 18, 19.)

2.1   There are reasons to believe that a specialist can indeed add to the wisdom of decisions and that the call experience is a sign of an ability to do so. A recent study indicates that persons who are especially successful in intuition—that is, in making correct judgments on the basis of a limited amount of explicit data—are relatively "unconventional and comfortable in their unconventionality" (Westcott: 141). Investigations of creative persons describe them as independent, rather androgenous (somewhat "feminine," if they are males), welcoming complexity (even messiness), and willing to tackle large issues (e.g., Bruner: 24; Barron: 192, 212, 220; Berlyne: 319). Sometimes, a prolonged "creative illness," primarily psychological, precedes a burst of insight (H. Ellenberger: 889). All of these characteristics have been observed among mediums and shamans and frequently constitute a sign to a community and to the individual concerned that a certain man or woman has been called. Specific signals include a distant gaze and special sensitivity (Bogoras: 415), running into the wilderness or nakedness (Harva: 453; Field: 61-66; Middleton, 1971:224), and, very commonly, illness with psychological overtones (as also in the Christian-influenced Handsome Lake, Parker: 9). Shamans and mediums may be impotent or homosexual, or dress transsexually (e.g., Schärer: 57; Eliade: 125: Burridge: 119). In some societies, they tend to be orphans or to have physical disabilities, such as blindness (Murphy: 75-76; Eder: 369, 373). They have been described as "individualists, odd, abnormal, queer," socially difficult persons, who live in "a hectic, excited manner and in a dangerous world which is not the world of everyday life" (Krader: 336). A call vision is received primarily in solitude—in other words, with some independence from social exchange /24/.

2.2   The dynamics of creative insight can be clarified to a considerable extent by referring to recent analyses of the process of communication. It is now recognized that only a situation with a large degree of uncertainty can provide much information to a recipient, since a stable condition is already known. For this reason, complexity as a high form of order stands in contrast to "orderliness" or predictability (Buss, 1979:13-15, 19). Creativity and fresh perception, then, involve a willingness to confront uncertainty and complexity and to stand loose in regard to established structures. Such a readiness appears to be facilitated by a receptive state, since an assertive goal-direction limits the information intake to patterns relevant to one's specific aim /25/. Sheer receptivity, it is true, does not reach a solution; but in conjunction with appropriate reasoning and information gathering, an open state of mind can lead to important results (Martindale and Armstrong: 311, 317; Field: 57; Tanner: 278; Fry: 35). Furthermore, imagination—including hallucination—is fostered by withdrawal from external input /26/. All in all, creative and prophetic persons are quite flexible in their facing of reality. Societies clearly have learned to give a place to such persons.

2.3   The guidance of a shaman or medium is usually sought for limited concerns, but a revelatory person can present a new general perspective or express social criticism /27/. A number of those propounding a new or special point of view have presented themselves as being called primarily to proclaim that particular message (e.g., Wallis: 136, 143; so, perhaps, also Amos). Innovations, however, are also included in the work of professionals with various revelations (Hori: 196-197; Horton: 43, 46; Reinhard: 288; Adas). The relative freedom of prophets in relation to social structure encourages an association and sympathy with lower levels of stratified societies and gives room to women, who may otherwise occupy a deprived position. Accordingly, revelations in ancient Israel and elsewhere exhibit a protesting or equalizing tendency /28/.

The Attribution of Cause and Assignment of Responsibility

3.0   It is important to give specific attention to the logic and practical implications of a belief that a call by a spiritual reality has taken place. This belief is a special case of the attribution of causes and thus the assignment of responsibility in human perception and expression (cf. Heider: 89, 114–118, 168–171; Harvey *et al.*). The narrative of a call declares that a spiritual power forms the basis of the activity of a revelatory person. It supports the truth or authority of prophetic declarations or demands and elicits in those who accept them appropriate emotional states and active responses (cf., for such consequences, E. Jones *et al.*: xi).

3.1   Of course, the fact that a story is told does not imply that a hearer or even the narrator believes the account. Indeed, there is widespread skepticism of prophetic claims and a fair amount of conscious deceit (sometimes rationalized as for the good of the other) among intermediaries (e.g., Evans-Pritchard, 1937:185–193; Beattie: 167; Tanner: 284). Therefore, a first-person account of a call does not in itself accomplish an authentication; the acceptance of a shaman or medium rests primarily on other grounds, such as recognition by an established diviner, appropriate behavior, and, especially, successful prediction or analysis of a problem (e.g., Anisimov: 120; Winkler: 248–249; Deut 18:20–22; Jer 28:9 /29/). Probably in large part for this reason, reports of receiving a prophetic call are not very plentiful and the primary emphasis in public pronouncements is laid on particular messages and recent or current inspiration /30/. It appears, however, that in many and perhaps most instances a sense of having been called informs the self-concept of a revelatory person (with J. Lindblom: 21, 182). The specific form of a call report is clearly shaped by cultural patterns /31/; it is likely, however, that the subjective experience is influenced by cultural expectation as well, so that no conscious deception need be implied by such stereotyping.

3.2   The theme of a spiritual origin of prophetic activity concerns the whole sequence of revelations initiated by a call and involves the issue of responsibility in prophecy. On the one hand, the attribution of messages to a source in the spirit world absolves human individuals from personal responsibility for presenting or accepting them. A value in this absolution lies in the fact that a medium can express an unpopular opinion (or one critical of authority) and a hearer can make a difficult (perhaps somewhat humiliating) decision, more readily than may be easily possible otherwise (Field: 76; Lewis: *passim*; Long: 6–7). On the other hand—in a more positive view—the orientation toward an overarching reality encourages an ethical outlook which incorporates a self-transcending concern for the larger human and nonhuman community. The assignment of responsibility to the spiritual realm then expresses an encompassing perspective wider than that of a private interest.

3.3   Thus a call is associated precisely with those tasks which, in actuality, bear a high degree of responsibility in that they require considerable discretion and have a major impact on individual and group existence /32/. For persons with such assignments, self-transcendence clearly does not stand in opposition to a strong selfhood but rather in a close connection with it—a situation which is symbolized by the fact that the initial summons sometimes consists in the calling of the recipient's name /33/. Although it may appear paradoxical, the high task to which a person is called provides major elements of freedom even as—in part, because—it is related to an ultimate reference point.

Concluding Reflections

4.0   There are several aspects of call experiences and narratives that can be explored further. Yet the observations that have been made are enough to show that major features of prophetic call accounts appear throughout the world and can be understood in terms of sociopsychological categories. Thus, although certain elements of individual stories may strain modern belief, the occurence of a call as such need not be dismissed as a superstition. Furthermore, the events and narratives fit human experience well enough so that one can conclude that divine communication does not violate common processes. Anthropological study of call phenomena, rather, reveals their specific place in human life. A call inducts the recipient into a highly responsible role; one that is received personally typically leads to a communicative task which provides guidance in decisions.

4.1   In regard to the relation of biblical accounts of a call to human history, a few tentative comments are in order. First, diffusion undoubtedly took place. Israelite prophecy received impulses from other traditions and had considerable influence on later cultures. Secondly, although the call narratives of the Bible resemble those found elsewhere, they also exhibit some special characteristics. Perhaps most notably, the Israelite call is represented as coming from a single and supreme deity, while in many traditions one or more lesser spirits are held responsible. A large part of the reason for this difference appears to lie in the situation of Israel among high societies of the ancient Near East without being, politically, one of them (cf. Gottwald for a discussion of this issue). Thirdly, Israelite society, at least since the beginning of kingship, was sufficiently specialized to differentiate between several roles, but it was not as diversified as were (and are) larger states. Thus a call in Israel stands intermediate between those of other groups in terms of comprehensiveness. Finally, the concrete nature of Israelite descriptions of a call, with voices and visions, is somewhat different from the way in which many persons of the present time sense their responsibility. Some of them, for instance, differentiate more sharply between ultimacy (or the dimension of commitment) and finite (or specifically describable) events.

4.2   If theology is inherently an inclusive discipline—as is likely—it needs to incorporate both structural and historical considerations. With the aid of philosophy, it can construct a general theory of dynamic relations including the particular categories employed here (role as the contribution of individuals to a group, communication as the content of a relationship, and origin as the ground of responsibility). An anthropological analysis cannot by itself establish a theological point of view, but it can contribute to one by shedding light on the process of faith.

NOTES

/1/   Wilson: 16 asks students of the Bible to "avoid the interpretive schema into which sociologists, anthropologists, and Near Eastern scholars have placed the data"; it is more appropriate to urge that they learn from, and seek to refine, such perspectives.

/2/   Thus, without taking account of comparative data, L. Schmidt: 46 argues that the reluctance theme in call stories did not arise in Israel before the monarchy. Early Israelite literature and religion cannot be reconstructed positively or negatively from the relatively late documents now available, but reasonable estimates can be derived through comparison with other traditions.

/3/   The concept of "role" is more open than that of "office," which Weber, 1956:125-126, set in contrast to "charismatic" activity; cf. Buss, 1980:3-8.

/4/   On the role of the shaman as the oldest specialization, cf. Chapple and Coon: 407; Hoebel: 414. For instance, the shaman is the only prominent specialist of any kind among Eskimos (Lewis: 163) and the only one among many South-American tribes (Métraux, 1949:596). A union of priest and seer in early Arabic society is described by Wellhausen: 134. Since no other useful term is available, the word "shaman" will here be used to designate a religious specialist with a quite comprehensive task (as Findeisen: 14 and Burridge: 117); such a broad specialty is found typically in small communities, which may be engaged in hunting or gathering (with Czaplicka: 191; Lommel: 69, 73, 100).

/5/   See, e.g., Bogoras: 413-414 and Ohlmarks: 276-292 (although differing in detail). In a number of societies—especially smaller ones—individuals engage in a quest for vision or possession and (if successful) receive spiritual insight and power, to a large extent for their own purposes rather than as an intermediary for others. Such an acquisition is not based on the initiative of the spirit world—in other words, not on a call—but it is understood as a gift. (Cf. Eliade: 109; McClintock: 252-253).

/6/   An absence of a call (cf. also Reinhard: 262, 268) is viewed by Cooper: 750 and Anisimov: 115 as the older procedure; but the theory of a call is certainly widespread in observable shamanism.

/7/   The ideology of a call is well-nigh universal for primarily revelatory persons. Apparently, however, a call is sometimes not reported for minor mediums; cf. Hori: 203. (The majority of the called intermediaries referred to in Wilson: 51-52 should be classed as "central possession mediums" in the sense of I. M. Lewis, while those described there without a personal call are ritualists or members of a cult). Heredity occasionally plays a part (e.g., Evans-Pritchard, 1940:186).

/8/ E.g., Horton: 24. M. Weber's "routinization of charisma" (1956:146) needs to be seen together with the simultaneous emergence of more purely charismatic prophetism and should be understood as a phenomenon of specialization.

/9/ A widespread form of the call involves illness (especially one with psychological problems); this is then often diagnosed by a diviner or shaman. See, e.g., Horton: 27; Colson: 73; Sagant: 85. Training by an established medium, to a greater or lesser extent, is very common. Cf. Wilson: 50, 60–61.

/10/ *ANET*: 119; Falkenstein and von Soden: 105, 114, 115, 120–21, 127 (Isa 6 may have an affinity with such elections, although it is not likely part of a royal designation, *pace* Schoors). The Accadian word translated "called one" is *nabium*—from which the Hebrew *nābî'* for prophet may be derived (see Wilson: 137, following W.F. Albright and others). The role and manner of divine designations of political leaders needs to be further investigated. It is certain, however, that "charismatic" leadership is not unique to early Israel (*pace* Noth: 25).

/11/ For data and analyses regarding Israelite call accounts, see Olmo Lete and Baltzer. The interrelationship between such stories has been discussed extensively. It is by no means clear (as G. von Rad: 68, Schmid: 20–22, and others have argued) that the story of Moses' call reflects specfically prophetic tradition and is thus derived from the latter (cf., on the motif of reluctance, nn. 19–20 below, and on Moses' role, Vater: 122–172. At the same time, it is unlikely that prophetic accounts (except perhaps that of Jeremiah, in a form that may be late) are deliberately connected with those of Moses or of political figures, as held by Habel: 316, since the pattern is old in shamanism and may be considered to be a living one in prophetic tradition as well. Richter, 1970:175, in attempting to relate prophetic and other calls, does not consider the possibility of a common heritage. A quasi-shamanic union of tasks is also reflected in the description of the craftsman Bezalel as imbued with divine spirit (Exod 31:3; 35:31); cf. Lommel.

/12/ Assignment to the sacred role is called "anointing" in 1 Kgs 19:16, as it is in relation to kings, priests, and cultic objects in other contexts. A vision confirms or grants the prophetic status, according to 2 Kgs 2:10–11.

/13/ Cf. Rowley: 111–120; Fichtner: 1085; and, for the royal element, e.g., Westermann: 79 (similarly, on Jeremiah, Reventlow: 43–45). An ambiguous figure—equivalent to the "Servant," including the prophet and Israel?—is given a call in Isa 40:6 (cf. Melugin: 84 and Vincent: 204–251 [a third-person reading here, accepted by Petersen: 20, is probably too specific, but Zion is to be a herald according to v. 9]; a closely related speaker appears in Isa 61:1).

/14/ At birth, upon an oracle or (reported) observation: Lehtisalo: 146; Nebesky-Wojkowitz: 451; G. Lindblom: 254; Fenton: 70. Before birth, such as in the womb: Rasmussen, 1929:116; Horton: 40; Tschopik: 226; Taylor: 110–11; Gilula: 114 (for an eighth-century Egyptian pharaoh); Judg 13:5; Jer 1:5; Isa 49:1; Luke 1:13–17, 31–35 (with entry of God's spirit).

/15/ Thus, whether Isa 6 represents a life-long call can hardly be decided on such grounds (*pace* Steck: 190–91; cf. n. 20 below). Quite a few of the biblical accounts may refer to a more or less limited task; even Moses' assignment is not clearly more than that.

/16/ There is no contradiction between engaging in a certain activity and disavowing one's being a specialist, or even a paid professional, in that line (*pace* Hoffmann: 212, and others;

better, Curtis:492). Occasionally among shamans or mediums, an absence of human training is valued (cf. Rassmussen, 1929: 115-19). Possibly Amos implies such absence; in any case he places stress on a divine initiative, an emphasis stylistically reflected in the repetition of the name "Yahweh."

/17/ Cf. Reinhard: 265; Tschopik: 285; Evans-Pritchard, 1937:253. The prophets at Mari included both cultic personnel and others ("lay" persons); it is not clear to what extent their revelatory activity was part-time or temporary, or both. Does the sending of hair and hem to authenticate their messages reflect the special garb and hair style of many shamans and ecstatics (cf., Eliade: 145-80, 407; Gouldsbury and Sheane: 87; the long hair of the Nazirites and the mantle of Israelite prophets [Carroll: 405])? Their sense of mission resembles a call (Hayes: 403), although no initial experience is related.

/18/ See, for different parts of Asia, Africa, and the Americas: Eliade: 72, 109; Harva: 453-54; W. Schmidt, XI:518; XII:653; Knoll-Greiling: 235; Elwin, 1939:137; Jordan: 71-73; Spiro: 208-10; R. Jones 47; Gelfand: 110; Landes: 208; Hamer: 395; Park: 26; Pressel: 304.

/19/ Gideon: Judg 6:15; Saul: 1 Sam 9:21; 10:22. Possible reluctance by Joshua is countered in the divine charge of Josh 1:9. Solomon expresses humility when God appears to him in a dream soon after becoming king: "I am a little child, not knowing how to come or go," 1 Kgs 3:7. Somewhat similarly, Thut-mose III in the report of his divine call to kingship describes himself in terms of "a puppy," and "weaned child" before his installation as "prophet," i.e., comprehensive religious leader (*ANET*, 446; his reference to a flight to heaven is reminiscent of shamanic accounts). Such an outlook is also reflected in the autobiography of this pharaoh's vizier, who speaks of his nature and abilities being changed (*ANET*: 213; Baltzer: 134-69 proposes, too specifically, that the prophetic call reflects that of a vizier). According to Zoroastrian tradition Yima, the first king, turned down a divine request to present the law (Vendidad 2.1.3).

/20/ Especially, Jer 1:6, perhaps influenced by Mosaic or royal traditions (cf. Holladay: 154-160; Schreiner: 142-143), but appropriate for the prophetic sense attested in the complaints (20:9). A sense of inadequacy in the face of God appears in Isa 6:5 (but not an objection; the prophet responds to the call for a volunteer, v. 8 [Engnell: 42]). Hesitation may be implied in Ezek 2:6, 8 (at least as a possibility [cf. 3:14, MT]), but probably not in Isa 40:6 or in 1 Kgs 19:20. Jonah's avoidance relates to a specific message. Zimmerli: 16-21 and Gouders: 183 envision two types of a prophetic call—one with, and one without, an expression of reluctance; although reality is richer than such a dual typology, it is true that reluctance is indeed not always, or specifically, a prophetic motif. It is also not related especially to a life-long call. In Accadian stories, temporary commissions may lead to disturbance or refusal (*ANET*: 110, 113 Buccellati: 69).

/21/ Similarly, Richter, 1966:148 (not repeated in 1970:21).

/22/ The problem of responsibility is mentioned also by Shirokogoroff: 380 (including the possibility of conflict) and Métraux, 1959:73. Self-doubt in the novice was observed by Bogoras: 420 (as well as apparent pretention, 421). For the more pragmatic considerations, cf. Wilson: 49.

/23/ Occasionally, persons consciously seek to attract the attention of spirits (Rasmussen, 1908:147; Colson: 73). The importance of an (unconscious) desire for successful operation as shaman is stressed by Shirokogoroff: 346-48. Sometimes, the acceptance of a call is viewed as strictly voluntary (Butt, 1966:41).

/24/ For solitude and travel to another society as part of training in receptivity and insight, see e.g., Butt, 1966:42, 45-46. According to an experimental investigation, shamans impose forms on ambiguous phenomena in a more varied and self-directed manner than do others in the same society (Shweder). Overholt: 531 and Wilson: 58 have rightly emphasized the social aspect of prophecy; it is important to note that societies acknowledge the value of independence, so that some individuals fulfil a social function precisely through not being fully immersed in common social operations. (On the interplay between society and individual in prophecy, see also Wallis: 255-263.)

/25/   See Martindale and Hines for an experimental analysis, and cf. Plato, *Phaedrus*, 244; Heschel: 381-389.

/26/   Some observers (e.g., Silverman: 26-27; Bourguignon: 241) have noted a similarity between the experiences of shamans or mediums and those that arise experimentally under conditions of sensory deprivation.

/27/   See, among others, Fuchs; Ray: 200, 208. Similarly, Wilson: 84 (although not with sufficient emphasis, so that Wilson regularly attributes sharp criticism to peripheral possession). On the inherent connection between authority and change, cf. Knuttson: 20, 134.

/28/   E.g., Linton: 129; Beattie: 169; Lannoy: 201-202; Lewis: 66-126 (with special attention to the deprived position of women); Fry: 37; Winkler: 247 and Macdonald: 318 (on indifference to caste). The role of women as shamans and mediums appears to be quite old—in small communities to a large extent as a matter of relative equality (cf., e.g., Czaplicka: 243-255); where heredity plays a part in the selection of shamans or mediums, it not infrequently takes place along matrilineal lines (e.g., W. Schmidt, XII:651; Kuper: 165; Leonard: 151; R. Jones: 49; Sagant: 71).

/29/   See, further, Long: 10, 14. Accuracy of prediction is a feature of the image of a "Mosaic" prophet, according to Wilson: 164, 186, 199, 240, 250; but it is not limited to that tradition.

/30/   The main point of Isa 6 and Mic 3:8 lies in their message (cf. Knierim: 68, and others). Amos 7:15, however, responds to a specific role challenge (Tucker: 431).

/31/   Buxton: 280; Tschopik: 227. The extent to which the motif of a call of a shepherd or peasant is literary, rather than reflecting historical actuality (Schult: 469), remains uncertain.

/32/   The task of personal healing, often associated with that of revelation, cannot be treated here in detail; midwifery is a quite responsible task, which may be included in a diviner's work (Middleton, 1969:225) or—if it is a separate role—can be viewed as assigned by a call (Rowe: 312; Dougherty: 152). On actual responsibility, cf. Ezek 3:16-21 and above, n. 22.

/33/   Cf. "Moses, Moses" in Exod 3:4, "Samuel, Samuel" in 1 Sam 3:10 (cf. vv. 4, 6), the voicing of a name as the substance of an Eskimo call (Spencer: 292), and the triple calling of a name in Nepal (Macdonald: 312). For the relation of self-transcendence to selfhood, see Buss, 1980: 9-10, on responsible individuality, Burridge: *passim*. Hölscher: 196 notes that Amos 7:14-15 is simultaneously modest and proud.

WORKS CONSULTED

Adas, Michael
1979   *Prophets of Rebellion.* Chapel Hill: University of North Carolina.

Anisimov, A. F.
1963   "The Shaman's Tent of the Evenks and the Origin of the Shamanistic Rite." Pp. 84–123 in *Studies in Siberian Shamanism.* Ed. H. N. Michael. Toronto: University of Toronto.

Baltzer, Klaus
1975   *Die Biographie der Propheten.* Neukirchen-Vluyn: Neukirchener.

Barron, Frank
1968   *Creativity and Personal Freedom.* Princeton: Van Nostrand.

Beattie, John
1969   "Spirit Mediumship in Bunyoro." Pp. 159–170 in *Spirit Mediumship and Society in Africa.* Eds. J. Beattie and J. Middleton. London: Routledge and Kegan Paul.

Beidelman, T. O.
1971   "Nuer Priests and Prophets." Pp. 375–415 in *The Translation of Culture: Essays to E. E. Evans-Pritchard.* Ed. T. O. Beidelman. London: Tavistock.

Berlyne, D. E.
1965   *Structure and Direction in Thinking.* New York: Wiley.

Bogoras, Vladimir G.
1909   *The Chukchee.* Leiden: Brill.

Bourguignon, Erika
1979   *Psychological Anthropology.* New York: Holt, Rinehart and Winston.

Bruner, Jerome S.
1962   *On Knowing: Essays for the Left Hand.* Cambridge: Harvard University.

Buccellati, Giorgio
1976   "Towards a Formal Typology of Akkadian Similies." Pp. 59–70 in *Kramer Anniversary Volume: Cuneiform Studies in Honor of Samuel Noah Kramer.* Ed. B. L. Eichler. Kevelaer: Butzon and Bercker.

Burridge, Kenelm O. L.
1979   *Someone, No One: An Essay on Individuality.* Princeton: Princeton University.

Buss, Martin J.
1979   "Understanding Communication." Pp. 3–44 in *Encounter With the Text.* Ed. M. J. Buss. Philadelphia: Fortress and Missoula: Scholars Press.
1980   "The Social Psychology of Prophecy." *Prophecy: Essays Presented to Georg Fohrer.* Ed. J. A. Emerton. Berlin: W. de Gruyter.

Butt, Audrey
1952   *The Nilotes of the Sudan and Uganda.* London: International African Institute.
1966   "Training to be a Shaman" and "A Solitary Among Mountains." Pp. 38–52 in *Trances.* By S. Wavell, *et al.* London: Allen and Unwin.

Buxton, Jean
1975   *Religion and Healing in Mandari.* Oxford: Clarendon.

Carroll, R.P.
1969   "The Elijah-Elisha Sagas." *VT* 19:400–415.

Chadwick, Nora Kershaw
1952   *Poetry and Prophecy.* Cambridge: Cambridge University.

Chapple, Eliot D., and Coon, Carleton S.
1942   *Principles of Anthropology.* New York: Holt.

Colson, Elizabeth
1969   "Spirit Possession Among the Tonga of Zambia." Pp. 69–103 in *Spirit Mediumship and Society in Africa.* Eds. J. Beattie and J. Middleton. London: Routledge and Kegan Paul.

Cooper, John M.
1946   "The Araucanians." *Bureau of American Ethnology Bulletin* 143, II:687–760.

Curtis, John Briggs
1979   "A folk etymology of nābî'." *VT 29:491–493.*

Czaplicka, M. A.
1914   *Aboriginal Siberia.* Oxford: Clarendon.

Dougherty, Molly C.
1978   "Southern Lay Midwives as Ritual Specialists." Pp. 151–164 in *Women in Ritual and Symbolic Roles.* Eds. J. Hoch-Smith and A. Spring. New York: Plenum.

Eder, Matthias
1954/58   "Shamanismus in Japan." *Paideuma* 6:367–380.

Eichhorn, W.
1976   *Die alte chinesische Religion und das Staatskulturwesen.* Leiden: Brill.

Eliade, Mircea
1964   *Shamanism: Archaic Techniques of Ecstasy.* New York: Bollingen Foundation.

Ellenberger, D. Fred., and McGregor, J. C.
1969   *History of the Basuto.* New York: Negro Universities.

Ellenberger, Henry F.
1970   *The Discovery of the Unconscious.* New York: Basic Books.

Elwin, Verrier
1939   *The Baiga.* London: Murray.
1955   *The Religion of an Indian Tribe.* London: Oxford University.

Engnell, Ivan
1949   *The Call of Isaiah.* Uppsala: Lundequistska Bokhandeln.

Evans-Pritchard, E. E.
1937   *Witchcraft, Oracles and Magic Among the Azande.* Oxford: Clarendon.
1940   *The Nuer.* London: Oxford University.

Falkenstein, A., and von Soden, W.
1953   *Sumerische und akkadische Hymnen und Gebete.* Zürich: Artemis.

Fenton, William N.
1953   *The Iroquois Eagle Dance*. Washington: Smithsonian Institution.

Fichtner, J.
1957   "Berufung II. Im AT." *RGG*, 3rd. ed., I:1084-86.

Field, M. J.
1960   *Search for Security: An ethno-psychiatric study of Rural Ghana*. Evanston, Northwestern University.

Findeisen, Hans
1957   *Shamanentum*. Stuttgart: Kohlhammer.

Fry, Peter
1976   *Spirits of Protest*. Cambridge: Cambridge University.

Fuchs, Stephen
1965   *Rebellious Prophets*. New York: Asia Publishing House.

Gelfand, Michael
1959   *Shona Ritual*. Cape Town: Juta.

Gilula, M.
1967   "An Egyptian Parallel to Jeremiah I 4-5." *VT* 17:114.

Gottwald, Norman K.
1979   *The Tribes of Yahweh: A Sociology of the Religion of Liberated Israel, 1250-1050 B.C.E.* Maryknoll: Orbis.

Gouders, Klaus
1972   "Die Berufung des Propheten Jesaja (Jes 6, 1-13)." *Bibel und Leben*, 13:172-184.

Gouldsbury, Cullen, and Sheane, Hubert
1911   *The Great Plateau of Northern Rhodesia*. London: Arnold.

de Groot, J. J. M.
1910   *The Religious System of China*, VI. Brill: Leyden.

Habel, N.
1965   "The Form and Significance of the Call Narratives." *ZAW*, 77:297-323.

Hamer, John and Irene
1966   "Spirit Possession and its Socio-Psychological Implications Among the Sidamo of Southwest Ethiopia." *Ethnology* 5:392-408.

Harva, Uno
1938   *Die religiösen Vorstellungen der altaischen Völker* (FF Communications, 125). Helsinki: Suamlainen Tiedeakatemia.

Harvey, John M., Ickes, William, and Kidd, Robert F.
1978   *New Directions in Attribution Research*, II. Hillsdale, NJ: Erlbaum.

Hayes, John H.
1967   "Prophetism at Mari and Old Testament Parallels." *ATR* 49:397-409.

Heider, Fritz
1958   *The Psychology of Interpersonal Relations*. New York: Wiley.

Heschel, Abraham J.
1962   *The Prophets*. New York: Harper & Row.

Hoebel, E. Adamson
1949   *Man in the Primitive World*. New York: McGraw-Hill.

Hölscher, Gustav
1914   Die Propheten. Leipzig: Hinrichs.

Hoffmann, Y.
1977   "Did Amos regard himself as a nābī'?" VT 27:209–112.

Holladay, William L.
1964   "The Background of Jeremiah's Self-Understanding: Moses, Samuel, and Psalm 22." JBL 83:153–164.

Hori, Ichiro
1968   Folk Religion in Japan. Chicago: University of Chicago.

Horton, Robin
1969   "Types of Spirit Possession in Kalabari Religion." Pp. 14–49 in Spirit Mediumship and Society in Africa. Eds. J. Beattie and J. Middleton. London: Routledge and Kegan Paul.

Jones, Edward E., et al.
1972   Attribution: Perceiving the Causes of Behavior. Morristown, NJ: General Learning.

Jones, Rex L.
1976   "Limbu Spirit Possession and Shamanism." Pp. 29–55 in Spirit Possession in the Nepal Himalayas. Eds. J. T. Hitchcock and R. L. Jones. Warminster: Aris and Phillips.

Jordan, David K.
1972   Gods, Ghosts, and Ancestors: The Folk Religion of a Taiwanese Village. Berkeley: University of California.

Knierim, Rolf
1968   "The Vocation of Isaiah." VT 18:47–68.

Knoll-Greiling, Ursula
1952/3   "Berufung und Berufungserlebnis bei den Schamanen." Tribus 2/3:227–238.

Knuttson, Karl Eric
1967   Authority and Change: A Study of the Kallu Institution Among the Macha Galla of Ethiopia. Göteborg: Elander.

Krader, Lawrence
1954   "Buryat Religion and Society," Southwestern Journal of Anthropology 10:322–351.

Kuper, Hilda
1947   African Aristocracy. New York: Oxford University.

Landes, Ruth
1968   Ojibwa Religion and the Medēwiwin. Madison: University of Wisconsin.

Lannoy, Richard
1971   The Speaking Tree. New York: Oxford University.

Lehtisalo, T.
1924   Entwurf einer Mythologie der Jurak-Samojeden. Helsinki: Société Finno-Ougrienne.

Leonard, Anne P.
1973   "Spirit Mediums in Palau: Transformations in a Traditional System." Pp. 129–177 in Religion, Altered States of Consciousness, and Social Change. Ed. E. Bourguignon. Columbus: Ohio State University.

Lewis, I. M.
1971   Ecstatic Religion. Baltimore: Penguin Books.

Lindblom, Gerhard
1920   The Akamba of British East Africa, 2nd ed. Uppsala: Appelberg.

Lindblom, Johannes
1962   Prophecy in Ancient Israel. Philadelphia: Fortress.

Linton, Ralph
1956   Culture and Mental Disorders. Springfield, IL: Thomas.

Lommel, Andreas
1966   Shamanism: The Beginnings of Art. New York: McGraw-Hill.

Long, Burke O.
1977   "Prophetic Authority as Social Reality." Pp. 3–20 in Canon and Authority. Eds. G.W. Coats and B. O. Long. Philadelphia: Fortress.

Macdonald, A.W.
1976   "Preliminary Report on Some Jhãkri of the Muglan." Pp. 309–341 in Spirit Possession in the Nepal Himalayas. Eds. J. T. Hitchcock and R. L. Jones. Warminster: Aris and Phillips.

Martindale, Colin, and Armstrong, James
1974   "The Relationship of Creativity to Cortical Activation and its Operant Control." Journal of Genetic Psychology 124:311–320.

Martindale, Colin, and Hines, Dwight
1975   "Creativity and Cortical Activation During Creative, Intellectual and EEG Feedback Tasks." Biological Psychology 3:91–100.

McClintock, Walter
1968   The Old North Trail: Life, Legends and Religions of the Blackfeet Indians. Lincoln: University of Nebraska.

Melugin, Roy F.
1976   The Formation of Isaiah 40–55. Berlin: W. de Gruyter.

Métraux, Alfred
1949   "Religion and Shamanism." Bureau of American Ethnology Bulletin 143, V:559–99.
1959   Voodoo in Haiti. New York: Oxford University.

Middleton, John
1969   "Spirit Possession Among the Lugbara." Pp. 220–231 in Spirit Mediumship and Society in Africa. Eds. J. Beattie and J. Middleton. London: Routledge and Kegan Paul.
1971   "Prophets and Rainmakers." Pp. 179–201 in The Translation of Culture: Essays to E. E. Evans-Pritchard. Ed. T. O. Beidelman. London: Tavistock.

Mühlbacher, Engelbert
1876   Die streitige Papstwahl des Jahres 1130. Innsbruck: Wagner.

Murphy, Jane M.
1964   "Psychotherapeutic Aspects of Shamanism on St. Lawrence Island, Alaska." Pp. 53–83 in Magic, Faith, and Healing. Ed. A. Kiev. New York: Free.

Nebesky-Wojkawitz, Réne de
1956   *Oracles and Demons of Tibet.* Mouton: 's-Gravenhage.

Noth, Martin
1958   *Amt und Berufung im Alten Testament.* Bonn: Hanstein. (Reprinted in *Gesammelte Studien*, 3rd ed. Munich: Kaiser.)

Ohlmarks, Åko
1939   *Studien zum Problem des Schamanismus.* Lund: Gleerup.

Olmo Lete, Gregorio del
1973   *La vocacion del lider en el antiguo Israel: Morfologia de los relatos biblicos de vocacion.* Salamanca: Universidad Pontificia, 1973.

Overholt, Thomas W.
1979   "Commanding the Prophets: Amos and the Problem of Prophetic Authority." *CBQ* 41:517–532.

Park, Willard Z.
1938   *Shamanism in Western North America.* Evanston: Northwestern University.

Parker, Arthur C.
1913   "The Code of Handsome Lake, the Seneca Prophet." *New York State Museum Bulletin*, No. 163. Albany: University of the State of New York.

Petersen, David L.
1977   *Late Israelite Prophecy.* Missoula, MT: Scholars Press.

Pressel, Esther
1973   "Umbanda in São Paulo: Religious Innovation in a Developing Society." Pp. 264–318 in *Religion, Altered States of Consciousness, and Social Change.* Ed. E. Bourguignon. Columbus: Ohio State University.

Rad, Gerhard von
1960   *Theologie des alten Testaments,* II. Munich: Kaiser.

Rasmussen, Knud
1908   *The People of the Polar North.* London: Kegan Paul, Trench, Trübner.
1929   *Intellectual Culture of the Iglulik Eskimos.* Copenhagen: Nordisk Forlag.

Ray, Benjamin C.
1976   *African Religions.* Englewood Cliffs, NJ: Prentice-Hall.

Reinhard, Johan
1976   "Shamanism Among the Raji of Southwest Nepal." Pp. 263–292 in *Spirit Possession in the Nepal Himalayas.* Eds. J. T. Hitchcock and R. L. Jones. Warminster: Aris and Phillips.

Reventlow, Henning Graf
1963   *Liturgie und prophetisches Ich bei Jeremia.* Gütersloh: Mohn.

Richter, Wolfgang
1966   *Traditionsgeschichtliche Untersuchungen zum Richterbuch.* Bonn: Hanstein.
1970   *Die sogenannten vorprophetischen Berufungsberichte.* Göttingen: Vandenhoeck & Ruprecht.

Rowe, John Howland
1946   "Inca Culture at the Time of the Spanish Conquest." *Bureau of American Ethnology Bulletin 143*, II:183–330.

Rowley, H. H.
1950   *The Biblical Doctrine of Election*. London: Lutterworth.

Sagant, Philippe
1976   "Becoming a Limbu Priest: Ethnographic Notes." Pp. 56–99 in *Spirit Possession in the Nepal Himalayas*. Eds. J. T. Hitchcock and R. L. Jones. Warminster: Aries and Phillips.

Schärer, Hans
1963   *Nagju Religion*. Trans. R. Needham. The Hague: Nijhoff.

Schenke, Hans-Martin
1963   "Orakelwesen im Alten Ägypten." *Altertum* 9:67–77.

Schmid, Hans Heinrich
1976   *Der sogenannte Jahwist*. Zürich: Theologischer Verlag.

Schmidt, Ludwig
1970   *Menschlicher Erfolg und Jahwes Initiative*. Neukirchen: Neukirchener Verlag.

Schmidt, Wilhelm
1954/55   *Der Ursprung der Gottesidee*, XI and XII. Münster: Aschendorff.

Schoors, A.
1977   "Isaiah, the Minister of Royal Appointment?" *OTS* 20:85–107.

Schreiner, J.
1975   "Jeremias Berufung (Jer 1, 4–19)." Pp. 131–145 in *Homenaje a Juan Prado*. Eds. L. Alvarez Verdes and E. Alonso Hernandez. Madrid: Consejo Superior de Investigaciones Cientificas.

Schult, Hermann
1971   "Amos 7:15a und die Legitimation des Aussenseiters." Pp. 462–478 in *Probleme biblischer Theologie: Gerhard von Rad zum 70. Geburtstag*. Ed. H. W. Wolff. Munich: Kaiser.

Shirokogoroff, S. M.
1935   *Psychomental Complex of the Tungus*. London: Kegan Paul, Trench, Trubner.

Shweder, Richard A.
1972   "Aspects of Cognition in Zincanteco Shamans: Experimental Results." Pp. 407–412 in *Reader in Comparative Religion*, 3rd ed. Eds. W. Lessa and E. Vogt. New York: Harper and Row.

Silverman, Julian
1967   "Shamans and Acute Schizophrenia." *American Anthropologist* 69:21–31.

Spencer, Robert F.
1959   *The North Alaskan Eskimo*. (Bureau of North American Ethnology Bulletin 171.) Washington: Government Printing Office.

Spiro, Melford E.
1967   *Burmese Supernaturalsim*. Englewood Cliffs, NJ: Prentice-Hall.

Steck, O. H.
1972 "Bemerkungen zu Jesaja 6." *BZ* 16:188–206.

Tanner, R. E. S.
1969 "The Theory and Practice of Sukuma Spirit Mediumship." Pp. 273–289 in *Spirit Mediumship and Society in Africa*. Eds. J. Beattie and J. Middleton. London: Routledge and Kegan Paul.

Taylor, Douglas MacRae
1951 *The Black Carib of British Honduras*. New York: Wenner-Gren Foundation.

Tschopik, Harry, Jr.
1951 "The Aymara of Chucuito, Peru. l. Magic." *Anthropological Papers of the American Museum of Natural History*, 44:133–308.

Tucker, Gene M.
1973 "Prophetic Authenticity." *Int* 27:423–434.

Turnbull, Colin M.
1965 *Wayward Servants: The Two Worlds of the African Pygmies*. Garden City, NY: The Natural History Press.

Underhill, Ruth M.
1969 *Papago Indian Religion*. New York: AMS Press (original, 1946).

Vater, Ann
1976 *The Communication of Messages and Oracles as a Narration Medium in the Old Testament* (Dissertation, Yale University). Ann Arbor: University Microfilms.

Vincent, Jean M.
1977 *Studien zur literarischen Eigenart und zur geistigen Heimat von Jesaja, Kap. 40–55*. Frankfurt a. M.: Lang.

Wallis, Wilson D.
1918 *Messiahs: Christian and Pagan*. Boston: Badger.

Weber, Max
1951 *The Religion of China*. Glencoe: Free Press.
1956 *Wirtschaft und Gesellschaft*. 4th ed. Tübingen: Mohr.

Wellhausen, J.
1897 *Reste arabischen Heidentums*. 2nd ed. Berlin: W. de Gruyter.

Westcott, Malcolm R.
1968 *Toward a Contemporary Psychology of Intuition*. New York: Holt, Rinehart and Winston.

Westermann, Claus
1966 *Das Buch Jesaja: Kapitel 40–66*. Göttingen: Vandenhoeck & Ruprecht.

Wilson, Robert R.
1980 *Prophecy and Society in Ancient Israel*. Philadelphia: Fortress.

Winkler, Walter F.
1976 "Spirit Possession in Far Western Nepal." Pp. 244–262 in *Spirit Possession in the Nepal Himalayas*. Eds. J. T. Hitchcock and R. L. Jones, Warminster: Aris and Phillips.

Wissler, Clark
    1912   *Ceremonial Bundles of the Blackfoot Indians.* New York: American Museum of Natural History.

Wright, G. Ernest
    1950   *The Old Testament Against its Environment.* Chicago: Regnery.

Zimmerli, Walther
    1979   *Ezechiel,* I. Neukirchen-Vluyn: Neukirchener Verlag.

SOCIAL DIMENSIONS OF PROPHETIC CONFLICT

Burke O. Long
Bowdoin College

ABSTRACT

Anthropological studies emphasize the importance of situation-specific social factors for understanding conflict among various types of prophetic figures. Conflict is normal, and complex; it involves personal, social, economic, and political dynamics as well as ideologies. We should weigh the importance of these factors relative to each other in any given situation. The social effects of conflict may be positive, negative, or both, depending on factors at work in a particular society and time.

Against this background, we look at a Biblical example of conflict (Jeremiah 26–29; 36–38) and explore the social dimensions relevant to both the *tradition* of conflict and the historically reconstructed *situations* of Jeremiah's day. (1) The Jeremiah traditions are paradigmatic. To survivors of national destruction, they explain the reason for exile, and lessen "cognitive dissonance," by reaffirming belief in God-given monarchy and prophecy; they seek vindication of "true" prophesying and "right" rule. The traditions of conflict transform a prophetic impulse into a text of implicit warning. The tradents may even assert a precedent within the advocacy of pure Yahwism for an exilic political policy favorable to co-existence with Babylonian rule. (2) There were few or no social (class) distinctions between Jeremiah and his opponents among the prophets, priests, and governmental officers. Jeremiah gained position and support from a network of blood and social relationships extending back into Josiah's court and into the highest reaches of contemporary royal and cultic service. Among people of high birth and professional connection, Jeremiah joined in a political struggle between "autonomist" and "coexistence" options for national policy. Partisans of both persuasions at various times exercised political authority, and continued their vicious struggles even after exile. Both options found ample Yahwistic, theological justification among prophets. Since Jeremiah was aligned with the "coexistence" policy, as were the later bearers of his tradition, this policy's attendant triumphalist religious ideology now dominates our vision.

0.1 The Hebrew Bible frequently alludes to conflict involving the prophets—conflict with each other and with various other people with whom they interacted, or to whom they addressed their oracles. At the same time, because of its viewpoint which champions an impeccable Yahwistic faith, the Bible tends to view these conflicts almost exclusively in ideological terms. It is a question of truth, and of a prophet truly sent by God: true religion, prediction, reading of events; true understanding of religious norms; true homily for a needy people, e.g., Ezek 13:1–19; Jer 23:9–15; Mic 3:5–8. Accordingly, the Bible tends to ignore, or to suppress, the societal aspects of conflict—those personal, political, social, and economic factors that would have been a part of any public display of rivalry. The Biblical traditions may even foster a slightly negative attitude toward conflict, which after all, interferes with a person's being a prophet. Conflict is something to be endured and suffered in the interest of a higher duty to one's holy calling (see I Kgs 22:24–28; Jer 1:7–8, 18–19; 20:7–12; Ezek 3:8–9).

0.2   Naturally, this perspective on the prophets' conflicts reflects the bias of those who collected and authored the Biblical materials. Careful study of the traditions has exposed therein a history of developing consensus among people who were convinced of the religious truth and value of *certain* individual prophets, and of the falsity of those who opposed them. We now see a stereotype in which *any* opposition to a prophet who came to be canonized is viewed simply, and simplisticly, as anti-prophetic, anti-Yahwistic, as a misguided and even virulent paganism (Hossfeld and Meyer: 113).

Despite a few neutralist voices among historians of religion (e.g., Ringgren: 215–16; Lindblom: 211–12), this theological interest and commitment have remained at the center of the studies on prophetic conflict. Consequently, for most critics, the canonical tilt toward ideologically drawn pictures persists.

In one form, the bias shows up in the fixation on truth and falsity as an issue, perhaps *the* issue, in the earliest translators (Septuagint and Targum) down to the latest historical critical investigations. This stream of discussion was brought to a modern watershed by G. Quell (1952), who moved beyond *a priori* and pejorative assumptions about the moral character, motivations, and intentions of so-called "false" prophets, and set the agenda for subsequent study. It is now widely held that criteria for distinguishing true from false were, and are, illusive and subjective, quite incapable of generalization (von Rad; Osswald; Hossfeld and Meyer; Crenshaw). Nevertheless, the quest goes on, dressed recently as a problem in hermeneutics. The (true) prophet was one who turned out in time to be flexible, alive to the shifting situation, and above all sensitive of Yahweh's transcendent freedom to do a new and surprising thing with his people Israel. In ancient Israel, true or false was a matter of correct or incorrect interpretation of authoritative Israelite traditions (Sanders, 1972: 73–90; 21–41; see Kaufmann: 278–79; Overholt: 43–44). Taking account of our skeptical and pluralistic times, one may say that in these recent discussions the Biblical claims of truth in all their boldness were suspended or, at least, muted for purposes of scholarly description, but the Biblical formulation of the problem posed by conflict was embraced. To this extent, the social, non-theological dimensions of the prophets' conflicts were largely, if not entirely, overlooked.

Even when the focus of study is on the prophets' conflicts with the royal houses, the canonical bias dominates scholarly imagination. For example, in an exhaustive study of I Kings 22, Simon de Vries not only ranks the prophet's problem with the king as the most important, but he defines the problem theologically—just as do the author-editor(s) of the Biblical traditions. Micaiah ben Imlah, the hero, emerges in our mind's eye as the defender of true Yahwism over against the hubristic, self-serving royal establishment.

> It is clear that the most central conflict was the constant polarity between the spiritual power of prophecy insisting on Yahweh's absolute priority, and the political establishment—theoretically instrumental but ever prone to forsake its status as servant to Yahweh and the people.... conflict is always between covenant integrity and political opportunism. (de Vries, 148; cf. Th.C Vriezen: 42–43.)

One last example. James Crenshaw has written an admirable book in which he emphasizes that the inevitable conflict among the prophets grew out of the nature of prophecy itself. Appeals to higher transcendent authority, charges and counter charges, the inner struggles of the prophets with self-doubt, all fueled controversy. For Crenshaw, it is a theological problem, theologically imagined:

> Within the two-fold task of the reception of the word of God in the experience of divine mystery and the articulation of that word to man in all its nuances and with persuasive cogency rest multiple possibilities for error and disbelief. (Crenshaw: 3)

And the outcome, the eventual collapse of prophecy as a viable religious institution, is evaluated theologically.

> ... the conflict between prophets so degraded the prophetic movement that its witness was weakened and prophetic theology was too burdensome to overcome such a weakenss. (Crenshaw: 108)

0.3   The theological approach to prophetic conflict is neither incorrect nor inappropriate. But like any method, it limits while illuminating. In order to engage overlooked, but important, aspects of the Israelite situation, we must be absolutely clear about the theological interests of both the Bible and the bulk of critical scholarship. Often in details that may escape the theologian's eye (that of the Biblical narrator as well as the commentator) lie hints of social, economic, and political currents helpful in giving us fuller historical understanding. In quest for this elusive and indirect evidence, we find some help in contemporary anthropological studies where access to a particular culture is not limited to literary texts. Such aid comes not in the form of directly comparative data, but as enriching stimulus to historical and sociological imagination. From anthropology we gain a wider range of questions, a heightened sense of the relative place of ideology (or theology) along side of other forms of social exprssion, and a feel for what might be worth investigating in ancient Israel.

This article is especially concerned with some social aspects of conflict among the Hebrew prophets. We will survey a few recent anthropological studies related to this sugject, and armed with this new background material, look again at selected Biblical traditions.

1.0   At the outset, we must realize that the word "prophet" has been used in a number of different ways by ethnographers. A broad range of material discusses diviners, priests, oracle givers, shamans, witches and mediums in rather culturally specific ways. These titles, if there is a corresponding native word for such, often overlap to a considerable degree in a given society, and religious functions may blend and separate in quite specific ways. To be able to gain from these studies, a flexible stance is helpful. We follow Wilson (27-28; see Fry: 30; Carley: 242-43) in speaking generally of an "intermediary," that is, of a religious specialist who works in contact with the divine reality, and who brings forth for his public direct or indirect messages through which others gain access to, and benefits from, the supranatural world. From this standpoint, then, we may mention a few relevant studies. I have been selective rather than exhaustive, citing works which illuminate the social dimensions of conflict among intermediaries, and which seem to me to be particularly useful to Biblical scholars because of the specific character and history of our discipline.

1.1   As part of a thorough study of the shaman (="master of the spirits," Eliade: 3-13; Shirokogoroff: 269) as a social and religious institution among the Evenks of Eastern Siberia, A. F. Anisimov provides a detailed description of a curative seance. After the disease spirit had been captured and expelled with raucous and aggressive ceremony, there followed the ritual "vengeance of the shaman and his spirits on the shaman of the hostile clan . . . (wherein) exclamations of indignation and threats descended from all sides onto the evil alien shaman" (Anisimov: 105). The alien shaman, seen as the cause of disease among clan members, naturally bears the brunt of this purgation (cf. the ritualized combat among the South American Yanomamö in Chagnon). This form of conflict received social reinforcement not only in the public ritual but in the cultural mythology about the shaman himself. The master healer possesses a *marylya*, a mythical fence consisting of those spirits controlled by the shaman and built to protect his clan from the invasion of evil spirits from alien sources. Some of the protective spirits are weak, however, and sometimes an evil spirit at the behest of an alien shaman breaks through the defenses, bringing disease or misfortune. Hence, the necessity of shamanizing, and the appropriateness of a curative procedure dramatizing conflict and power; the shaman aims to drive off the spirit, and to repair the protective fence around the clan (Anisimov: 111-12). Thus ritual conflict among shamans is fully expected. It is thought to be essential and is explainable in the society's world view.

Conflict is also a positive world-maintaining social force because it is connected with healing and maintaining the equilibrium of the Evenk clan. Such social functions are entirely consistent with the highly professional, specialistic, and status conscious role of the shaman among the Evenks. Winning these important battles with the alien spirits (and their shamans) is a way to defend power and position through public works—all part of the shaman's social network which offers an extraordinarily privileged status to a chosen few (Anisimov: 114–15).

1.11 Asen Balikci (1967; 1970) paints a similar picture for Netsilik Eskimo shamans. Based in part on the North American expedition reports of Rasmussen, Balikci (1967) interprets the shaman's powers and rituals as means to (1) deal with environmental threats which endangered the clan; (2) mitigate individual or group crises; (3) control interpersonal relations, including the aggressive and competitive acts by shamans against others; and (4) support and enhance the shaman's own prestige among the clan members.

Where the shaman is in conflict with members of his clan or with other shamans, it becomes a matter of competition for superior status, power, and recognition. Informants told Balikci about contests of supernatural strength which sometimes involved aggressive behavior, and often the working of miracles before an appreciative audience. People who claim to have seen such performances speak with awe and admiration about the ability of the shamans; folk tales, particularly, remember the power of some great shamans of the past (Balikci, 1967: 203–204). /1/

As in the Evenk groups, this aggressive behavior seems to have been supported by belief in a hostile cosmos from which one needed powerful protection. Shamanizing and shamanistic conflict not only were expected, but in a dramatic way mirrored the hidden world of the spirits. Conflict seems therefore to reinforce both the clan's world view and the shaman's central position in society. Nevertheless, discreet criticism and skepticism of particular practitioners may be privately expressed by a few (Rasmussen; 54–55).

1.12 Shirokogoroff gives us a much fuller picture of the shaman's social position among the Tungus of Siberia. In the days before extensive Russian European influence, the shaman was an important figure who stood at the head of a network of social relations built out of contacts and dealings with clients. As with the Evenks and the Netsilik Eskimos, the Tungus shaman carried out his profession against the ideological backdrop of a spirit filled cosmos from which mankind needed protection. Ironically, while regulating the social and psychological equilibrium of the clan, the shaman's own social position was, according to Shirokogoroff, delicate and in need of constant fine tuning. Lacking the absolute authority of the priest, and the political position of the clan "chief," the shaman was dependent upon public opinion, which monitored his every step. His shamanizing in public, while supported by the group's liking for social gatherings, nevertheless faced a range of reactions—from full approval to hostile interference. Success in curing and bringing on a kind of group "ecstasy" brought him status. Failure, brought lowered prestige, perhaps disuse. Such public evaluations were individual matters, however, and need not weaken confidence in the institution of shamanism. Even individual failure could sometimes be explained ideologically by pointing to evil spirits which could not be fought, or to an evil shaman, a "bad person," whose aggressive and hostile powers proved too strong (Shirokogoroff: 332–378; 342–344; 376–378; 332–334).

In this context of fragile reputations and guarded positions, the Tungus knew a much more dangerous form of shamanic conflict: the "wars" between shamans who were personal rivals for power and influence, or representatives of clan hostilities. Battles in the form of competition in art and murder took place while dreaming or awake. But the results were thought to be tangible indeed—mystifying deaths, illness, bodily mutilations, intractable disease, and the like. Among certain groups of Tungus, these shamanic conflicts had a decidedly negative effect on the public attitude toward shamanizing. For most groups, however, negative feelings were directed only at individual practitioners. These "bad persons" were feared, not consulted, and in other ways were socially isolated by clansmen. They were also fought by ritual means. Shamanism as an institution thereby remained intact, supported by ideologies and social forces more powerful than individual competing shamans (Shirokogoroff: 371–372).

1.2   A thorough and substantial study of mediums (=a human channel of communication from the spirits, the god, or the gods) among the Zezuru in southern Rhodesia provides yet another picture of social authority, status, and conflict (Fry). For the Zezuru medium, as among many other peoples, public success depends upon an ability to articulate common consensus, especially in politics (i.e., African nationalism), and his day to day "capacity as a diviner, his ability to foster a wide circle of adherence, his ability as a showman, and a certain amount of luck" (Fry: 33–42).

Conflict with the public is built into the social order. Insofar as status rests upon public opinion, undergirded of course by certain ideologies relating to spirits and the specialists' role in mediating their influence, conflict with members of the public including other mediums may result in being dismissed as a fraud or simply down-graded. More rarely, a Zezuru medium might be *totally* discredited because of a flagrant violation of social norms (Fry: 43). He might be only *partially* discredited when suspected of feigning his "trance" (Fry: 44) or on the basis of a public challenge to the identity of his spirit presentation, rather than a more radical challenge to his mediumship (Fry: 68–106). A particularly interesting case involved one called "Wild Man," who claimed to be the medium of the legendary spirit,

Chaminuka, a famous Shona oracle-giver and rainmaker (see Cripps). Another person, one Muchatera, claimed also to be *Chaminuka's* medium, and pointedly observed that it was impossible for two people to act as hosts for the same spirit. A public meeting was thereby arranged. According to *Drum* magazine, the two claimants exchanged deprecatory comments with one another, and Muchatera challenged the "Wild Man" to make rain, whereupon he climbed up a small rock, waved his arms, and rain clouds appeared. The "Wild Man" and his supporters demanded the withdrawal of Muchatera, who did in fact leave, disgraced. Later, the "Wild Man" announced that Muchatera was not the medium of *Chaminuka*, but of another spirit, *Zhanje*. Fry's analysis follows:

> The import of the *Drum* article was that the 'Wild Man' was the true *Chaminuka* medium whereas Muchatera was a fraud. However, such questions are relative, for the status of a particular medium depends on the population which supports him. In this case, Muchatera's authority was based on his followers who were far away in Rusape. The 'Wild Man's' status as the true medium of *Chaminuka* was guaranteed by the presence of his followers at Chitungwiza [where the meeting took place]. Muchatera was partially discredited because he was 'playing away' and it is quite probable that the outcome would have been reversed had the meeting taken place in Rusape [Muchatera's home]. (Fry: 43–44).

Conflict primarily with other mediums rather than the general public is built into the social order because claims of supernatural warrant and proper ritual initiations, even successful mediation with the spirits, are not sufficient in themselves to guarantee success and social status, both of which—contrary to the Zezuru ideology of mediumship—are in fact important to individuals (Fry: 36). In practice, authority is built and maintained by creating a network of client and peer relationships. In this situation, endemic rivalry among mediums is a given, as they compete for positions of power and status relative to various factions in the populace. In Fry's words:

> The overall situation is best described in terms of networks and spheres of influence. Each medium, on being initiated, incorporates himself into the ritual network of the mediums who are involved in the initiation. If he is successful as a high level medium he in his turn will initiate new mediums who join the wider network through joining his, and so on. In this way successful mediums are able to build up networks which ramify continuously and which are not bounded. These spheres of influence reach the lay public through their contact with the mediums as clients, as attenders of rituals, but these ritual networks are not stable or exclusive. Their stability is threatened by the competition between mediums which is endemic to the system and which may bring a medium to challenge the authority of the medium who initiated him, in order to alter relationships within the network or to establish a new network with him as center. (Fry: 45).

A good deal of Fry's book is in fact given over to intensive case study material which penetrates the complexities of these social networks. He was a close observer of the entry of his assistant, Thomas Mutero, into high-level spirit mediumship, and witnessed a long and difficult process in which Mutero met not only considerable opposition in the village from the senior low level mediums in the village, but became embroiled in a long standing dispute between his full and paternal half-brother. Eventually the personal, village level disputes touched on the larger Black nationalist movement in Rhodesia, the support of which was a major source for the social strength of mediumship (Fry: 68–106; 107–123).

1.3   It is clear from Fry's analysis that competition, public rivalry, and conflict were as much a part of the Zezuru medium's life as ritual performances. And equally important. Conflict served to destroy and to build status and influence, to challenge a social situation, and to adapt to changing situations—including the political movements in Rhodesia. Conflict was a constant and positive means of adjusting the "system" to the rise and fall of various mediums in the society. It seemed to have less to do with ideological differences than with social and political dynamics.

But is not conflict among intermediaries divisive rather than upbuilding? The answer must be in some cases, yes, in others, no, in others, both yes and no. Certainly for the Zezuru medium, conflict both builds and tears social fabric. For the Nuba peoples, of the southern Sudan, whom Nadel (1946) studied, conflict seemed more clearly divisive. Highest ranking shamans were remembered as leaders in the widest sense; they were appealed to regularly, and looked to for leadership in war. They would advise on blood feuds between clans and ordain wars to be fought. Equally, they might recommend peace and reconciliation, and negotiate on behalf of communities or kinship groups. But shamanistic leadership was fluid, irregular, localized, and often conflicting. The shamans were rivals of one another, and frequently divided the people. In Nadel's words:

> One shaman, entrusted with the supervision of some ceremonial, would unite the community in one way and on certain occasions; the war shaman would unite it in a different way and for different purposes. The leadership of each would last only while he was alive or unrivalled by the priest [shaman] of a stronger spirit. Rival war shamans and other *kujurs* frequently divided the people. The Nyima rebellion of 1918 collapsed so easily because a *kurjur* prophesying the downfall of its leader caused a large section of the community to desert the cause (Nadel: 31).

Similarly, Kingsley Garbett (1977) has noted for modern Zimbabwe the divisive effect of competition among factions which claim rival intermediaries and spiritual sanctions for their political programs (Garbett: 86–87). On the other hand, Elizabeth Colson (1977) observed a more complex situation among the Tonga peoples of Zambia. She studied conflict and tension between prophets ("possessed" oracle-givers) and custodians of local shrines (ritual officiants carrying out seasonal religious duties). In the situation following government resettlement of large numbers of people, however, this tension had a double effect. When resettled prophets criticized a shrine or its custodian, disputing, for example, matters of shrine maintenance, the prophets emphasized by their actions their freedom to reassert innovative leadership in a new geographic area. On the other hand, this public conflict indirectly highlighted the "social maintenance" role of traditional shrines, and their importance in meeting needs for continuity among the resettled prophets. Thus, conflict affirmed both the prophetic "free" role and status, while underlining the important conservative social functions of shrines (Colson: 119-139, esp. 128-135).

1.4   Reviewing these various studies with due caution and allowing for the uneven quality of data and interpretation, we may venture a few summarizing comments. First, conflict among intermediaries is obviously a complex, little-studied, imcompletely understood social phenomenon. Second, conflict is highly situational—that is, related to, and expressive of social dynamics in particular societies. Full understanding requires more information than we usually have for a given example. Third, conflict in the mediational process is certainly normal, if not inevitable. /2/ The potential for disputes lies in the claim to supernatural mediation—spirit possession, manipulation of the spirits, disputes over the value of, and interpretations given to, messages from these spirits. The potential for conflict lies also in the social components of such ideological matters: competition for status, influence, and power in situations where religious authority tends to be pragmatically given and removed by public concensus (Fry). Fourth, it is important to conceive of such conflicts in both their ideological and social aspects. Given the variety in the examples we have seen, we may recognize, according to the weight given to various factors, different *kinds* of conflict among intermediaries, such as personal, ideological, and political. But no typology should fail to take into account the degree and extent of overlap in characteristic features and social involvements. /3/ It seems appropriate always to ask about the relative weight these factors may have, and how this may differ from express comments made by participants.

The social effects of conflict among intermediaries is also complex, shifting, and varied. Although Nadel and Garbett mentioned in passing the divisive, negative consequences of disputes among shamans and mediums, other studies clarified more positive effects as well. Depending on the situation, and a given society's basic view of reality, conflict might be supportive and protective of community (Anisimov; Balikci), somewhat disruptive (Shirokogoroff), or expressive of a socially healthy and upbuilding tension between need for innovation and conservation of religious values (Colson). Disputes among intermediaries may also be important to an individual's maintaining both social position and adaptability in changing circumstances (Fry). Finally conflict may, but need not, undermine public acceptance of the mediation process (Shirokogoroff), although it may have something to do with an individual's credibility among his peers. (Fry) /4/

2.0   In the light of these anthropological studies, some of the special problems associated with trying to reconstruct social aspects of conflict among Biblical prophets are all the more obvious. The historical and social distance between text and situation to which text might refer, a point of view more theological than sociological, a one-sided, Yahweh-triumphant perspective on conflict and opposition—these are the main problems to be dealt with, but not entirely overcome. I have chosen to comment on a few major scenes of conflict in Jeremiah 26-29 and 37-38, which, because of their fullness of detail, offer the best hope of adding some important information to our understanding.

2.1   There is widespread agreement among critics that early exilic Deuteronomistic (Dtr) editors had a determinative hand in shaping the materials in Jeremiah 26; 27-29; 37-38. There is less agreement when it comes to spelling out details of that editing or isolating original traditions (see Hossfeld and Meyer; Nicholson; Seidl; Kessler). It seems the safest course, therefore, to consider first the matter of conflict from the perspective of these latest editors.

2.11   Jeremiah 26 highlights the fate of the divine word as spoken by Jeremiah and as resisted by King Jehoiakim. It is this king who by implication acquiesces to the priests, opposition prophets, and all the people in the hostile rejection of Jeremiah (vv 7-9). And this same Jehoiakim is explicitly said to have spurned the word and person of yet another prophet (vv 20-23; cf. Jer 22:13-19). These two pictures of conflict and rejection now frame a scene of apparent reprieve for Jeremiah: "This man does not deserve the sentence of death, for he has spoken to us in the name of Yahweh our God." (v 16). The point seems to be a double one: Jeremiah is spared (vv 16-19, 24) and yet the hopes raised in v 3 that the divine word might achieve its end are dashed. The tradents cite no repentance by this king, but only a second instance of obstinate hostility toward a Yahweh prophet.

In Jeremiah 27-29, despite problems in some details, it is clear that we are meant to see a unit of thematic consistency. The tradition develops two events: chaps. 27-28, Jeremiah's word about the inevitable Babylonian conquest in King Zedekiah's day (after a first deportation to Babylon of certain leaders in 597 B.C.E.), and chap. 29, a letter from the prophet to these same exiles. These two events, linked by the symbol of ox yoke and Jeremiah's word, are now woven together as material about Jeremiah and prophets who rejected his message. The effect is to dramatize the singularity of Jeremiah's view—speaking for Yahweh over against many whose heads and hearts were turned to others—and to maintain the correctness and eventual triumph of Jeremiah's position. Having focused in this way on the rejection of the divine word in chaps. 26-29, the text goes on to tell of Jeremiah's rejection and violent treatment during Zedekiah's reign (Jer 37-38), and his ultimate vindication in events of exile (Jer 39:1-10) and rescue (Jer 39:11-14).

2.12   Clearly, we are reading in all these chapters a Dtr vision of the failure of a nation and its religion, focused like a prism on the actions of Kings Jehoiakim and Zedekiah, princes, and prophets (principally Hananiah and Shemaiah) /5/. In Jeremiah 26, the issue is not so much conflict among the prophets or between Jeremiah and his public as it is the fate of Jeremiah's message, seen now as the true word of God. Will the word be heeded or ignored? True, the message provoked hostile reactions, and eventually Jeremiah escaped harm, but in the eyes of the final editors this incident along with Jehoiakim's treatment of another prophet, Uriah ben Shemaiah, seems to have been treated as illustrative of the failure of a people to turn to Yahweh alone for guidance. These scenes are paradigmatic for the editor and perhaps for his audience. One cannot ignore Jeremiah and his words, preserved of course in tradition, nor should one ignore the "type" of the pious king, represented in Hezekiah (26:18–19; cf. the Dtr evaluation of Hezekiah in 2 Kings 18:1–18).

Similarly, chaps. 27–29 defend the correctness of Jeremiah's word and the legitimacy of this particular prophet in the long line of those prophets who were sent as messengers of warning to a stubborn people (28:8–9; 29:19; cf. 2 Kgs 17:13–14, a classic Dtr text). For the editor, it is not the institution of prophecy which is on trial, but certain practitioners, just as the monarchy is not in itself religiously misguided, only certain kings. Indeed, in Jeremiah 26, the value of prophecy as a means of mediation with the deity is affirmed by citing as a positive model the earlier incident involving Micah and King Hezekiah (26:18–19). And in chap. 28, the editor must have defended Jeremiah over against his look-alike Yahweh prophet Hananiah by succinctly showing Jeremiah's word of death to Hananiah fulfilled ("In that same year, in the seventh month, the prophet Hananiah died." v 17) and by repeating Hananiah's prophecy of a short exile (v 3) in a tradition aimed at an exilic prople who had already experienced its disconfirmation. The perspective is no different in chap. 27, where Jeremiah opposes other prophets, and where the Dtr ideology of the legitimate prophet is applied to the opposition (27:18). The institution is not questioned, but a number of practitioners *en masse* are measured and found wanting.

2.13   In this later editorial context, the *traditions* of Jeremiah's conflict functioned obviously to explain the catastrophe of exile in terms of the transgressions of king and people, mainly their refusal to heed the consistent warnings of Yahweh's messengers, especially the one called Jeremiah whom hindsight and devotion now deemed to be among those truly sent to a misguided people. The *tradition* of conflict, therefore, carried with it certain ideological claims, and this probably meant that it also was addressed to a situation of ideological confusion and or competition following the demise of temple, monarchy, and cult in 587 B.C.E. If we might apply the categories of "cognitive dissonance" (Festinger; cf. R. P. Carroll), we might suggest that when the basic social, political, and religious institutions were destroyed, and consequently their religious underpinnings called into question, the Dtr editors could have lessened dissonance over disconfirming facts by reinterpreting tradition in the light of new circumstances. Belief in monarchy, Yahwism, and prophecy is reaffirmed by remembering paradigmatic examples of "true" prophesying, and "right" rule, and by attributing present circumstances to improper handling of these God-given trusts. /6/

The traditions of conflict may also have served as a kind of homily in this exilic period. As paradigmatic literature, they represented a transformation of the prophetic impulse into a textual tradition of implicit warning to a later generation—those who bore and those who heard the filtered memory of the events spiraling to disaster. The Dtr ideology of prophet, as reflected in 2 Kgs 17:13-15, is embodied as it were in Jeremiah 26, 27-29. These incidents become warnings, therefore, and carry with them a "prophetic" exhortation—as do the prose traditions dealing with law in the Book of Jeremiah—"turn again (to *Tôrāh*) and live" (Jer 7-8:3; 17:19-27; 18:1-12; 24:4-7; 29:10-14; Nicholson: 57-93). Whether or not conflict among prophets was a live issue for the Dtr editor(s) remains uncertain. The self-serving assertions found in Zechariah, " . . . you shall know that Yahweh of hosts has sent me . . . " might suggest that such conflict among intermediaries was not unknown in the exile and post exilic periods (Zech 2:15 [= 2:11 RSV]; 6:15; see Petersen).

2.2   Can we see anything of these conflicts other than what the Dtr editor wanted us to see? Perhaps so, by focusing on elements in the tradition not directly expressive of the editor(s) apologetic and homiletic interests.

2.21   The prophet delivers oracles to Israelite kings, priests, princes and people, as well as to the kings of neighboring states (Jer 27:4-11). Even allowing for exaggeration, it seems justified to say that Jeremiah at the least worked as a highly placed oracle-giver (cf. Jer 37:3, 17; 38:14-28), who enjoyed certain influence with at least one King (Zedekiah) (37:17-20), but who was opposed by certain of Zedekiah's high ranking men (Jer 38:1-6) and sometimes even the king (such as Jehoiakim [Jeremiah 26 and 36]). We get some indication of the social and political status of these opponents from Jeremiah 38. The text, as usual, has been pointed by later interest in the eventual rescue and vindication of Jeremiah (vv 7-13; cf. 39:15-18), but the details of name and family in 38:1 ring truly. The "princes" (*sārîm*) who plot against Jeremiah are among the elite in the land. Gedaliah is the son of Pashhur, presumably the priest who was in charge of the temple (he is *pāqîd nāgîd bĕbêt YHWH* in 20:1) and who was an opponent of Jeremiah (20:1-6). Jehucal (Jucal) turns up elsewhere in a delegation of two persons, one of whom is a priest, sent by King Zedekiah to Jeremiah for divinatory consultation during the military siege of Jerusalem (37:3). Similarly Pashhur, son of Malchiah, is one of two persons, and again the second is a priest, sent by King Zedekiah to Jeremiah for consultation when the Babylonians first attacked the city (21:1). In both instances, the priest is Zephaniah ben Maaseiah, who is the second ranking priest in the kingdom (Jer 52:24), and who possesses some kind of supervisory power over prophets in the temple compound (Jer 29:25). Shephatiah is unknown.

2.22   If there was some presumed difference in social status between Jeremiah and the princes who opposed him, there is little or no evidence that he differed in any way from his prophetic opponents. Jeremiah is opposed by another Yahweh prophet, Hananiah, in chap. 28, without any hint of social distinction. They speak with similar language, using typical prophetic forms of discourse, and ply their trade inside the temple compound in the presence of priests. In chap. 29, it is a Yahweh prophet in exile, Shemaiah, who complains to a priest in Jerusalem about Jeremiah's activities; and they are Yahweh prophets who are said by the people to have been "raised up by Yahweh" in Babylon, and who are condemned by Jeremiah (29:15, 21-22). Furthermore, both Jeremiah and his prophetic opponents are pictured as delivering oracles to the king (Jer 27:12-15). Moreover, both Jeremiah and his prophetic opponents share the common characteristic of being native to villages outside the royal and religious capital. Hananiah comes from Gibeon (28:1), Jeremiah himself from Anathoth (1:1), and Shemaiah from Nehelan. Even those prophets cited in the traditions as ideologically akin to Jeremiah, are similarly remembered to have been non-Jerusalemites (Uriah, 26:20; Micah, 26:18). None of these prophets, including Jeremiah, claim a special status because of place of birth or family associations. But they may in fact have had in common the social background and culture of village life.

2.23   Jeremiah and his prophetic opponents also appear to have been associated with priests and their cultic affairs. The Dtr editors pictured the prophets as oracle givers to both king and priest (27:16b; 28:1). They viewed Jeremiah in exactly the same way (27:16a; 28:5; 29:1). As far as we can tell, this view of the editor(s) is consistent with historical fact. In Jer 29:26, a Yahweh prophet who opposes Jeremiah appeals to a priest, Zephaniah, and thereby implies that the latter has some authority over, or at least working association with, prophets who prophesy in the temple. The exact nature of Zephaniah's authority is unclear. At the least, the tradition assumes a relationship that made a complaint before a priest a sensible course of action for disputing prophets.

From other texts, we may sketch something more of this association of priest and prophet. Jeremiah enjoyed free access to the temple (26:1; 35:2-4) /7/ and speaks in the temple before priests (28:5); so does his rival, Hananiah (28:1). According to Jer 26:7, Jeremiah's temple audience consists of priests, prophets, and "all the people." These references may be nothing more than narrative stereotyping, however. A more reliable indication is the oracle in 23:11, which implies that both priest and prophet regularly operate within the temple:

> Both prophet and priest are ungodly;
>   even in my house I have found their wickedness,
>   says the LORD (Jer 23:11; cf. Lam 2:20)

Or again, Jeremiah says:

> The prophets prophesy falsely,
>   while priests make rulings /8/
>   at their direction. (Jer 5:30–31)

Quite without tendentiousness, Jer 35:4 mentions a special chamber in the temple set aside for the "sons of Hanan ben Igdaliah, the man of God," that is, for a guild of prophets attached to Hanan ben Igdaliah. We recall, too, that Nathan, the prophet, and Zadok, the priest, worked together in the coronation of Solomon (I Kgs 1:26, 32–40). Similarly, in Zech 7:1–14, both priest and prophet are involved in a cooperative effort at rebuilding the temple. All these passages suggest a long-standing association of priest and prophet (Johnson: 60–64). They further suggest no important distinction between Jeremiah and his rival prophets in this regard. The details escape us. But apparently Jeremiah, his rivals, and the priests are functionaries in associated systems for dealing with the national deity.

2.24   In sum, the evidence suggests that there was little social distinction between Jeremiah and his prophetic rivals, and they had much in common. A typology of "peripheral" and "central" to describe and/or contrast their relationships to central governmental authority does not seem appropriate (against Wilson). On the other hand, the Dtr perspective gives the distinct impression that Jeremiah is something of an outsider. For example, he addresses King Zedekiah and refers to other prophets who speak to that king as though he, Jeremiah, is not a part of the group of prophets who regularly have the royal ear. And in that same chapter, Jeremiah speaks to priests as though he is not regularly used to working with the cultic officials (v 16). But, given the ample indication of Jeremiah's activities within the temple before the priests and his associations with and solicitation by royalty (37:3–5; 38:14–28; 22:1; 34:6), the impression that Jeremiah was something of an outsider likely means only that in the view of the Dtr editor Jeremiah was pitted *ideologically* against others in the society.

2.3   Precisely because of this editorial interest, it is very difficult to gain a sure sense of the ideologies of Jeremiah's opponents, or even the full range of issues in any given incident of conflict. For the prophets, we unfortunately see this matter only through the eyes of editors, who by and large have Jeremiah speak for the opposition. Any picture we have of their beliefs is very likely to be simplified, exaggerated, and hardly able to be generalized into an ideological portrait of the opposition, despite efforts to the contrary (e.g., van der Woude; Crenshaw).

According to tradition, the opposition prophets spoke of Yahweh's unshakable attachment to Jerusalem and its well-being, šalôm (Jer 5:12-13; 6:14 = 8:11; cf. 14:13). This characterization of the prophets' message seems consistent with a kind of royal theology evidenced in Isaiah 36-38, a theology which rested the defense of Jerusalem of Yahweh's protective care and covenant with the Davidic monarchy (cf. Isaiah 7:1-9 and 2 Sam 7:1-14). However, the matter is put this way partly, perhaps largely, because the collectors of the traditions focus Jeremiah's distinctiveness in his predictions of destruction for Jerusalem, which in hindsight turned out to be correct. We really have very little basis on which to reconstruct an opposing ideological position. My guess is that the conflict between Jeremiah and these other prophets was, as the anthropological evidence would suggest, highly situational, highly geared toward particular events and circumstances to which all of these prophets addressed themselves. There must have been ideological disagreements on specific issues, and in the Book of Jeremiah we see these issues by editorial choice circling around the threat of Babylonian conquest and the fate of Jerusalem and its exiles.

2.31   We can be even less assured of the ideological positions of those princes who opposed Jeremiah. Presumably they were active in positions of authority with Zedekiah, son of Josiah. The Babylonians had taken Jehoiachin and the queen mother into exile, and instead of installing a successor in the normal line, put Zedekiah, Jehoiachin's uncle, on the throne (37:1). If not exactly a puppet government, it was a regime which stood at the pleasure of the Babylonian King Nebuchadrezzar. It must have been a government naturally sensitive to its precarious position, and to judge from Jer 38:4; 52:3, apparently secretly nationalistic as well. Perhaps it was a sign of the times that the house of a high ranking royal official, the scribe (sôpēr) had become a prison in Zedekiah's reign (37:15) /9/. We might surmise that the princes (śārîm) were jealously guarding the hope of eventually resisting the Babylonian threat and surviving the siege (Jer 38). Presumably, it was this reading of the situation that Jeremiah opposed (38:2-3). Here again, we must allow for the Dtr editor's filtering of the situation for his own apologetic and homiletic purposes.

2.4   What of those who supported Jeremiah in the midst of conflict? We have only indirect information of a general sort, and no information for specific situations of conflict in chaps. 26, 27-29, 37-38. According to Jer 1:1, the prophet came from Anathoth, a city which by tradition was given to the Levites (Josh 20:18). Jeremiah was possibley a descendant of the priest Abiathar, who was an early supporter of the Davidic house and part of a line of priests nearly wiped out by King Saul (I Sam 22:11-23). Abiathar was one of David's chief priests who had been later banished by King Solomon to Anathoth for aiding Adonijah's rebellious claim to the throne (I Kgs 2:26–27). There at Anathoth, the priestly family continued, perhaps as earlier, variously supportive of and opposed to the monarchy. Jeremiah's father was Hilkiah, and we may wonder if this is the same Hilkiah who was the chief priest intimately connected with Josiah's reform of Israelite religion (2 Kings 22). Perhaps he was not. But in any case, Jeremiah's uncle, Shallum, was a property owner at Anathoth (Jer 32:7), and thus presumably a member of the landed Levites in that village. Shallum might be the husband of Huldah, the prophetess who was instrumental in Josiah's reform (2 Kgs 22:14). Thus one may see that tradition assigns Jeremiah blood relationships with a prominent priestly house, a house moreover that was linked to events of religious reform highly praised by the Dtr editors of the Books of Kings and Jeremiah.

The tradition also indicates that Jeremiah was closely associated with the family of Shaphan, a family also linked to the Josianic reforms. Jeremiah is protected by Shaphan's son Ahikam, who had been at court in Josiah's time (Jer 26:24; 2 Kgs 22:11, 14). The letter which Jeremiah sent to the exiles (Jer 29) was carried by Elasah, a second son of Shaphan (Jer 29:3). The scroll which Baruch read to King Jehoiakim was read from the house of Gemariah, another son of Shaphan (Jer 36:10–12). From this particular passage, we learn that Shaphan himself held royal office as the king's scribe (sôpēr), and indeed must be the same Shaphan who bore that title for King Josiah (2 Kgs 22:3, 8). Finally, when the Babylonians crushed the Israelite monarchy, they put Jeremiah into the custody of Gedaliah, a grandson of Shaphan (Jer 39:14; 40:5).

As we have seen, Jeremiah's uncle, Shallum, was a property owner at Anathoth and presumably a Levite. His son, Maaseiah, Jeremiah's second cousin, was a priestly official, the "keeper of the threshold" (Jer 35:4; see 2 Kgs 25:18 = Jer 52:24; 2 Kgs 12:9). One of Maaseiah's sons, and second cousin to Jeremiah, was the second ranking high priest, Zephaniah (Jer 21:1; 37:3; 52:24). This same Zephaniah presumably supported Jeremiah on at least one occasion, to judge from his refusal to take Shemiah's side in opposing Jeremiah (29:24–32).

Finally, Elnathan ben Achbor, a prince (śar) in Jehoiakim's court (36:12), is among Jeremiah's sympathizers. At least, he was not openly hostile to the message of Jeremiah when it was presented at court (Jer 36:25). Now Elnathan's father was linked to Josiah's reform (2 Kgs 22:12,14). Also, this same Elnathan may have fathered Jehoiakim's queen (2 Kgs 24:8).

Thus we may catch the barest suggestion of a network of family relationships supportive of Jeremiah, and extending into the highest levels of royal and cultic service. Jeremiah is born into a priestly house, is kinsman to at least two prominent priests—the second ranking high priest and one of the three "keepers of the threshold." Jeremiah finds support with this high ranking priest Zephaniah in a dispute with another Yahweh prophet. He also is surrounded by supporters from families whose connections with the royal court are intimate and extensive, and whose links to the religious reform movement under King Josiah are deep. Jeremiah may have been born a rural non-Jerusalemite, but his blood and social relationships are anything but lower class.

2.5   We now have another perspective on the conflicts reflected in chaps. 26; 27-29; 37-38. A scene of conflict between Jeremiah and royal princes with priests (Jer 26) is essentially repeated in the following regime with a new king, and many of the same royal officials (chaps. 27-29; 37-38). We have a picture of a relatively weak king (Zedekiah) who is said to have rebelled against the Babylonians and hence to have brought on a siege of the capital city (Jer 52:3). But this king is dominated by a group of princes (śārîm), who at least want to offer strong resistance to the Babylonians and may stand in a general tradition of protecting national autonomy at all costs (Jer 38:5, 7-16, 24-38). Presumably, the Yahwistic theology which would have accompanied such political sentiments is reflected in the royalist theology of the Davidic dynasty (2 Samuel 7) and the divinely chosen and protected city, Jerusalem (Isaiah 36-38). On the other side, we may think of Jeremiah and his supporters from members of an aristocratic family (Shaphan) and official, priestly ranks in Judean society. Because Gedaliah, a grandson of Shaphan and a protector of Jeremiah, was eventually chosen by conquering Babylonian authorities to be a Judean provencial governor instead of other princes in Zedekiah's court (Jeremiah 39-40), we may presume that he and his family associates were perceived as more or less amenable to Babylonian authority. If so, the basis for the Babylonian perception may have lain in their earlier political action and opinions which would have argued for cooperation and co-existence with Babylon: ride out the storm, cooperate with the foreign domination, make the best of Judah's position of weakness following a first deportation in 597 B.C.E. In fact, Jeremiah is accused of going over to the Babylonians during the siege (37:11-15) and of counselling others to do the same (38:2). In 29:4-9 he was said to have advised the first deportation exiles to support their new Babylonian masters. Presumably, the theological justification for this political persuasion would have roots in the ideals of Josianic reform, as now reflected in 2 Kings 22-23, since Jeremiah and his supporters had such deep and intimate ties with that movement. But these ideals in this particular moment in history may have been cast in terms of allegiance to Yahweh alone and turning away from what was deemed a religiously apostate and foolhardy course set by the noblemen around Zedekiah, the "autonomists" who apparently hoped to resist (Jer 26:4-6; 36:29). Thus within the royal court, among people of high familial and professional connection, including Jeremiah the prophet, there apparently raged a political struggle for the future of the nation. How much, or how little, a role personal ambitions may have played in the conflict, we cannot know.

The struggle did not cease with the final blow to the monarchy in 587 B.C.E. The Babylonians crushed the resistance, sweeping away, presumably, Zedekiah and many of those who supported the "autonomist" position. They also chose Gedaliah, a grandson of Shaphan, and presumably heir to all those associations stretching back through Shaphan to Josiah's reign, to be the provincial governor at Mizpah (Jeremiah 39; 52). This same Gedaliah was given custody of Jeremiah as well (39:11-14). It looks as though the political figures who were more or less amenable to living with, rather than resisting, Babylonian power were now placed in authority. But the remnant of Zedekiah's court resisted and finally murdered Gedaliah (Jer 41:1-10), provoking counter violence (Jer 41:11-12) and a plan to flee to Egypt out of fear of Babylonian reprisals for Gedaliah's murder. In this new situation of political division, Jeremiah apparently was aligned with Gedaliah and the remnant in the land who had accepted existence under Babylonian supervision as a positive, desirable state (40:7-12). And he counsels them even in the wake of this murder to remain where they are, not to flee to Egypt. His line is as it was before 587: roll with the Babylonians, do not resist them, or in this case, do not flee to Egypt.

2.51   These same basic political divisions must have been at work in the dispute between Hananiah and Jeremiah. Hananiah counsels that exile (the first deportation) will be short, that the Babylonian power is short-lived, that autonomy will be regained within two years. Jeremiah, representing the political option of "co-existence," has a different prophecy: servitude to Babylon is inevitable (28:14; cf. 27:7-8). Both men stand for opposing political options in the kingdom; both may have been closely involved in the struggles for influence. At least we know that Jeremiah was well connected; possibly Hananiah's grandson accused Jeremiah of deserting to the Babylonians (37:13); both, as Yahweh prophets, cover or reinforce their political persuasion with oracles from Yahweh.

2.52   We may see something similar in Jeremiah 29. Jeremiah's letter to the exiles, victims of the first deportation, counsels "co-existence" as a command from Yahweh:

> Build houses and live in them; plant gardens and eat their produce.... seek the welfare of the city where I have sent you into exile, and pray to the LORD on its behalf, for in its welfare you will find your welfare. (29:5-7)

Apparently what we have is an attempt by Jeremiah to extend his sphere of influence to the exiles who are in Babylon—done at close to the time that he advocated to those in Jerusalem a similar conciliatory posture toward Babylon (Jer 38). And just as his political advice met with opposition in the capital, so too, his advice by letter to the exiles drew forth resistance in the person and words of Shemaiah, the Babylonian Yahweh prophet (29:24-32). Again, the matter seems not to be just that two prophets opposed one another on a specific theological issue, but that they—at least we may say this for Jeremiah—were part of a larger struggle between factions for "autonomist" or "co-existence" political action. Both factions evidently sought support in prophetic oracles.

2.6   It is surely no accident that the struggles of Jeremiah are preserved and presented so fully by the Dtr editors. We may presume from the thoroughly Dtr composition in chap. 44 that the editors were unsympathetic to those Israelites who insisted upon fleeing to Egypt after the murder of Gedaliah. Translated into political terms, the editors in hindsight favored the counsel put in the mouth of Jeremiah, that one should remain in Judah, wait out this period of exile while Jerusalem lay in ruins, and get along with the Babylonians (42:7-17; 44:1-14; 26-30). It may be that these editors were themselves survivors of that group which before exile had counselled moderation and co-existence. In any case, it appears that now, in exile, the traditions of conflict between Jeremiah and his public were serving yet another function besides explanation and homily for Yahwistic religion. Tradition of conflict may have reinforced the social and political position of the editors as well. We might suppose that they wished to mount a political argument against those who went to Egypt, sanctioned of course with theological reprobation, because their own situation in exile demanded that they remain on amicable terms with their Babylonian masters. Such a pro-Babylonian posture was in fact to be elaborated more fully by the Chronicler (Ackroyd).

3.0   We have come full circle—beginning with the latest editorial perspectives on these traditions, back to what we could learn of Jeremiah's situation, now returning to the environment of the editors. There remains much that we would wish to know: the group with which Jeremiah apparently was aligned seems hardly distinguishable in socio-economic terms from those "autonomists" around Zedekiah. But were there in fact "class" distinctions? Were there social, economic, material bases for the political options we have seen? The personal dimension remains closed to us—those human strivings for power and influence that one might imagine to be at work are never mentioned or hinted at. And the effects of those conflicts, whether over theological warrants for political action or political programs themselves, are invisible. It is difficult to say who the victors and the victims finally were, unless one assumes the story to be written by the victors, i.e., that the Dtr editor(s) carried on that earlier tradition of cooperation with Babylonian powers.

In any case, what we can see has enabled us to gain a somewhat fuller picture of the social dimensions of conflict between one prophet and his public. And certainly from the point of view of the editors, conflict in itself was not viewed as a problem, but part of a renewed proclamation of religion and (implicitly) political posture. It may have been that a consistent literary portrait of conflict along with the vindication of spokesmen for certain political views would have been served as part of the Dtr editor(s) response to a new need in Babylonian exile, viz., to establish that there was precedent within the advocacy of pure Yahwism for a policy which, if not pro-Babylonian, was at least favorable to co-existence with that nation.

The textual tradition, tendentious as it is, nevertheless allows us a glimpse of the complex social and political situation in which this example of prophetic conflict was played out. Anthropological studies help us realize that conflict is a vital element in prophetic activity, and that it is both deeper and broader than disputes over religious beliefs. Thus, anthropological study helps us compensate for distortions which arise from isolating religious ideology from other forms of social expression.

NOTES

/1/ Many of the tales have been collected and translated in Rasmussen. Note also legends in Bogoras. Cf. the public shows of power and prestige among shamans in the Pacific islands (Berndt: 338–344) and conflicts for status among shamans of west Nepal (Winkler: 257–258).

/2/ Note, however, that absence of conflicts between prophets is noted by Tamoane (205) for Melanesia, and that Evans-Pritchard (1956:305) emphasized the absence of conflict between priests and prophets among the Nuer.

/3/ In contrast to a focus on ideology, see the study of "possession" as a social fact by Lewis and also Beattie and Middleton.

/4/ Evans-Pritchard (1937:181–201; 245–257) was of this opinion for the healing specialists (witch doctors) among the Azande.

/5/ Nicholson (52–53, 93–100) argues that these traditions were actually composed by the Dtr editors of Jeremiah.

/6/ This Dtr perspective is consistent with that of Chronicles. Cf. 2 Chron 20:20, 36:11–21.

/7/ Jer 36:5 does not necessarily imply a legal restriction on Jeremiah's movements into the temple, as RSV "I am debarred from going to the house of the LORD" might suggest. The Hebrew is better translated, "I am imprisoned; I am not able to go to the house of the LORD." (Cf. 33:1 and 39:15, where the verb, 'āṣûr, "be imprisoned, bound, shut up," is used in an identical way. Cf. 32:2; Neh 6:10.)

/8/ The meaning is uncertain, but demands some association between priest and prophet.

/9/ On the royal scribe or secretary (sôpēr), see Mettinger: 25–51

WORKS CONSULTED

Ackroyd, Peter
1968   *Exile and Restoration*. Philadelphia: Westminster.

Anisimov, A. F.
1963   "The Shaman's Tent of the Evenks and the Origin of the Shamanistic Rite." Pp. 84–123 in *Studies in Siberian Shamanism*. Ed. H. N. Michael. Toronto: University of Toronto.

Balikci, Asen
1967   "Shamanistic Behaviour among the Netsilik Eskimos." Pp. 191–209 in *Magic, Witchcraft, and Curing*. Ed. John Middleton. New York: Natural History Press.
1970   *The Netsilik Eskimo*. Garden City: American Museum of Natural History.

Beattie, John and J. Middleton, eds.
1969   *Spirit Mediumship and Society in Africa*. New York: Africana Publishing Corporation.

Berndt, R. M.
1946–48   "Wuradjeri Magic and 'Clever Men.'" *Oceania* 17: 327–365; 18: 60–86.

Bogoras, Vladimir G.
1910   *Chuckchee Mythology*. The Jesup North Pacific Expedition. Vol 8, Parts 1–2. New York: American Museum of Natural History.

Carley, Keith
1977   "Prophets Old and New." Pp. 238–266 in *Prophets of Melanesia*. Ed. G. Trompf. Port Moresby: Institute of Papua New Guinea Studies.

Carroll, Robert P.
1977   "Ancient Israelite Prophecy and Dissonance Theory." *Numen* 24: 135–151.
1979   *When Prophecy Failed: Cognitive Dissonance in the Prophetic Traditions of the Old Testament*. New York: Seabury.

Chagnon, N. A.
1968   *Yanomamö: The Fierce People*. New York: Holt, Rinehart, and Winston.

Colson, Elizabeth
1977   "A Continuing Dialogue: Prophets and Local Shrines Among the Tonga of Zambia." Pp. 119–139 in *Regional Cults*. Ed. R. P. Werbner. Association of Social Anthropologists Monograph 16. London: Academic Press.

Crenshaw, James L.
1971   *Prophetic Conflict: Its Effect Upon Israelite Religion*. BZAW 124. Berlin: W. de Gruyter.

Cripps, A. S.
1928   *Chaminuka*. London: Sheldon Press.

De Vries, Simon
1978   *Prophet Against Prophet*. Grand Rapids: Eerdmans.

Eliade, Mircea
1964   *Shamanism. Archaic Techniques of Ecstasy*. Princeton: Princeton University.

Evans-Pritchard, E. E.
1937 *Witchcraft, Oracles, and Magic Among the Aznade.* Oxford: Clarendon.
1956 *Nuer Religion.* Oxford: Clarendon.

Festinger, Leon; Henry W. Riecken; and Stanley Schachter.
1956 *When Prophecy Fails.* Minneapolis: University of Minnesota.

Fohrer, G.
1972 *History of Israelite Religion.* Nashville: Abingdon.

Fry, Peter
1976 *Spirits of Protest.* Cambridge: Cambridge University.

Hossfeld, F. L. and I. Meyer
1973 *Prophet Gegen Prophet.* BibB 9. Fribourg: Schweizerisches Katholisches Bibelwerk.

Johnson, Aubrey
1962, 2nd edition *The Cultic Prophet in Ancient Israel.* Cardiff: University of Wales.

Kaufmann, Yehezkel
1960 *The Religion of Israel, From its Beginnings to the Babylonian Exile.* Chicago: University of Chicago.

Kessler, Martin
1968 "Jeremiah Chapters 26–45 Reconsidered." *JNES* 27: 81–88.

Kingsley, Garbett
1977 "Disparate Regional Cults and a Unitary Ritual Field in Zimbabwe" Pp. 55–92 in *Regional Cults.* Ed. R. P. Werbner. London: Academic Press.

Lewis, I. M.
1971 *Ecstatic Religion.* Baltimore: Penguin.

Lindblom, Johannes
1962 *Prophecy in Ancient Israel.* Philadelphia: Fortress.

Martin-Achard, R.
1977 "Hanania contre Jeremie. Quelques remarques sur Jeremie 28." *Bulletin du Centre Protestant d'Etudes* 29: 51–57.

Mettinger, T.N.D.
1971 *Solomonic State Officials.* Lund: Gleerup.

Meyer, Ivo
1977 *Jeremia und die falschen Propheten.* Göttingen: Vandenhoeck and Ruprecht.

Nadel, S. F.
1946 "A Study of Shamanism in the Nuba Mountains." *Journal of the Royal Anthropological Institute* 76: 25–37.

Nicholson, E. W.
1970 *Preaching to the Exiles. A Study of the Prose Tradition in the Book of Jeremiah.* Oxford: Blackwell.

Osswald, E.
1962 *Falsche Prophetie im Alten Testament.* Tübingen: Mohr.

Overholt, Thomas
1970 *The Threat of Falsehood: A Study in the Theology of the Book of Jeremiah.* Napierville: Allenson.

Petersen, David L.
1977 *Late Israelite Prophecy.* Missoula: Scholars.

Quell, G.
1952 *Wahre und falsche Propheten.* Gütersloh: Bertelmann.

Rad, Gerhard von
1933 "Die falschen Propheten." *ZAW* 51: 109–120.

Rasmussen, Knud
1931 *The Netsilik Eskimos.* Report of Fifth Thule Expedition, 8. Copenhagen: Nordisk Forlag.

Ringgren, Helmer
1966 *Israelite Religion.* Philadelphia: Fortress.

Sanders, James A.
1972 *Torah and Canon.* Philadelphia: Fortress.
1977 "Hermeneutics in True and False Prophecy." Pp. 21–41 in *Canon and Authority: Essays in Old Testament Religion and Theology.* Eds. George W. Coats and Burke O. Long. Philadelphia: Fortress.

Seidl, Theodor
1977 *Texte und Einheiten in Jeremia 27–29: Literaturwissenschaftliche Studie.* St. Ottilien: EOS Verlag.
1978 *Formen und Formeln in Jeremia 27–29: Eine literaturwissenschaftliche Studie.* St. Ottilien: EOS Verlag.

Shirokogoroff, S. M.
1935 *Psychomental Complex of the Tungus.* London: Kegan Paul, Trench & Trubner.

Tamoane, Matthew
1977 "Kamoi of Darapap and the Legend of Jari." Pp. 174–211 in *Prophets of Melanesia.* Ed. G. Trompf. Port Moresby: Institute of Papua New Guinea Studies.

van der Woude
1969 "Micah in Dispute with the Pseudo-Prophets." *VT* 19: 244–260.

Vriezen, Th.C.
1970, 2nd edition *An Outline of Old Testament Theology.* Oxford: Blackwell.

Wilson, Robert R.
1980 *Prophecy and Society in Ancient Israel.* Philadelphia: Fortress.

Winkler, Walter F.
1976 "Spirit Possession in Far Western Nepal." Pp. 244–262 in *Spirit Possession in the Nepal Himalayas.* Eds. J. T. Hitchcock and R. L. Jones. Warminster: Aris and Phillips.

Zimmerli, W.
1978 *Old Testament Theology in Outline.* Atlanta: Knox.

PROPHECY: THE PROBLEM OF CROSS-CULTURAL COMPARISON

Thomas W. Overholt
University of Wisconsin-Stevens Point

ABSTRACT

Prophets have been widely distributed throughout human societies and they and their movements have been extensively studied. Because of difficulties related to the sometimes vastly different patterns of cultural adjustment represented by the various groups among which they have appeared, however, there have been few attempts at a broadly cross-cultural analysis of the nature of the prophetic process. The paper suggests a model in terms of which such an analysis and comparison can be made, and applies it to a discussion of two specific prophets, Jeremiah, a Judean of the late 7th and early 6th centuries B.C.E., and Handsome Lake, a Seneca Indian of the late 18th and early 19th centuries C.E. In conclusion some implications of the comparison are suggested for three interrelated problems which are important for any attempt to understand prophecy: the nature of the situation in which the prophet operates, the nature of prophetic authority, and the problem of how the content of a prophet's proclamation relates to the cultural tradition in which he stands.

0.1   The phenomenon of prophecy has been widely distributed throughout human societies. We have recorded instances of prophetic activity from an impressive range of times and places, from the ancient Mesopotamian city-state of Mari, where in the 18th century B.C.E. prophets confronted royal administrators with the demands and promises of the god (Malamat, 1966; Huffmon; Hayes; Moran), to the New Yorker Joseph Smith, whose revelation and message have formed the basis for the development of Mormonism. The Saint-Simon movement of early 19th century France is another of the many instances of prophecy that have arisen within the Western stream of tradition (Talmon), but prophetic activity has also been widespread outside that tradition. Since the late 19th century the peoples of Melanesia have produced a whole series of cargo cult movements in most of which prophetic figures were of central importance (see Worsley). There were Tokerua, the "prophet of Milne Bay" (Papua, 1893), Saibai, the prophet of the German Wislin movement (Torres Straits, 1913; see Chinnery and Haddon; Eckert), Evara and Biere of the Vailala Madness (Papua, 1919; see Williams, 1923 and 1934), and Manehevi and his successors in the John Frum movement (Tanna, 1939–present; see Guiart, 1951 and 1956; Barrow), to name but a few. Prophets have appeared in Africa (Lanternari, Sundkler), wartime Japan (May), among various American Indian groups (see Mooney: 657–763), and in other parts of the world as well.

Nor has the appearance of prophets been confined to a particular kind of cultural adjustment. To be sure, the term "prophet" is likely first to call to mind the great high civilizations of the ancient Near East and figures like Isaiah, Jeremiah, and Muhammad. But Wovoka, the prophet of the Ghost Dance religion of 1890, was a Nevada Paiute, a tribe whose simple hunting and gathering culture had only recently come into close contact with European civilization. Navosavakadua, the first prophet of the new Tuka religion among Fijians, began his movement about 1885 in an interior region where there were as yet no white settlements (Sutherland, Thomson).

0.2   As one begins to explore the vast literature on prophecy, certain tendencies appear /1/. For one thing, data from primitive and higher cultures are usually dealt with separately. Studies of the Old Testament prophets, for example, normally make reference to extra-Israelite phenomena only to the extent that they bear directly on the development of Israelite prophecy. Much of the continuing discussion of the Mari prophets has centered on the question of the extent to which they were parallel in nature and function to the Israelite prophets, and one finds a similar concern mirrored in discussions of cult prophecy (Johnson, Pedersen), and other possible institutional analogues to Old Testament prophecy such as the royal messenger (Ross) and royal vizier (Baltzer). On the other hand, one finds studies of prophecy that are confined to its appearance within "lower cultures" (Schlosser or among "colonial peoples" (Fabian, Lanternari).

0.3   Another tendency of the literature is to discuss prophecy less for its own sake than as an element in some larger process. Studies of the Old Testament prophets have been very much preoccupied with the content of what these men proclaimed, and have found their message useful in helping to define the nature of Yahweh and his relationship to his people, as well as the general development of Israelite culture and religion. Thus we have discussions of "prophecy and covenant" (Clements, 1965) and of the relationship of prophecy to certain specific aspects of Israelite culture (e.g., Donner, Koch). This inclination to be more interested in the theological content of the proclamation than in the prophetic process itself is particularly evident in some of the well-known "theologies" of the Old Testament /2/.

When one turns to extra-Israelite phenomena, the situation is similar. The focus is not so much on prophecy itself as on the broader sociocultural movements of which the prophets are a part, a concern which Anthony F. C. Wallace makes clear in his now-famous essay, when he defines a "revitalization movement" as "a deliberate, organized, conscious effort by members of a society to construct a more satisfying culture"

(1956:265). Beginning with Ralph Linton's essay on "nativistic movements" (1943), there has been a continuing effort to classify these cults in terms of their beliefs and goals (Guariglia, Koppers, Kobben), as well as numerous attempts to define their causes (in general see LeBarre). There have, of course, been many studies of individual movements, and these often take their departure from the kinds of theoretical analyses just mentioned (Zenner, following Festinger; Griffin, following Wallace, 1956). On the whole the same conditions persist in all these studies which led Jarvie to protest, with specific reference to theories of Cargo cults, that the prophetic leader himself has been unjustifiably neglected (1963:131).

0.4 Now it must be acknowledged that there are good reasons for these two tendencies, for real stumbling-blocks to the comparison of prophets arise from at least three sources. The first has to do with the nature of the given group's cultural adjustment. There are obvious and striking differences, say, between stone age, tribal men of aboriginal New Guinea or North America and iron age, urban men of the ancient Near East, which complicate the task of comparison. And these differences do not stop with the material culture, but extend to world-views as well. One can think of the Judeo-Christian "historical" tradition as opposed to native mythological traditions and observe that persons who write about prophets tend to come out of the former and spend time discussing the "irrationality" of the latter. A second and closely related stumbling-block involves the content of the prophecies themselves, which in all cases is culturally conditioned. Separate movements may share a general hope for the eventual appearance or return of some valued person or thing, but to what extent are the specific objects of hope (e.g., Jesus, the buffalo, the ancestors bringing cargo) comparable? Finally, there is a real danger that the investigator will fall prey to ethnocentricity and evaluate more highly what to him is more familiar or intelligible or "rational."

0.5 The difficulty of overcoming these barriers may be seen by glancing briefly at several attempts to do so. J. Lindblom, for example, approaches his study of ancient Israelite prophecy on the assumption that prophecy is a universal human phenomenon (1962). Early in the book he discusses extra-Israelite prophets and suggests what he considers to be the three defining characteristics of prophecy in general, namely that the prophet is a person who is conscious of having received a special call from his god, who has had revelatory experiences, and who proclaims to the people the message received through revelation. He then discusses the Old Testament materials with reference to these characteristics. But the extra-Israelite prophets are not again brought into the discussion for purposes of comparison, and it is clear that one of Lindblom's main interests, to which he devotes the last third of the book, is the specific theological content of the ancient Israelite prophetic messages.

James Mooney's classic study of the Ghost Dance of 1890 is another case in point (1896). Mooney was not satisfied simply to describe the origin and development of this one prophetic movement, but attempted to set it in the context of a number of others which he took to be similar in character. Thus the first eight chapters of his book are devoted to descriptions of prophetic activity among various North American Indian groups, beginning with the Pueblo Revolt of 1680 and culminating with John Slocum and the Shakers of Puget Sound in the late 19th century. In addition a later chapter is devoted to "parallels in other systems" and discusses examples of such activity from the biblical period, Islam, and Christian sects and movements from the Middle Ages to the 19th century. Mooney does not elaborate any theorectical structure in terms of which he makes his comparisons, but one can find occasional statements that indicate he was using two general criteria in the selection of his materials. The first was the notion that messianic doctrines, wherever they are found, "... are essentially the same and have their origin in a hope and longing common to all humanity" (1896:657). The second is a list of traits—inspiration via dreams, dancing, ecstasy, and trance—which are taken to "... have formed a part of every great religious development of which we have knowledge from the beginning of history" (1896:928; see 719, 947). Because of its scope, Mooney's study is important and interesting, but it is more a listing of movements than a systematic comparison. It avoids the stumbling-blocks mentioned above by not acknowledging their presence, and throws little theoretical light on the nature of the prophetic process.

1.1   It is clear that the effort to compare prophecy cross-culturally would be greatly facilitated if one could arrive at some basis for comparison that was as much as possible free from culturally-conditioned content. With this in mind I want to propose a model of how the prophetic process works, apply this model to the discussion of two specific prophets, Jeremiah and Handsome Lake, and then suggest several implications that seem to me to follow from this approach to prophecy. The claim I wish to make is that although the specific *content* of their respective messages is culturally conditioned and, therefore, quite dissimilar, the prophetic *activity* of the two conforms to the same general pattern.

1.2   Before introducing the model itself, a word seems in order regarding its genesis. My own training has been in biblical studies, and my primary interest OT prophecy. I gradually became aware of and interested in what appeared to be prophetic movements among American Indians, and a post-doctoral fellowship which allowed me to spend a year studying anthropology afforded the opportunity for an extensive investigation of one such, the Ghost Dance of 1890. Though a formal cross-cultural comparison was not part of my original intention, it eventually became evident that the Ghost Dance as well as other prophetic movements and figures that I studied had important features in common with OT prophecy. Reflection on this fact led to the development of the model, which I first proposed in a study of the Ghost Dance (Overholt, 1974). I view the model, then, as the natural outgrowth of my study of Israelite and non-Israelite prophetic movements and of the important interpretive literature that has been generated by the scholarly investigation of both /3/.

1.3   Figure 1 states in the form of a diagram a way of understanding the nature of the prophetic process. The basic components of this model are two: a set of three actors and a pattern of interrelationships among them involving revelation (r), proclamation (p), feedback (f), and expectations of confirmation (e).

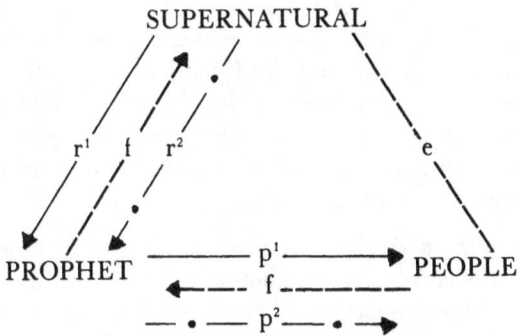

Figure 1.

1.4   The focus on interrelationships that is evident here calls for some enlargement of traditional notions concerning a prophet's authority. Since the prophet functions as the messenger of the god, it seems justifiable to view his revelatory experiences as the primary source of his authority. In all instances of which I am aware it is simply assumed that a person who is truly functioning as a prophet has been the recipient of some such communication. These experiences are essentially private, and form the theological justification for his activity. They are also inevitably culturally-conditioned, since both his perception and later articulation of them will be affected by the cultural and historical context in which he stands. In addition to this, however, there is a more public aspect of a prophet's authority which displays itself in various reactions to his message by the people to whom it is addressed. Since the act of prophecy must necessarily take place in a social context, these reactions are both inevitable and of critical importance. For the prophet seeks to move his audience to action, and his hearers may be said to attribute authority to him insofar as they acknowledge and are prepared to act upon the "truth" of his formulation. In their response the hearers in effect judge the cultural "competence" of the prophet by deciding whether or not his message makes sense in the context of their cultural and religious traditions and is relevant to the current socio-political situation. As Peter Worsley has put it, "Charisma is thus a function of recognition: the prophet without honor cannot be a charismatic prophet" (1969: xii; cf. also Overholt, 1977:144f.). We will return to this point below.

Though most of the prophet's audience will be members of his own cultural community, we can expect that they will not all be of one mind in their evaluation of his message. But whether individuals accept, reject, or are indifferent to it, they will react to the prophet in some fashion, and it is this "feedback" and the prophet's response to it that defines the dynamic interrelationship between actors that is central to the model. Similarly, the prophet will assess his own message against his perception of the events going on around him and the feedback he gets from his audience. Since in his understanding the message he delivers is not strictly his own but is revealed to him by the god, we also need to assume the possibility of feedback from the prophet to god and an eventual new revelation either confirming or altering the original message.

1.5   Operating on the basis of this model, we can now list in a more systematic way the component elements that we would expect to find in any given example of the prophetic process. The minimum number of elements necessary for the operation and identification of the process are three: 1. The prophet's revelation. 2. A proclamation based on that revelation, which will have the following general characteristic: though it will inevitably contain innovative features, the message will nonetheless "make sense" in light of the cultural traditions of the prophet and his audience and the current social and historical situation in which they find themselves (cf. Barnett: 181–266). 3. an audience to whom the proclamation is addressed and whose reactions to it—positive, negative, or indifferent—will be determined in large part by how well the message is perceived to meet the criterion suggested above. Additional components (prophetic feedback to the source of revelation; additional revelations; additional messages; certain experiences, here labeled "expectations of confirmation," which tend to independently confirm the god-given task of the prophet and strengthen the conviction of his authenticity) are possible, in fact even probable, although our ability to discover them will depend largely on the amount of data extant for any given instance of prophecy. Sometimes a fourth "actor," in the form of one or more disciples who serve as intermediaries between the prophet and his audience, may be added to the basic model sketched in Figure 1.

2.1   Because a prophet speaks in a concrete historical situation and elicits a response from his audience partly on the basis of their judgments concerning what he says about it, it is necessary to preface the discussion of our two prophets with a brief sketch of the contexts within which they operated. The known public activity of the prophet Jeremiah spans approximately the last forty years of the existence of the Palestinian state of Judah (626–586 B.C.E.) /4/. For the century prior to this period Judah had been an Assyrian vassal state, but by the time Jeremiah appeared on the scene the power of the Assyrians had begun to wane, particularly in the outlying regions of their empire. Under King Josiah (640–609 B.C.E.) Judah began to reassert her independence. Her political influence was extended northward into the Assyrian provinces of Samaria and Galilee, and accompanying this rebellion there was a major reform of the Yahweh cult. Based on an old lawbook found during the remodeling of the temple in 622, this reform sought to reassert the traditional form of the covenant relationship between Yahweh and his people.

But though independent, Judah's geographical position placed her in the middle of an international struggle for power that made her situation precarious. Revolts in both Egypt and Babylon had contributed to the weakening of the Assyrian empire, but as the pressure on the Assyrians by Medes and Babylonians became more intense (614–610), Egypt, hopeful of preserving a buffer state between herself and these new threatening powers, came to the aid of her old enemy and joined Assyria in an abortive attempt to recapture the city of Haran near the headwaters of the Euphrates. It was while he was on his way to this rendezvous in 609 that Pharaoh Neco met and killed Josiah in battle, and on his return from the Euphrates three months later deposed Josiah's successor and placed a Judean of his own choice, Jehoiakim, on the throne in Jerusalem. Four years later in 605 the Babylonian king Nebuchadnezzar decisively defeated the Egyptian army at Carchemish on the Euphrates, and Judah again found herself squarely between two opposing powers.

As one might expect, there was considerable factionalism in Judah over how best to respond to this situation. During his reign, Jehoiakim and his supporters among the princes adhered to a pro-Egypt policy and came into open conflict with Jeremiah /5/. The king eventually revolted against Nebuchadnezzar, and the result of this action was the capture of Jerusalem and the deportation of persons and property to Babylon in the year 597. Under Zedekiah, the last king of Judah, the same party dispute continued. The majority of the princes seemed to have been solidly pro-Egyptian, while the proclamations of Jeremiah became explicitly pro-Babylonian in the sense that he interpreted Nebuchadnezzar's conquest of Jerusalem as Yahweh's will and instructed the people to be obedient to their Babylonian overlord (cf. Jer 27–29). The king wavered, but ultimately threw in with the former group. Judah revolted again, and Jerusalem was again besieged and captured. More of the population was exiled, and the city itself was destroyed and the temple of Yahweh burned. The prophet elected to stay in Judah, but shortly was carried away to Egypt against his will by a group of fleeing Judeans (cf. Jer 37–44).

This series of events presented the participants in them with a complex political and theological problem. Decisions were required concerning concrete and appropriate political and military actions, and in this critical time some looked to the religious traditions of the people for guidance. But prophets differed (cf. Jer 28), and no single answer satisfactory to all emerged.

2.2   Turning now to the New World, the Seneca tribe of North America Indians to which the prophet Handsome Lake belonged had been a member of the famed Iroquois League, a closely knit confederation of tribes whose origin predates the arrival of Columbus /6/. During much of the 18th century, this confederation was able, through a system of playing off the British against the French, both to maintain its territory and security and benefit from the material goods of European culture. But all that ended during the Revolution, which split the confederacy. Neutrality was abandoned, and most of the Iroquois gave their loyalty to the British. The ultimate result was that nearly all of their villages from the Mohawk River to the Ohio country were destroyed and they were cut off from their allies to the west, who established their own confederacy separate from the Iroquois.

The reservation system which was gradually imposed upon the Iroquois during the last decades of the century created what Wallace calls "slums in the wilderness, where no traditional Indian culture could long survive and where only the least useful aspects of white culture could easily penetrate" (1972:184). The Cornplanter grant on the Allegheny River in northern Pennsylvania was somewhat unique among the reservations because of its relative isolation from white settlement. Though the influences of European material culture were considerable, many of the old social and political customs survived and the annual cycle of traditional religious ceremonials was still observed. It was there that Handsome Lake, Cornplanter's half-brother, resided. Of course, such isolation could only be relative, and the social pathologies that had been making inroads among the Iroquois for years were found also in Cornplanter's town. Drinking was a particularly serious problem /7/.

As in the case of Judah in Jeremiah's day, there was no unanimity of opinion among the Iroquois as to how to confront the problems inherent in their historical and cultural situation. Each reservation had its factions, the progressives "advocating the assimilation of white culture" and the conservatives "the preservation of Indian ways" (Wallace, 1972:202, Berkhofer). Cornplanter may be reckoned with the former group, and by the time of Handsome Lake's vision his village had already come under the influence of Quaker missionaries. These men were non-dogmatic in their approach to religion, and chose to concentrate on offering positive assistance to the Cornplanter Seneca in such practical areas as farming, carpentry, and education. By May of 1799 they had also persuaded the council to ban the use of whiskey in the village (Deardorff; Wallace, 1972:221–236).

3. The model outlined above assumes that for the prophetic process to occur there is required, first of all, a set of three actors designated the supernatural, the prophet, and the people. In the pages that follow we will be dealing with two such sets. The prophets are Jeremiah, a Judean of the late 7th and early 6th centuries B.C.E., and Handsome Lake, a Seneca who lived in the late 18th and early 19th centuries C.E. Jeremiah addressed his message to Judeans, primarily the inhabitants of the royal city of Jerusalem. Handsome Lake's message was directed to the Seneca of Cornplanter's band and, subsequently, other groups of Iroquois. The supernatural powers from whom each received his revelation were those familar to the people: Yahweh, the ancestral God of Israel, and the Iroquois Creator.

The second basic component of the prophetic process is a pattern of inter-relationships among these actors. I have termed the modes of this interaction revelation, proclamation, expectations of confirmation and feedback. The latter is especially important, since it allows us to understand what has sometimes been conceived of as a one-way informational flow as a dynamic, two-way process. For the sake of brevity the following discussion will center mainly on two sequences of action involving revelation, proclamation and feedback.

3.1 The prophetic process involves what we might call a *revelation-feedback-revelation sequence*. The Book of Jeremiah opens with an account of an experience that Jeremiah understood to be a revelation from Yahweh commissioning him to be a prophet (1:4–10). Both from the style in which the various utterances of the prophet are framed and reports of other visionary or auditory experiences (1:11–12, 13–19: 13:1–11; 18:1–11; 19:1–15; 24:1–10), it seems clear that Jeremiah continued to receive revelations. But this communication with Yahweh was not all one-way. In the call vision itself Jeremiah is pictured as protesting against the role that was being put upon him (1:6), and these protests continued in a series of six "laments" or "complaints" in which he lashed out against his enemies (11:20, 12:1–4, 15:5, 17:18, 18:21–23), complained about the burdens of his office (20:7–9, 14–18), and accused Yahweh himself of acting unfaithfully (15:18, 20:7–9) /8/.

It is important to point out that one of the factors in the mutual hostility between Jeremiah and some of his hearers was the question of the validity of his revelation and the message derived from it. Because he understood it to be part of what had been revealed to him, Jeremiah continually announced that disaster would befall the nation of Judah (cf. 1:10, 13–19; 17:16). But the people, who in any case would not have been overjoyed at such a message, at some point began to subject him to intense ridicule because the threatened calamity had failed to occur (17:15, 20:7f). The prophet also seems to have had his doubts about the revelation (15:18, 20:7), and these formed one element in his feedback to Yahweh.

The book also provides us with two examples of Yahwheh's rejoinder to the prophet's feedback (12:5f., 15:19-23), and these can be considered "additional revelations" which in effect confirmed the prophet's original message. By implication we can assume that a similar feedback-response sequence lies behind that portion of the Hananiah episode (chapter 28) in which Jeremiah was temporarily unable to dispute the message of his opponent, but "sometime later" returned to condemn him as a liar. Further, it seems necessary to assume that, given the nature of prophecy, any alteration in message would be understood by the prophet to be grounded in an additional revelation from god, and therefore insofar as the announcement of a "new covenant" (31:31-34) and other passages of a more "positive" tone (e.g., 32:1-15) can be taken to reflect a genuine element of Jeremiah's message, they also imply further revelations.

The Gaiwiio ("Good Message"), a record of Handsome Lake's teachings which is still in use among followers of the "Longhouse way" (see Shimony), begins by describing a "time of troubles" in Cornplanter village. The scene is at first community-wide. A party of Indians had just returned from Pittsburg, where they had traded skins and game for whiskey. A wild drinking party followed in which village life was disrupted and some families moved away for safety. The focus then shifts to a single sick man, who was held in the grip of "some strong power" and feared that he might die. Realizing that the cause of his illness was whiskey, he resolved never to use it again. Afraid that he would not have the strength to do this, he prayed to the "Great Ruler" and began to be confident that his prayer had been heard and he would live. The sick man was Handsome Lake (Parker: 20-22).

On June 17, 1799, the sick man appeared to die. His body was prepared for burial and relatives summoned, but he revived and reported he had had a vision of three messengers who had been sent to reveal to him the Creator's will and instruct him to carry it to the people. The vision also contained a threat, for Handsome Lake was shown the steaming grave of a man who had formerly been commissioned "to proclaim that message to the world," but had "refused to obey." On August 7 of the same year the prophet received his second revelation in which he was guided on a journey through heaven and hell and given moral instruction. A third revelation occurred on February 5, 1800. Each of these visions was reported and discussed in a council of the people /9/.

Several passages in the Gaiwiio make it clear that Handsome Lake expected to receive further revelations. In his initial vision the three messengers promised, "We shall continually reveal things unto you," and this promise was repeated in 1809 when in the midst of a personal crisis the messengers came to the prophet and said, "We understand your thoughts. We will visit you more frequently and converse with you" (Parker: 25, 47; Wallace 1972:293f.). Although the present form of the Gaiwiio makes it difficult to date specific revelations, there is some internal evidence of such a continuing sequence. Most conspicuous are the place names. The Gaiwiio specifically sets the initial vision in Cornplanter's village, but subsequent sections are said to derive from Cold Spring, Tonawanda, and Onondaga (all in New York; Parker: 20, 46, 47 ,57, 60-62, 76-80). These localities correspond to known periods of the prophet's activity. Furthermore, there are at least four sections of the Code that Wallace links to specific, dateable events: a derogatory reference to Chief Red Jacket arising out of a dispute over the sale of reservation land in 1801, a prophecy intended to discourage Iroquois participation in the "war in the west" (1811), and a composite section mentioning the people's reviling of Handsome Lake and his meeting with the Spirit of the Corn which seems to mirror events that took place in the years 1809 and 1815 (Parker: 68, 65f., 47; Wallace, 1972:260, 293f., 318). The final sections of the Code deal with the revelations and events immediately preceding the prophet's death, which occurred on August 10, 1815, at Onondaga (Parker: 76-80). It is clear that these revelations did not simply repeat what had gone before. They arose out of Handsome Lake's attempt to deal with new situations, and were doubtless seen by him to be divine responses to his own quest for a solution.

3.2 The prophetic process involves as well a *proclamation-feedback-proclamation sequence*. Throughout his long career Jeremiah seems to have proclaimed a fairly consistent message, viz., that because of their actions and the "falsehood" that pervaded their existence the people were standing on the brink of a great national catastrophe (Overholt, 1970). This message evoked both positive and negative responses from the people, though judging from the material available to us, the latter predominated. The negative feedback was sometimes stated in terms of derision because the destruction he proclaimed had not yet come to pass (17:15, 20:7f.). In addition there are reports that he was at various times of his life threatened (11:18-23; 18:18, 22; 20:10), put in the stocks and beaten (20:1-6; cf. 29:26-28), brought to trial on a trumped-up charge (26:7-19), thrown into an abandoned cistern in hopes that he would die (38:1-6), charged with treason (37:13f., 38:1-4), and imprisoned (32:2f; 37:15f., 20f.).

A further negative response to his proclamation can be seen in the numerous references to prophetic opponents whose message of "peace" contradicted that of Jeremiah (cf. 6:9-15, 23:9-40). A classic example because of its richness in narrative detail is the conflict with the prophet Hananiah recounted in chapter 28. We also have references to persons simply refusing to obey instructions conveyed to them by Jeremiah as the will of Yahweh (43:1-7, 44:15-19). On the other hand, there are instances of positive feedback. There were individuals and groups which supported the prophet (26:16-19, 24; 36:13-19; 39:11-14; 40:1-6), as well as occasions on which he was sought out by someone who wished to learn Yahweh's will for the current situation (21:1f., 38:14-16, 42:1-3).

I have already suggested that the response of the people to a prophet will depend largely upon whether they perceive his message to be in continuity with their cultural and religious traditions and relevent to the current sociopolitical situation. But this is a rather flexible criterion, and not likely to lead to complete unanimity of opinion. It puts a tremendous burden upon the hearers, each of whom will be tempted to view the matter in terms of his own self-interests. It is evident that both Jeremiah and Hananiah had a following, and that the supporters of each could find some legitimate grounds for believing that their man's message was faithful to the tradition and relevant to the situation. I have dealt specifically with this problem in another place, and will not repeat that discussion here (1970, chaps. II and V). It is sufficient for our present purposes to point out the intensity and significance of this feedback from the people to the prophet and suggest the mechanism by which it works.

As to whether the content of Jeremiah's message was affected by this feedback, the data are not so clear. In the Hananiah episode we have reference to a specific occasion on which the prophet was at least temporarily blocked and forced to retreat for some reconsideration and/or renewal of his message (28:11-16). Taken in conjunction with other passages in which he expresses doubts about his revelation (15:18, 20:7), it would seem reasonable to conclude that the intensity of the negative feedback Jeremiah experienced from time to time caused him to reconsider both the content of what he said and his own continuance in the prophetic office (cf. 20:9). Beyond that, the passages of more positive tone referred to above may indicate a response to a changing historical situation (looking beyond the destruction of Judah and Jerusalem) and mark the beginning of a substantive change in the prophet's long-standing proclamation of doom.

A summary of Handsome Lake's proclamation to the Iroquois has come down to us in the Gaiwiio. This narrative begins with an account of an episode of drunkenness and destruction in Cornplanter's village and of the prophet's sickness, death, and resurrection. It is in connection with the latter experience that the main themes of Handsome Lake's proclamation assert themselves, for the messengers revealed to him the four great wrongs by which "men spoil the laws the Great Ruler has made and thereby make him angry": drinking whiskey, using witchcraft, using "compelling charms," and practicing abortion. In the remaining sections considerable space is given to positive commands relating to social behavior (gossip, drunkenness, sharing, mourning customs, etc.), family life (the care of children, husband-wife relationships, the care of elders), and religion (the medicine societies were ordered to disband, but a number of the traditional ceremonies are specifically sanctioned and regulated). In addition the Code deals in several places with the relationship between Indians and whites (agriculture, schooling, and the Creator's protection of his people against extermination by the whites) and with the status of the prophet (disbelief is said to be due to the operation of an evil spirit, and will be punished). A number of these themes are reinforced in the sections recounting the second revelation (the "sky journey"), where Handsome Lake witnessed the suffering of a variety of sinners (drunkard, wife-beater, gambler, etc.) in the house of the "punisher." Finally, there is reference to the apocalyptic themes of the sin of the world and the world's end and renewal.

Wallace understands the preaching of Handsome Lake to fall into two distinct phases. The first, covering the years 1799 to 1801, was characterized by an "apocalyptic gospel" in which the people were summoned to repentance and the recurring themes were world destruction, sin, and salvation. The second phase began in 1801 and featured a "social gospel" in which the main values that were stressed were "temperance, peace and unity, land retention, acculturation, and a revised domestic morality" (Wallace, 1972:278, cf. 239-302). As in the case of Jeremiah the response to this message was mixed. In the early years he was able to exercise both political and religious power, and the council at Buffalo Creek in 1801 prohibited the use of liquor and appointed him "High Priest, and principal Sachem in all things Civil and Religious." Over the next few years, however, his political influence declined. In 1807 the Iroquois confederacy was reorganized and the great council fire established at Buffalo Creek, where one of the prophet's chief rivals, Red Jacket, was influential. Handsome Lake and Cornplanter also quarreled, and factions developed in the Allegany band, causing the prophet to move out and locate first at Cold Spring and later at Tonawanda. But his religious influence remained strong. He made an annual circuit of visitations to other reservations preaching his gospel and winning converts (Wallace, 1972:260f., 286ff., 296ff.). As Wallace describes it, "these conversions were not casual matters. The Indians traversed the same mystic path to Gaiwiio as white converts to Christianity; the converts retained an intense devotion to the prophet who gave them strength to achieve salvation. 'One of the Onondagas, when asked why they did not leave their drunken habits before, since they were often urged to do it, and saw the ruinous consequences of such conduct replied, they had no power; but when the Great Spirit forbid such conduct by their prophet, he gave them the power to comply with their request" (1972:301).

What one notices about the Gaiwiio is how directly it spoke to the situation that plagued the Iroquois of Handsome Lake's day. Addressing a people debauched and demoralized by contact with white culture and the loss of their own traditional ways, the Gaiwiio accused them of wrong-doing /10/, laying heavy stress on evils disruptive of harmonious community life (strong drink, witchcraft, charms, and abortion, Parker: 27-30). In its commandments great emphasis was placed on the strengthening of family relationships and the regulation of social behavior /11/. In response to the growing influence of white culture there was explicit approval of farming, house-building, animal husbandry, and, to a limited extent, education "in English schools" (Parker: 38).

In real life parts of this message evoked a negative response and caused the prophet trouble, particularly his determined attacks against witchcraft and supposed witch-inspired conspiracies. Reaction to the execution of one witch in 1809 caused him to have to leave Cold Spring, a situation reflected in the Gaiwiio: "Now it was that when the people reviled me, the proclaimer of the prophecy, the impression came to me that it would be well to depart and go to Tonawanda. In that place I had relatives and friends and thought that my bones might find a resting place there" (Parker: 47, cf. Wallace, 1972: 254-262, 291-294). Other sections which mirror responses to feedback in specific situations have been mentioned above.

The Gaiwiio spoke to the current situation, advocating such important cultural innovations as the involvement of men in farm labor, limited acceptance of white education, and the dissolution of the totem animal societies. But for all that, the Gaiwiio "made sense" in light of the traditions of the past. Social solidarity was stressed in the ethical commandments of the Code, and in particular the old religious values and ceremonies were for the most part retained. Its major new religious concept, the notion of judgment and afterlife in heaven or hell, was compatible with the old beliefs and was introduced "to insure the dedication of the people to conservative ritual." Handsome Lake "was in his own eyes as the messenger of God, necessarily the defender of the faith" (Wallace, 1972:318; cf. 251-254, 315-318). As Parker puts it, "Handsome Lake sought to destroy the ancient folk-ways of the people and to substitute a new system, *built of course upon the framework of the old*" (114; emphasis added). Eventually, a myth even developed to account for the origin of the conditions that made the Gaiwiio necessary and fix its place in the overall order of things (see note 7).

The position taken in this paper is that feedback from the people to the prophet is important both because of its potential for helping to shape the latter's message and because their acceptance forms one of the bases of his prophetic authority. That the message of Handsome Lake gained such wide acceptance among the Iroquois in his own day would seem to be due largely to the skill with which he utilized the old traditions of the people in addressing himself to the crucial problems of the present. And when after his death (1815) some of the traditional Iroquois leaders sought a way to counter the threats of both sectarian Christian and disruptive nativists, they found it convenient to call upon the memory of Handsome Lake in attempting to define the form and spirit of the old religion. At the religious council at Tonawanda in the summer of 1818 John Sky repeated a version of Handsome Lake's teaching and a minor prophet recounted a vision of confirming it. Similar incidents occurred over the next two decades, and by the 1840s the text of the Code, which continues to this day to be an important force in Iroquois life, was fixed (Wallace, 1969: 330-37).

3.3   In discussing specific instances of prophecy we are always dependent upon the vicissitudes of historical reporting for our information. This is especially evident in the case of the final interactive element of the model, *expectations of confirmation*. We are dealing here largely with beliefs based upon circulating reports of individual experiences of a "supernatural" character, and such pious tales easily escape the attention of the chroniclers of prophetic movements. Nevertheless, enough examples are available to suggest that this element was of importance in the people's response to a prophet. Faith in Wovoka, the prophet of the Ghost Dance of 1890, was certainly enhanced by Indians returning from visits to his camp with tales of how he could control the weather and miraculously "shorten" the homeward journey of those who made the long trip from the northern Plains to western Nevada to visit him (Overholt, 1974:47-48). With respect to Handsome Lake the same dynamics can be seen at work in the Onondagas crediting the Great Spirit with giving them the power to give up alcohol and follow the Gaiwiio, as well as in the visions of other prophets confirming his message. If it is difficult to find such clear examples as this in Jeremiah (20:7-8 and 44:16-19 rather seem to echo disconfirming experiences), that is perhaps because the book as we have it is preoccupied with the negative reactions of Jeremiah's audience to him.

4.   It seems fair to conclude on the basis of the foregoing summary of evidence that the model which I have proposed for understanding the nature of the prophetic process "works" cross-culturally. That is to say, it provides us with categories in terms of which to compare the activity of two such culturally disparate holy men as Jeremiah and Handsome Lake in a fashion not unduly prejudiced by the obvious differences in their respective messages. This is an important conclusion in several respects. In the first place it has been pointed out above that the processes of interaction which lie at the heart of the prophetic act have for the most part not been given their due by students of prophetic movements. Moreover, it would seem that adopting this view of prophecy enables us to put into satisfactory perspective three interrelated problems which are important for any attempt to understand prophecy: the nature of the situation in which the prophet operates, the nature of prophetic authority, and the problem of how the content of a prophet's proclamation relates to the cultural tradition in which he stands.

4.1   The prophetic process has its locus in a specific situation. This means that any discussion of a prophet's activity will need to be informed by details of the cultural context and historical moment in which he operated. The question is whether in comparing situations which gave rise to prophecy one can say anything beyond the widely recognized fact that they are invariably times of "crisis." Let me briefly suggest, with the aid of concepts borrowed from Kenelm Burridge and Clifford Geertz, that it is possible to understand these situations more fully.

Burridge's view of the prophetic situation derives from his notion that religion is "the redemptive process indicated by the activities, moral rules, and assumptions about power which, pertinent to the moral order and taken on faith, not only enable a people to perceive the truth of things, but guarantee that they are indeed perceiving the truth of things" (6–7). Religion thus establishes a prestige system in which the criteria of one's integrity within the social order are well-known and consistent with everyday experience. The crisis of the prophetic situation resides specifically in the fact that events have taken place (usually involving contact with another culture) which have posed a serious challenge to these assumptions. The result is that the experience of a loss of prestige and integrity and the need for regeneration are widely felt among the populace. In a similar fashion Geertz speaks of a religious system as a cluster of sacred symbols woven into an ordered whole which supports a certain view of morality "by picturing a world in which such conduct is only common sense" (1973:129). Religion creates a synthesis of ethos (the moral and aesthetic tone of a culture) and world view (a culture's picture of the way things are in sheer actuality). Either of these elements taken by itself "is arbitrary, but taken together they form a gestalt with a peculiar kind of inevitability" (1973:130). Above all, such symbolic activities are "attempts to provide orientation for an organism which cannot live in a world it is unable to understand" (1973:140–141). The prophetic situation, then, is one in which the basic religio-cultural understanding has been undermined. In what did the integrity of the Seneca male reside, now that the game animals were depleted and he could no longer go to war? To be able to subsist more emphasis had to be put on farming, but that was woman's work! And what could be more damaging to the system of beliefs about Yahweh's election and protection of his people Israel than the death of "good king Josiah" and the first Babylonian conquest of Jerusalem (597 B.C.E.) and exiling of its inhabitants? In these situations men found chaos breaking in upon them (cf. Geertz, 1966:12–24), but heard as well prophets like Jeremiah and Handsome Lake proclaiming an interpretation which promised a new order.

4.2   This leads to a second problem, viz. how one is to understand the basis or source of a prophet's authority. My main concern here has been to avoid a one-way interpretation of the prophet's activity, that is to say, an interpretation of the power of the prophet over others which dwells too exclusively on the presumed divine source of his message. The divine revelation which the prophet claims is, of course, important to his understanding of himself (cf. Amos 3:8), and can be used to justify his utterances (Jer 26:12–15) and condemn his opponents (Jer 28:15–16). It is also an important element in the people's understanding of a prophet. But despite this fact the prophet's exercise of his role cannot be effective unless his message is met with a positive response on the part of at least some of his hearers.

Thus there are two aspects to the prophet's authority. On the one hand, the prophet makes the claim that the deity has authorized the proclamation of a certain message. The basis of this claim is usually a religious experience which is private and therefore essentially intangible and unverifiable by the members of his audience, who nevertheless assume that a genuine prophet will have had such an experience. I wish to be emphatic about this, since the "call" of a deity is an absolutely crucial element in the constitution of a given occurrence of prophecy, not only in the OT but in other cultures as well. On the other hand, the prophet cannot be effective, cannot function as a prophet, unless the people acknowledge his claim to authority by their reaction to his words, and the social reality of prophecy depends upon this act. The brute fact behind the words of Peter Worsley quoted above is that the members of the prophet's audience are free to choose whom they will follow. Burke Long has summarized the matter in this way:

> The authority of a prophet was a vulnerable, shifting social reality—closely tied to acceptance and belief. It was supported by concrete deeds of power. . . . But the authority rested upon acceptance of those appeals (19).

To speak of authority in terms of acceptance is to acknowledge that, from the point of view of the hearers, a particular instance of prophecy will be deemed "authoritative" on the basis of certain tangible marks. One such mark is the prophet's ability to clarify and articulate what the people who follow him have themselves begun to feel about their particular situation. His utterances are experienced as having explanatory power. Burridge in fact sees the task of the prophet as one of organizing and articulating a new set of assumptions which suggest a way of making sense out of the chaos of the present situation (11-14). In doing so he concentrates in himself the people's own probings, and his revelation usually "echoes the theorizing and experimentation that has gone before" (111). The prophet is thus a transitional figure in a redemptive process the goal of which is the regeneration of the people as a group, i.e., the creation of new assumptions about power in the broad sense, a new politico-economic framework, a new mode of measuring man, new criteria of integrity, a new community. The people choose their prophets, that is they attribute authority to them, because they perceive in their proclamation continuity with the cultural traditions sufficient to make what they say intelligible and at the same time innovations sufficient to offer the possibility of a new interpretation that will bring order out of chaos. Thus, a second and closely-related mark of a prophet's authority is the effectiveness, real or imagined, which seems to characterize his activities. This effectiveness is perhaps most often experienced in the form of rhetorical skill (to his followers the prophet's message "makes sense" out of the current crisis situation), but marvelous acts, including instances of fulfilled prophecy, may also play a role (cf. Long: 13-16). Such seemingly supernatural occurrences help to confirm the authenticity of the prophet. They are accounted for in the model under the rubric "expectations of confirmation."

From the point of view of audience reaction, then, the general criterion for the attribution of authority to a prophet might be expressed as "perceived effectiveness." The hearers do not by their act of attributing authority to a prophet confer his powers on him, since, from one point of view, the claim to supernatural designation means that he already has or is perceived to have these powers. What they do, in effect, is confirm him in his role. Their affirmative response, necessary for his exercise of that role, is an act of commitment based on their recognition of that power. It must be stressed, however, that while some positive response to his message appears to be necessary for the operation of prophecy, large numbers are not. Crenshaw has shown with respect to the OT prophets that conflict with perhaps the great majority of those who heard them (even other prophets) was "inevitable" and that on the whole they had little impact upon their contemporaries. That they had some support, however, is shown both by references to specific instances (Isaiah's mention of his disciples, 8:16; the aid Jeremiah received from various members of the house of Shaphan, 26:4, chap. 36) and by the very fact that their utterances were preserved, collected, and eventually committed to writing.

Perhaps one of the most striking examples of this role of the people is the case of Yali, a native leader in post-World War II New Guinea. Though he made no supernatural claims for himself, his audience began to attribute prophetic authority to him, in effect making him a prophet even in the absence of any claims to revelatory experience. Without their reaction he would neither have claimed to be nor functioned as a prophet (Lawrence). Since prophecy is always situation-bound and public, private revelation alone is insufficient to establish its authority /12/.

4.3   This leads, finally, to the problem of how much "old" and how much "new" we might expect to find in a prophet's message. There can, of course, be no neat formula. Clearly, the message must have enough recognizable roots in the traditional but now threatened cultural synthesis for it to be understood and acceptable. In Burridge's scheme the millenial prophet is central to a process by which a people moves from a time when the "old rules" of the society remained intact, through an interim time of "no rules," and to a final synthesis of a set of "new rules" (165-169). Thus a consistent theme in Handsome Lake's preaching was condemnation of the individual autonomy and glorification that had been characteristic of the old Iroquois way, lately fallen into the chaos of social pathology, while advocating in its place restraint in social affairs. Elizabeth Tooker has suggested that what the prophet was trying to do was "to introduce a value system . . . consistent with the economic system that was also introduced at the same time" (187). With the collapse of the old hunting-trading system the Iroquois were forced into more intensive agriculture, but plow agriculture is a man's work and the yearly agricultural schedule demands a stable social order. Therefore, the values he selected emphasized communal order over individual gratification. If these values were similar to those of the white society, it was primarily because both were agrarian.

That the message of the OT prophets arises out of and is in dialogue with the religious traditions of their people is well-known (cf. Clements, 1965, 1975). For his part Jeremiah stood within the old exodus-election tradition of Judah (cf. for example, 2:1–8). His accusations against the people make it clear that from his viewpoint (i.e., that of a "pure" Yahwist; one wonders how many such there were among his compatriots) the present period was one of "no" rules, at least in the sense that the people had chosen to ignore important aspects of their covenant with Yahweh. Put differently, we might say that he was interpreting the fruits of a long process of acculturation in the land of Canaan as apostasy. Yet in the future he saw the institution of a "new covenant," one recognizable in terms of the old but operating on the basis of new assumptions about the nature of the relationship between Yahweh and Israel (31:31–34).

5. Almost inevitably when we look at a prophet we consider first the content of his proclamation, and having adopted this approach we are likely to be most impressed by his differences from all other prophets about whom we know. The argument of this paper has been that when we go beneath the level of content to that of process significant similarities begin to emerge. And having learned something about the underlying similarities of two specific prophets, Jeremiah and Handsome Lake, we have, I believe, gained at least some understanding of all other prophets as well.

NOTES

/1/ The temporal vicissitudes of scholarly publishing make a note on chronology appropriate. This paper brings to completion a series of interconnected studies of the "prophetic process" which includes Overholt 1974 and 1977. In recent years there has been increasing interest in the "social location" of Israelite prophecy, and in the interval between the final revisions of this paper and its publication an important book-length study of the dynamic interrelationship between the Israelite prophets and their society has appeared which is limited by neither of the tendencies described in the following paragraphs (Wilson).

/2/ W. Eichrodt's emphasis is on the covenant, the continuity through time of the Mosaic religion, and the personal quality of the divine-human relationship, G. von Rad is concerned with the larger process by which Israel's traditions underwent a series of reinterpretations, and L. Köhler mines the prophetic literature to construct a theological position conceived in Western categories.

/3/ A note on terminology is in order. In his recent work on the phenomenon Robert R. Wilson has chosen not to speak of "prophets," but rather of varieties of "intermediaries" who can be located with relation to each other along a continuum (Wilson). The figures I have been studying under the rubric "prophet" are the OT prophets and leaders of non-Israelite "nativistic" movements. A millenarian component is often important in the proclamation of these persons, but that term alone does not provide a sufficient explanatory framework for understanding the process characteristic of their activity.

/4/ This date has been disputed. For a discussion of the evidence cf. Overholt, 1971. On the history of this period cf. 2 Kings 15-25; M. Noth: 253-298, J. Bright: 259-319, A Malamat, 1968:137-156, and J. McKay.

/5/ Cf. Jer 26 and 36. In all of this Jeremiah, too, had his supporters in high places. Note particularly the references to members of the house of Shaphan in Jer 26:24; 29:3; 36:10-13; 25; 40:5f.; 41:2. Cf. Wilcoxen.

/6/ This brief historical sketch depends mainly on Wallace, 1972, especially pp. 21-236.

/7/ The followers of Handsome lake recounted a legend of how the "evil one" enticed an unsuspecting young European to bring a bundle of "five things" (a flask of rum, a pack of playing cards, some coins, a violin, and a decaying leg bone) across the ocean to the Indians. This gift resulted in great misery and made necessary the "Good Message" or Gaiwiio (Parker: 16-19). On drinking at Cornplanter's village cf. Parker: 20-22, and Wallace, 1972:193f., 228-236.

/8/ For a somewhat more detailed analysis of the Jeremiah materials from the point of view of this model cf. Overholt, 1977.

/9/ This chronology was reconstructed by Wallace on the basis of the Simmons journal and other sources. The present form of the Code as represented in Parker has some of the revelations out of context. Cf. Wallace, 1972:359f., n. 5.

/10/ "The Creator is sad because of the sins of the beings that he created. He ordained that mankind should live as social beings in communities." Parker: 36.

/11/ It is clear that Burke Long and I have been thinking about the problem of prophetic authority for several years now, and along similar lines. An earlier statement of the position taken here (Overholt, 1977:144-45) and the original draft of this paper were written before I had access to his 1976 study, but I want to acknowledge the influence of that study and of personal communications from Prof. Long on the final wording of these pages. One difference in our formulations is my suggestion that "perceived effectiveness" is likely to have been a general criterion for the hearers' attribution of authority to a prophet. Cf. also Overholt, 1979.

/12/ On the matter of the prophet's authority cf. also Overholt, 1979.

WORKS CONSULTED

Baltzer, K.
1968 "Considerations Regarding the Office and Calling of the Prophet." *HTR* 61: 567-81.

Barnett, Homer G.
1953 *Innovation:The Basis of Cultural Change*. New York: McGraw-Hill.

Barrow, G. L.
1951 "The Story of Jonfrum." *Corona* 3: 379-382.

Berkhofer, Robert F.
1965 "Faith and Factionalsim among the Seneca." *Ethnohistory* 12: 99-112.

Bright, John
1959 *A History of Israel*. Philadelphia: Westminster.

Burridge, Kenelm O. L.
1969 *New Heaven, New Earth*. New York: Schocken.

Chinnery, E. W. P. and A. C. Haddon
1916-17 "Five New Religious Cults in British New Guinea." *HibJ* 15: 448-463.

Clements, R. E.
1965 *Prophecy and Covenant*. London, SCM.
1975 *Prophecy and Tradition*. Oxford: Blackwell.

Crenshaw, James L.
1971 *Prophetic Conflict: Its Effect Upon Israelite Religion*. BZAW 124. Berlin: de Gruyter.

Deardorff, M. H.
1951 "The Religion of Handsome Lake: Its Origin and Development." Pp. 79-107 in *Symposium on Local Diversity in Iroquois Culture*. Ed. W. N. Fenton. Bureau of American Ethnology, Bulletin 149. Washington: Government Printing Office.

Donner, H.
1963 "Die soziale Botschaft der Propheten in Lichte der Gesellschaftsordnung in Israel." *OrAnt* 2: 229-245.

Eckert, Georg
1937 "Prophetentum in Melanesien." *Zeitschrift für Ethnologie* 69: 135-140.

Eichrodt, Walter
1961 *Theology of the Old Testament*. Vol. 1. London: SCM.

Fabian, J.
1963 "Führer und Führung in den prophetisch-messianischen Bewegungen der (ehemaligen) Kolonialvölker." *Anthropos* 58: 773-809.

Festinger, Leon; Henry W. Riecken; and Stanley Schachter
1956 *When Prophecy Fails*. Minneapolis: University of Minnesota.

Geertz, Clifford
1966 "Religion as a Cultural System." Pp. 1-46 in *Anthropological Approaches to the Study of Religion*. Ed. M. Barton. London: Tavistock.
1973 "Ethos, World-View, and the Analysis of Sacred Symbols." Pp.126-141 in *The Interpretation of Cultures*. New York: Basic Books. (Originally published in 1957.)

Griffin, William B.
1970 "A North Mexican Nativistic Movement." *Ethnohistory* 17: 95-116.

Guariglia, G.
1958 "Prophetismus and Heilserwartungsbewegungen in niedern Kulturen." *Numen* 5: 180-198.

Guiart, Jean
1951 "John Frum Movement in Tanna." *Oceania* 22: 165-175.
1956 "Culture Contact and the 'John Frum' Movement on Tanna." *Southwestern Journal of Anthropology* 12: 105-116.

Hayes, John H.
1969 "Prophetism at Mari and Old Testament Parallels." *Trinity University Studies in Religion* 9: 31-41.

Huffmon, H. B.
1968 "Prophecy in the Mari Letters." *Biblical Archaeologist* 31:101-124.

Jarvie, I. C.
1963   "Theories of Cargo Cults: a Critical Analysis." *Oceania* 34: 1–31, 108–136.

Johnson, A. R.
1962   *The Cultic Prophet in Ancient Israel.* 2nd Ed. Cardiff, University of Wales.

Köbben, A. J. F.
1960   "Prophetic Movements as an Expression of Social Protest." *International Archives of Ethnography* 44: 117–164.

Koch, Klaus
1971   "Die Entstehung der sozialen Kritik bei den Profeten." Pp. 236–257 in *Probleme Biblischer Theologie: Gerhard von Rad zum 70. Geburtstag am 21.10.1971.* Ed. H. W. Wolf. Munich: Kaiser.

Köhler, L.
1957   *Old Testament Theology.* London: Lutterworth.

Koppers, W.
1959   "Prophetismus und Messianismus als völkerkundliches und universalgeschichtliches Problem." *Saeculum* 10: 38–47.

La Barre, Weston
1971   "Materials for a History of Studies of Crisis Cults: A Bibliographic Essay." *Current Anthropology* 12: 3–44.

Lanternari, Vittorio
1963   *The Religions of the Oppressed.* New York: Knopt.

Lawrence, Peter
1964   *Road Belong Cargo: A Study of the Cargo Movement in the Southern Madang District, New Guinea.* Manchester: Manchester University.

Lindblom, J
1962   *Prophecy in Ancient Israel.* Oxford: Blackwell.

Linton, Ralph
1943   "Nativistic Movements." *American Anthropologist* 45: 230–240.

Long, Burke O.
1977   "Prophetic Authority as Social Reality." Pp. 3–20 in *Canon and Authority.* Eds. G. W. Coats and B. O. Long. Philadelphia: Fortress.

McKay, John
1973   *Religion in Judah under the Assyrians.* London: SCM.

Malamat, A.
1966   "Prophetic Revelations in New Documents from Mari and the Bible." *VTSup* 15: 207–27.

1968   "The Last Kings of Judah and the Fall of Jerusalem, An Historical-Chronological Study." *IEJ* 18: 137–156.

May, L. Carlyle
1954   "The Dancing Religion: A Japanese Messianic Sect." *Southwestern Journal of Anthropology* 10: 119–137.

Mooney, James
1896   "The Ghost-Dance Religion and the Sioux Outbreak of 1890." *Annual Report of the Bureau of American Ethnology* 14. Washington: Government Printing Office.

Moran, W. L.
1969   "New Evidence from Mari on the History of Prophecy." *Bib* 50: 15–56.

Noth, Martin
1958   *The History of Israel*. New York: Harper.

Overholt, Thomas W.
1970   *The Threat of Falsehood: A Study in the Theology of the Book of Jeremiah*. London: SCM.
1971   "Some Reflections on the Date of Jeremiah's Call." *CBQ* 33: 165–184.
1974   "The Ghost Dance of 1890 and the Nature of the Prophetic Process." *Ethnohistory* 21: 37–63.
1977   "Jeremiah and the Nature of the Prophetic Process." Pp. 129–150 in *Scripture in History and Theology: Essays in Honor of J. Coert Rylaarsdam*. Eds. Arthur L. Merrill and Thomas W. Overholt. Pittsburgh: Pickwick.
1979   "Commanding the Prophets: Amos and the Problem of Prophetic Authority." *CBQ* 41: 517–532.

Parker, Arthur C.
1913   "The Code of Handsome Lake, the Seneca Prophet." *New York State Museum* Bulletin. No. 163. Albany: University of the State of New York Press. Reprinted in W. N. Fenton, ed. *Parker on the Iroquois*. Syracuse: Syracuse University, 1968.

Pedersen, J.
1946   "The Role Played by Inspired Persons among the Israelites and the Arabs." Pp. 127–142 in *Studies in Old Testament Prophecy*. Ed. H. H. Rowley. Edinburgh: T. & T. Clark.

Rad, Gerhard von
1965   *Old Testament Theology*. Vol. 2. New York: Harper and Row.

Ross, J. R.
1962   "The Prophet as Yahweh's Messenger." Pp. 89–107 in *Israel's Prophetic Heritage*. Eds. B. W. Anderson and W. Harrelson. New York: Harper.

Schlosser, K.
1950   "Prophetismus in niederen Kulturen." *Zeitschrift für Ethnologie* 75: 60–72.

Shimony, Annemarie
1961   *Conservatism Among the Iroquois at the Six Nations Reserve*. Yale University Publications in Anthropology 65. New Haven: Department of Anthropology, Yale University.

Sundkler, B.G.M.
1961   *Bantu Prophets in South Africa*. 2d ed. Oxford: Oxford University Press.

Sutherland, W.
1910   "The 'Tuka' Religion." *Transactions of the Fijian Society, 1908–1910*: 51–57.

Talmon, J. L.
1958   "Social Prophetism in 19th Century France." *Commentary* 26: 158–172.

Thompson, Basil
1895   "The Kalou-Vu (ancestor-gods) of the Fijians and A New Religion: The Tuka Cult." *Journal of the Anthropological Institute of Great Britain and Ireland* 24: 340–359.

Tooker, Elizabeth
1968 "On the New Religion of Handsome Lake." *Anthropological Quarterly* 41: 187–200.

Wallace, Anthony F. C.
1956 "Revitalization Movements." *American Anthropologist* 58: 264–281.
1972 *The Death and Rebirth of the Seneca*. New York: Vintage.

Wilcoxen, Jay A.
1977 "The Political Background of Jeremiah's Temple Sermon." Pp. 151–166 in *Scripture in History and Theology: Essays in Honor of J. Coert Rylaarsdam*. Eds. Arthur L. Merrill and Thomas W. Overholt. Pittsburgh: Pickwick.

Williams, F. E.
1923 *The Vailala Madness and the Destruction of Native Ceremonies in the Gulf Division*. Port Moresby, Papuan Anthropology Reports, No. 4.
1934 "The Vailala Madness in Retrospect." Pp. 369–379 in *Essays Presented to C. G. Seligman*. Eds. E. E. Evans-Pritchard, Raymond Firth, Bronislaw Malinowski, and Isaac Schapera. London: Routledge & Kegan Paul.

Wilson, Robert R.
1980 *Prophecy and Society*. Philadelphia: Fortress Press.

Worsley, Peter
1968 *The Trumpet Shall Sound*. 2d ed. New York: Schocken.

Zenner, Walter P.
1966 "The Case of the Apostate Messiah: A Reconsideration of the 'Failure of Prophecy.'" *Archives de Sociologie des Religions* 21: 111–118.

FROM PROPHECY TO APOCALYPTIC: REFLECTIONS ON THE SHAPE OF ISRAELITE RELIGION

Robert R. Wilson
Yale University

ABSTRACT

Recent attempts to tie Israelite apocalyptic to a particular tradition stream such as prophecy or wisdom appear to be unable to accommodate all of the biblical evidence. Both prophetic and priestly elements appear in some of the so-called proto-apocalyptic passages in the prophetic books, and the Book of Daniel, the best example of early Israelite apocalyptic, contains explicit allusions to the prophetic traditions but at the same time employs wisdom motifs and vocabulary. New light on the problem of Israelite apocalyptic comes from recent anthropological studies of apocalyptic groups. The anthropological evidence indicates that any group can develop into an apocalyptic group if the right sociological conditions are present. However, the shape of the group's apocalyptic program will depend on the cultural background of the group's members. When this insight is applied to the Book of Daniel, a unique apocalyptic group emerges, a group not related exclusively to a single Israelite theological tradition. When other apocalyptic writings are analyzed in this way, it may be possible to understand more fully the complex character of apocalyptic religion in Israel.

0.1   Since the beginning of the critical study of the Hebrew Bible in the late nineteenth century, scholars have had trouble dealing with apocalyptic religion and literature. While pre-critical scholars were able to view books like Daniel as genuine and historically accurate sources of divine revelation about future events, critical scholars faced the task of analyzing apocalyptic as a religious phenomenon rooted in a particular historical setting and influenced by a variety of social, political, and theological forces. The results of this research then had to be integrated into the history of biblical religion and literature. However, many researchers found it difficult to fit apocalyptic into the religious and literary histories that they were reconstructing. In the opinion of these early scholars, apocalyptic religion was completely alien to preexilic Israelite Yahwism and had nothing to do with the profound theological insights of the prophets. For this reason some scholars ignored apocalyptic completely, while others regarded it as a late, degenerate feature of Israelite popular religion which was not originally Israelite at all but which was imported into Israel from outside sources. A number of external sources were suggested, but by the early twentieth century there was general agreement that most biblical apocalyptic ultimately had Persian roots. It was therefore a foreign import which did not originally grow on Israelite soil.

0.2　Having solved the problem of the origins of apocalyptic religion in Israel, early critical scholars turned their attention to the study of apocalyptic literature itself. Their normal approach to this topic was simply to catalogue the literary features and theological motifs to be found in the apocalyptic portions of the Bible. Over the years these lists have varied somewhat, but they have usually included items such as the notion of divine transcendence, the presence of a developed angelology, fantastic symbolism, cosmic imagery, the use of foreign mythology, reinterpretation of prophecy, references to cataclysm, judgment, the Day of the Lord, the destruction of hostile nations, the coming of the messianic age, and the resurrection of the dead (Russell: 91).

0.3　The early scholarly consensus about the origin of apocalyptic religion and the nature of apocalyptic literature was preserved largely intact for a number of years, and little new work was done on the subject. To be sure, the discovery of an almost archetypical apocalyptic community at Qumran forced a reevaluation of the apocalyptic roots of early Christianity and intertestamental Judaism, but students of ancient Israelite religion were not really touched by this activity. The new evidence from Qumran was later than the Hebrew Bible and could easily be accommodated in the standard view that apocalyptic religion was a late development in Israel and came about under Persian influence.

1.1　However, within the last ten years Israelite apocalyptic has once again become a subject for scholarly debate, and numerous new studies have appeared (Nicholson: 189–213). Included among them are at least two challenges to scholarly orthodoxy about the origins of Israelite apocalyptic. The first of these challenges came from Gerhard von Rad, who, in his attempt to fit apocalyptic into Israel's religious traditions, came to the conclusion that apocalyptic was the product of the wisdom movement in Israel. The keystone of von Rad's argument is the observation that time and the determination of time play an important role in apocalyptic literature such as Daniel, which contains several cosmic timetables purporting to sketch out in some detail the future events which are to occur. This information about the future course of history is hidden from ordinary people and can be uncovered only by the wise, who have been granted divinely revealed knowledge. Apocalyptic thus necessarily moves beyond the historical realm and deals with an unknown future which is in the process of being shaped by supernatural forces. According to von Rad, this move places apocalyptic outside of the mainstream of Israelite religion, which stresses God's saving activities in history and which celebrates those activities in its historical and prophetic traditions and in its cult (1965:301–308). Von Rad finds the closest analogues to apocalyptic views in Israel's wisdom writings, which, according to von Rad, are also concerned with the proper determination of times and with the acquisition of knowledge about the future (1972:278–282).

1.2   A second major challenge to the orthodox scholarly view of apocalyptic has recently been presented by Paul Hanson. In a major book and a series of articles, Hanson criticizes the standard view because it cannot adequately comprehend all apocalyptic literature. The lists of apocalyptic features which scholars have collected do not actually correspond completely to any given apocalypse. Hanson also criticizes von Rad for unnecessarily driving a wedge between apocalyptic and Israel's other traditions, particularly the prophetic tradition. Rather, Hanson argues, Israelite apocalyptic was a natural outgrowth of Israelite prophecy, and it is therefore not necessary to resort to theories of outside influence to explain the existence of apocalyptic in Israel. The basic elements of Hanson's own view can be outlined as follows:

> (1) The sources of apocalyptic eschatology lie solidly within the prophetic tradition of Israel; (2) the period of origin is in the sixth to the fifth centuries; (3) the essential nature of apocalyptic is found in the abandonment of the prophetic task of translating the vision of the divine council into historical terms; (4) the historical and sociological matrix of apocalyptic is found in an inner-community struggle in the period of the Second Temple between visionary [prophetic] and hierocratic [priestly] elements. (1975:29)

Hanson supports his position with a careful analysis of Second and Third Isaiah and Zechariah 9–14 and is able to demonstrate conclusively that in these instances apocalyptic did indeed grow out of prophecy.

1.3   Although Hanson's views are a much needed corrective to the orthodox scholarly position, there are hints that he has not completely solved the problem of biblical apocalyptic. First, although Hanson's detailed work does indeed uncover links between apocalyptic and prophecy, his thesis, at least in its classic form, has difficulty explaining the presence of non-prophetic elements in Israelite apocalyptic. In this respect the Book of Daniel is a particular problem, for here von Rad's discovery of wisdom motifs cannot easily be dismissed. Daniel does concern itself with timetables, and what appears to be wisdom terminology also occurs, particularly in the vision reports of chaps. 7–12. For example, in Dan 9:22 the angel Gabriel appears to Daniel and prefaces an interpretation of Daniel's vision with the remark, "I have come to make you understand." Furthermore, the title "the wise" *(maśkîlîm)* appears in the vision report in Dan10:1–12:4 and in the epilogue (12:5–13) as a designation of a human group. In 11:33–35 it is said that when there is oppression by the evil power, "the wise of the people will cause many to understand." As a result of the oppression, some of the wise will fall, but the oppression will serve to purify the wise because the time of the end has not yet come. In Dan 12:3 it is said that the wise will shine like the firmament. They will understand the future course of events, in contrast to the wicked, who will not understand. In the vision chapters, then, the apocalyptic group apparently characterizes itself as "the wise," who understand the meaning of events and who have the responsibility of making others understand. In this connection it is important to remember that in chaps. 1–6 Daniel and his companions are not usually portrayed as prophets or visionaries but as wise men. In 1:3–19 the Israelites are to be trained to join the royal wise men, while in chap. 2 Daniel and his friends are included among the wise who are condemned to slaughter because they cannot reconstruct and interpret the king's dream. In Daniel 5 Daniel is described by the queen as one having the wisdom and understanding necessary to interpret the handwriting on the wall, and both in chap. 4 and in chap. 5 Daniel is apparently able to provide interpretations on the basis of his own wisdom, without being dependent on divine aid. In short, there is evidence that von Rad was correct in seeing wisdom motifs and vocabulary in Daniel, and the reasons for the presence of this material must be investigated. Such an investigation has recently been undertaken by John P. Collins, who supports Hanson's thesis of the prophetic origins of apocalyptic but who also argues for a closer connection between "mantic wisdom" and prophecy, as well as for later apocalyptic influence on Israelite wisdom writers (Collins: 54–59). At the very least Collins's perceptive discussion suggests that the interrelationships between prophecy, wisdom, and apocalyptic may have been more complex than scholars have previously thought. His work also raises questions about the possibility of tracing Israelite apocalyptic to a single religio-historical source.

1.4   A second difficulty with Hanson's thesis is the sharp distinction which he seeks to draw between the visionary (prophetic) elements in Israel that gave rise to apocalyptic and the hierocratic (priestly) elements that opposed the prophetic apocalyptists. The problem here is that some apocalyptic passages, which according to Hanson's theory should reflect prophetic visionary eschatology, in fact seem concerned with priestly matters. For example, Ezekiel 38–39 immediately precedes a detailed account of the reconstruction of the temple (Ezekiel 40–48), an account which Hanson himself convincingly analyzes as a Zadokite priestly reconstruction program. Hanson seeks to solve this problem by analyzing Ezekiel 38–39 as a very late addition concerned with the failure of the prophetic promises to come true (1975:71–74, 234). He is thus able to eliminate the Ezekiel apocalypse from his discussion of the origins of apocalyptic eschatology, but by making this move he leaves unanswered the question of why what appears to be a piece of prophetic apocalyptic literature also has strong links with priestly language and theology. In this connection it is worth noting that Zadokite theology appears elsewhere in Ezekiel and is not confined to chaps. 40–48 (Hanson, 1975:240–242). Hanson experiences similar difficulties in his treatment of Zechariah 1–8, which he admits contains the literary features of apocalyptic but which he wishes to analyze as a series of visions supporting the Zadokite reform program. He is therefore forced to argue that Zechariah 1–8 does not reflect apocalyptic eschatology, even though the visions contain apoclyptic motifs (1975:250–262). This distinction seems difficult to maintain.

1.5   Hanson himself has recognized some of the difficulties with his analysis, and in his most recent treatment of apocalyptic he seeks to clarify his position by making several potentially useful distinctions. According to Hanson, in discussing apocalyptic it is necessary to distinguish an apocalypse (a distinctive literary genre) from apocalyptic eschatology and apocalypticism. Hanson defines apocalyptic eschatology as "a religious perspective, a way of viewing divine plans in relation to mundane realities" (1976:29). In Israel apocalyptic eschatology developed out of prophetic eschatology. In contrast to apocalyptic eschatology, apocalypticism is "the symbolic universe in which an apocalyptic movement codifies its identity and interpretation of reality" (1976:30). According to Hanson, the symbols used by apocalyptists can come from any number of sources, including earlier biblical traditions, Canaanite myth, Zoroastrianism, Greek myth, and wisdom. In Hanson's view, apocalypticism grows out of apocalyptic eschatology, although he does not explain exactly how this process works. Both are products of apocalyptic movements which are composed of alienated individuals and which appear in times of social disintegration.

1.6   While this distinction between apocalyptic eschatology and apocalypticism seems to solve some of the problems in Hanson's earlier work, two fundamental difficulties remain. First, Hanson ultimately provides no explanation for the origin of apocalyptic religion in Israel. Hanson refuses to equate apocalyptic eschatology with apocalyptic religion (1976:29), so the latter is not really considered at all in his discussion. Second, Hanson is unclear about the relation between apocalyptic religion and the various symbolic expressions of that religion. To put the matter in Hanson's own terms, he does not clearly relate apocalyptic religion either to apocalyptic eschatology or to apocalypticism.

2.1   In order to deal with some of the questions that remain after the important work of Hanson and Collins, it may be helpful to approach the problem of apocalyptic from a different direction. In the past, biblical scholars have tried to relate apocalyptic religion and the concrete expressions of that religion by beginning with the apocalyptic literature of the Bible and then by moving behind the literature to the apocalyptic religion that the literature reflects. Ultimately this approach is the only possible one to use in studying an ancient religion. Every theory about the religion must finally be judged against the available evidence, in this case the biblical text. But the way in which scholars have applied this approach in the past has assumed a direct and uncomplicated correlation between the written expression of apocalyptic religion (apocalyptic literature such as Daniel) and the apocalyptic religion itself. Thus, wisdom vocabulary, motifs, and concepts are said to indicate a wisdom origin for apocalyptic religion, and prophetic vocabulary, motifs, and concepts are said to indicate a prophetic origin for apocalyptic religion. This approach will work *only if* the relation between apocalyptic religion and its written expression is in fact direct and uncomplicated. Both apocalyptic religion and apocalyptic literature have been studied separately, but more attention needs to be given to the interrelationship between the two. Therefore, it may be helpful to outline in general terms the nature of apocalyptic religion as it is known from contemporary anthropological sources, where the relation between the religion and its concrete expressions can be studied. This information will illustrate the sorts of factors that cause apocalyptic groups to shape their literature in a particular way. Against the background of the modern evidence, it will then be possible to explore more fully the interrelation between apocalyptic religion and literature in Israel.

2.2   At the outset it is important to note that apocalyptic religion is always characterized by group formation. Apocalyptic religion is not an individualistic phenomenon but one which always appears in the context of a cohesive and relatively well organized group. Members of the group think of themselves as a group and seek to maintain and preserve its structure. They share common feelings and goals and may recognize the authority of a single leader (Lewis: 322–329). It is therefore necessary to approach the problem of apocalyptic religion by examining the groups connected with it.

2.30   Anthropologists are still debating the precise nature of apocalyptic groups, and in fact there is not even any agreement about the titles that should be given to such groups (La Barre, 1971:3–44). However, there does seem to be a consensus on the general sociological characteristics that all successful apocalyptic groups possess (B. Wilson: 1973; La Barre: 1972; Jarvie; Lawrence; Worsley; Cohn; Lofland). It is not necessary to deal with all of these characteristics here, but it is important to notice three of them.

2.31   First, apocalyptic groups are made up of people who are on the periphery of society. They lack political, religious, and social power and have little social status. Furthermore, they *know* that they are on the periphery. They feel repressed and deprived of something which they might reasonably expect to possess. The feelings of deprivation that these people experience may come from various sources. Peripheral individuals may lack food, clothing, useful work, or adequate housing. They may be politically powerless or socially ostracized, feeling that they no longer have a voice in the way in which the society or the government is run. They may even believe that they can no longer control their own lives and destinies. On the other hand, they may simply have the vague feeling that the quality of their lives is poorer than it was in a real or imagined past.

The sort of deprivation involved in apocalyptic groups is rarely absolute but is usually measured in relation to something else. People may measure their present situation against the situation of others in the same culture or in neighboring cultures, or they may measure their present situation against their own past situation.

Although it is normal for some feelings of deprivation to exist in every society, certain conditions tend to intensify those feelings and to create larger numbers of dissatisfied and deprived individuals. Such conditions are present particularly in times of rapid social change. Wars, famines, climatic changes, national economic reversals, and the shock of sudden cross-cultural contact can all lead to unusually widespread and severe feelings of deprivation. Not only do such periods of social upheaval produce political and social inequities that lead to genuine cases of deprivation, but crises such as wars and clashes with other cultures provide opportunities for people to compare their own situation with that of outsiders. These comparisons may lead to feelings of relative deprivation and fuel social unrest. Times of social crises frequently give rise to apocalyptic groups, for in such times feelings of deprivation are increased beyond tolerable levels.

Although members of apocalyptic groups are peripheral individuals, it is important to note that they normally remain physically within the larger society. They may sense a gap of some sort between themselves and the rest of the society, but this gap is usually more psychological than spatial. Participants in apocalyptic groups do not always separate themselves from the society as a whole, nor do they always cut their ties to other groups in which they participate. They may remain within the larger society and still feel that they are a minority within it (Aberle: 209–214; Burridge: 9–10; Barber: 664–668; Lanternari: 243–249; Spier, Suttles, Herskovits: 84–88).

2.32   A second feature of apocalyptic groups is that they have some sort of program for meeting the difficulties experienced by group members. The program expresses in concrete terms the group's analysis of the present state of society (and perhaps even the present state of the entire cosmos) and then outlines the course of future events that will lead to the solution of the group's problems. Apocalyptic programs usually look both forward and backward. The primary concern of apocalyptic groups is with the future, for they look forward to the solution of their present difficulties either in the present world or in a supernatural realm that lies beyond the world of time and space. However, if an apocalyptic program is to be made successful, it must deal with the immediate future as well as with the distant future and must provide group members with immediate realistic goals. If this is not done, the group may lose faith in its comprehensive program and eventually dissolve. However, apocalyptic programs have a historical dimension as well as a future dimension, for apocalyptic groups often tend to shape their picture of the future on the basis of what existed in the past. Sometimes they preserve threatened remnants of the past by incorporating them into the picture of an ideal future, while at other times groups seek to revive conditions believed to have existed before the present time of deprivation.

The nature of the language used to express an apocalyptic group's plan for salvation depends on the backgrounds of group members. They will use symbols, motifs, concepts, and language drawn from their own tradition and cultural experience in order to analyze society and to describe the anxiously awaited future. This means that apocalyptic groups within the same society may use different terms to articulate their programs. The shape of the program depends ultimately on the cultural and traditio-historical context of the group. Thus, while an apocalyptic group may form in any society where the proper sociological conditions are present, the written or oral expression of the group's religious beliefs will be at least partially determined by the backgrounds of the members of the group (Wallace: 270–278; Linton: 230–240; Talmon: 130–133; B. Wilson, 1963:93–114; R. Wilson: 62–68).

2.33   A third characteristic of apocalyptic groups is that they provide their members with some practical means of realizing group programs. These means may be active or passive. If an apocalyptic group uses active means, it will outline specific, usually rational, steps which group members can take to move the group toward its goals. If the group adopts a passive stance, it will take no direct action at all but will simply wait for the achievement of its goals by supernatural means (Wallace: 273–278; B. Wilson, 1963:93–114; Zygmunt: 245–268).

3.1   The anthropological evidence suggests that apocalyptic religion can arise at any time when the necessary sociological conditions are present. For this reason apocalyptic religion might have appeared during any of the times of political, social, and religious upheaval that dotted Israel's long history. However, sociological conditions were particularly favorable for the development of apocalyptic religion during the postexilic period. In recent years a number of scholarly studies have documented the political and religious chaos into which Israel plunged in the wake of the destruction of Jerusalem and the exile. The work of Paul Hanson, O. H. Steck, Morton Smith, and Otto Plöger, among others, has indicated that during and after the exile Israel was increasingly marked by factionalism, with well-formed groups articulating divergent views. Tension and disagreement grew as the postexilic period wore on, and religious problems were made worse by a deteriorating political situation. No matter whose reconstruction of late Israelite political and religious conditions is accepted, the picture is one of inter-group conflict and shifting group fortunes. As some groups accumulated more social, political, and religious power, others must have been pushed out of the religious and political establishments and onto the fringes of society. Hanson has clearly demonstrated that some prophetic groups occupied this position, and at various times priestly groups may have suffered the same fate. The Zadokites responsible for the first version of the temple reconstruction in Ezekiel 40-48 and for the programs advocated in Zechariah 1-8 may have considered themselves a frustrated minority when their plans failed to materialize. In any case, the chaos of the postexilic period set the stage for the formation of various types of apocalyptic groups. Some may have been composed of prophets who were disturbed by the diminution of their authority and by the failure of their prophecies to come true. Other groups may have been made up of former priests who were unhappy with the ascendancy of the Deuteronomic theology and the departure from pure Zadokite views. Still other groups may have been formed by members of the Jerusalemite establishment who were unhappy with the course of political and religious events. Members of these dissident groups would have found themselves increasingly estranged from the central religious and political establishments, with no access to positions of power. In short, these people would have experienced the feelings of deprivation typical of members of apocalyptic groups, and the stage would have been set for the development of such groups.

3.2 The specific shape that these groups gave to their apocalyptic programs would have depended on the backgrounds of their members. Group members coming from prophetic backgrounds would naturally have expressed their views by using symbols, motifs, concepts, and terms drawn from Israel's prophetic traditions. Similarly, former members of the Jerusalemite establishment would have used the distinctive language of their environment, the language of the royal court, which may have been similar to what is commonly called wisdom language. Groups of former priests would have expressed their apocalyptic programs in priestly language. Each group would have simply reflected the language and outlook of its members.

3.3 This brief survey of the anthropological evidence suggests new questions that might be asked of the biblical apocalyptic literature in an attempt to uncover more information about the religious views of the Israelite authors. In particular, the anthropological material indicates that biblical scholars should no longer concern themselves exclusively with the question, "why did apocalyptic religion and literature come into being in Israel?" That question has sociological and historical answers that have already been examined. Rather, scholars should also consider the question, "why did *this particular kind* of apocalyptic religion and literature come into existence?" "What sort of group would have produced literature having this particular shape?"

4.1   In order to illustrate the usefulness of phrasing the interpretive question in this way, we will now reexamine the Book of Daniel, paying particular attention to the way in which this distinctive literature may provide clues to the nature of the group or groups that produced it. However, at the outset two assumptions about the literary history of Daniel need to be stated. First, it is assumed that chaps. 1–6 antedate the Maccabean period and in general reflect a time when persecution was not a major problem (Collins: 8–11). Some of the stories in these chapters, particularly those in chaps. 3 and 6, may be quite old, although it is impossible to date them with any certainty. If one assumes that persecution became more of a problem as the Maccabean period approached, then it would appear that the oldest of the stories are those in which the relationship between the Jews and the government is the most benign (chaps. 3 and 6). Using this criterion, one might suspect that chaps. 4, 5, and 2 were created somewhat later than chaps. 3 and 6. The visions in the last chapters (7–12) are much later and in their final form date from Maccabean times. Second, it is assumed that the entire book was created over a period of time by a single group, although there is really no way to prove or disprove this assumption.

4.2   If one assumes that the earliest material, whenever it is to be dated, is found in the court tales in chaps. 3 and 6, then it is reasonable to accept the narrative's own description of the group involved. On this point the texts are fairly clear. Daniel and his companions are said to have been Jews who were trained for service in the government of the Babylonian and Persian empires. If so, then we might guess that the apocalyptic group that produced the Book of Daniel was composed, at least initially, of upper-class Jews who remained in Babylon after the exile. There they began to work in the government bureaucracy and at least partially assimilated to Persian culture, although they maintained their identity as Jews and saw themselves as a peripheral group within the Persian empire. Because the government was not particularly antagonistic toward foreigners, this cross-cultural interaction presented group members only with the problem of advancing in the bureaucracy without losing their distinctive group identity and compromising the basic elements of their ancestral faith.

4.3   The group expressed its analysis of its current situation and outlined its plans for survival in the familiar stories of the three young men in the fiery furnace (Daniel 3) and Daniel in the lion's den (Daniel 6). Both of these stories are told in language characteristic of the royal court, and both have roughly the same structure. The first story (Daniel 3) begins with the note that Nebuchadnezzar, the king of Babylon, set up a statue and commanded all of the government employees to worship it. There is nothing malicious about this command. It is simply the normal type of capricious behavior which one can expect from a king, and it will cause the government officials only a certain amount of inconvenience. The sensitive reader, however, already realizes that the king's command creates a potentially dangerous situation for the Jewish officials, whose faith demands that they worship only their own God. The Jews are suddenly thrown into the middle of this dangerous situation when some Babylonians inform the king that the Jews are not obeying his command. The king becomes angry and summons the three Jewish officials. He asks them if they intend to obey his command by worshiping the statue, and they reply that they will not. They will maintain their distinctive Jewish identity by obeying the law of their God, even if doing so leads to their deaths. The king then orders them to be thrown into a furnace. They are miraculously saved from death, and in the end the king praises the God of the Jews and promotes them in the bureaucracy.

4.4   The structure of the second story (Daniel 6) is similar to the structure of the first one. At the beginning of the story, the king promotes Daniel to a high government position, an act which angers some of the Persian bureaucrats. To retaliate, they convince the king to command that he alone is to be worshiped for a period of thirty days. The king apparently sees nothing unusual in this proposition, and so he innocently agrees to it. The king's command immediately poses a threat to Daniel, who, as a faithful Jew, can worship only the true God. Daniel persists in praying to his God, a fact which the Persians immediately point out to the king. Because of their urging, the king reluctantly orders Daniel thrown into a den of lions. But Daniel is saved through miraculous divine intervention, and the story ends with the king praising Daniel's God and confirming Daniel's power in the bureaucracy.

4.5   Both of these stories are not only told in language which is characteristic of the group that created them, the language of the royal court, but they also follow a structural pattern commonly found in the bureaucratic or "wisdom" circles in which the group moved. As Walter Baumgartner pointed out long ago, the stories have the basic structure of a typical martyr story. Stories of this type, which are found in many ancient and modern cultures, are didactic in their intent and are designed to inspire and strengthen the faithful so that they will not depart from their faith in times of persecution. However, in this particular case the authors or editors of Daniel 3 and 6 modified the structure of the traditional martyr story to reflect their perception of their current situation. The stories in Daniel are no longer typical martyr stories, for in fact they do not deal with martyrdom. The stories now end with the heroes being protected from death rather than being killed. This change in the ending of the traditional story not only reflects the group's belief that martyrdom is not a current threat but also expresses clearly the group's program for maintaining its distinct religious identity in the midst of an alien and potentially threatening culture. In their present form, the stories in Daniel 3 and 6 both convey the same message. As members of a foreign bureaucracy, group members will sometimes be faced with situations which might tempt them to give up their ancestral faith. But if they retain their faith in the face of outside threats, they will be protected, by supernatural means if necessary. They may suffer some inconveniences, but they will not lose their lives. They will be able to keep their jobs and in fact may even be promoted because of their faithfulness. It is possible to work for the government and still keep the ancestral faith. In this case the group's program is preservationist, for the group seeks to preserve its old religious values in the face of a new cultural situation.

4.6   Unfortunately, the relatively trouble-free conditions described in these stories did not survive the end of Persian rule. Gradually the political situation grew more oppressive, and peaceful coexistence with the government became an impossibility. The group which produced Daniel therefore became more alienated from the surrounding society and began to move in a more clearly apocalyptic direction. This change in the group's perception of its current situation naturally required a revision of the program designed to solve the group's difficulties. The outlines of this revised program can be seen in Daniel 2, 4, and 5. Again all of these chapters have a similar structure and present essentially the same message. In each of the three chapters the king has a dream full of obscure symbolism. He calls in the court astrologers and wise men to interpret the dream, but they are not able to do so. Then Daniel, who in these chapters is portrayed as the wisest and most skillful dream interpreter in the kingdom, is summoned, and he interprets the dream for the king. The details of the interpretation vary from chapter to chapter, but the point of the interpretation is the same in all three chapters. The kingdom will eventually be destroyed, and power will be given to the members of the apocalyptic group. At this stage the apocalyptic group apparently still looked for the perpetuation of their political power and religious autonomy within a normal political system.

4.7   The background of the royal court is again apparent in the language in which these chapters are written. "Wisdom" concepts and vocabulary abound. Furthermore, the chapters contain motifs that are also found in other ancient Near Eastern literatures. Particularly noticeable is the concept of four world empires (Daniel 2), a concept which seems to have had a long history in the Greek and Persian worlds (Collins: 37–43; Lambert: 7–9; Flusser: 148–175). Of course it would have been possible for any Jewish group to have been influenced by extrabiblical literature, but such influences would have been particularly likely in the case of upper-class bureaucrats, who were well educated, cosmopolitan, and in regular contact with people of other cultures.

4.8   The bureaucratic background of the group may also be reflected in the basic structure of the chapters, which bear a striking resemblance to some of the so-called Egyptian prophetic texts. These texts—which are not prophetic in the strict sense of the term since they do not claim to recount divine revelations—all follow a pattern which is roughly similar to the one found in Daniel 2, 4, and 5. All of the texts picture a wise speaker standing in the presence of the king and delivering messages dealing with present and future social and political conditions. For example, in "King Cheops and the Magicians" (Papyrus Westcar), the king is being entertained by a succession of his sons, each of whom tells a miraculous story. The series of stories ends when one son tells of an old man named Dedi, who possesses secret and particularly miraculous powers. The king visits Dedi, who predicts the birth of three kings, who will found a new dynasty and bring an end to Cheops's reign. A similar structure is exhibited by "The Admonitions of an Egyptian Sage," in which the wise Ipuwer berates the king for permitting lawlessness and chaos in the land and then describes the ideal society, exhorting the king to improve conditions. The "Prophecies of Neferti," the "Prophecy of the Lamb," the "Oracle of the Potter," and the "Demotic Chronicle" are all much more explicit. They describe in great detail the political and social chaos that will befall Egypt in the future and then predict the coming of a good ruler who will put an end to the turmoil (R. Wilson: 124-128). The stress which the Egyptian texts place on wisdom and perception, the court setting of the speaker's activities, and the predominant political concerns of the texts all suggest that this material was produced by scribes or other members of the Egyptian royal court. It is therefore precisely the sort of material that Israelite scribes and bureaucrats might have known, so it would not be surprising if the writers of Daniel were influenced by it when they produced Daniel 2, 4, and 5.

4.9   However, social, political, and religious conditions apparently deteriorated even further after Daniel 2, 4, and 5 were written. Government repression seemed to have grown more harsh, and opposing factions began to grow within the Jewish community itself. The group which produced Daniel therefore developed a third apocalyptic program now found in Daniel 7-12. The new program, expressed in a complicated series of visions, called for the revival of older political and religious ideals, but this revival was to be cosmic in its scope. Divine intervention would destroy *all* repressive foreign rulers and give both political and religious power to those who had remained faithful to the old Israelite ideals. The faithfulness of group members would be rewarded when they became the ruling elite in the new world order. According to the apocalyptists, the future could be predicted because it was unfolding according to a predetermined cosmic timetable and was heading for a predestined goal. The present sufferings of the group and its future exaltation were all part of a divine plan.

4.10   In Daniel 7-12 the language, symbols, and motifs continue to be drawn from the "wisdom" circles out of which the group came. Again foreign motifs can be traced in these chapters, and the shape of the chapters themselves may have been influenced by the so-called Akkadian apocalypses, a little-understood genre of texts in chronicle form containing "predictions" of future events. These prophecies, which are clearly *vaticinia ex eventu*, are given by a divine (or deified human) speaker, who gives an overview of coming political events. This historical survey is expressed by the repeated use of a formula such as "a prince will arise." The rulers are never explicitly named, but sometimes their countries are identified and the exact length of their reigns indicated. Each reign is evaluated positively or negatively in stereotypical terms. The texts seem to have ended with an elaboration of the reign of the ruler who was the real focus of the writer's interest, although this point is uncertain because of the fragmentary state of the texts. The exact function of these texts is not always clear, but they are certainly scribal creations, so it would not be surprising if they influenced the bureaucratic creators of cosmic timetables such as Daniel 11 (Lambert: 9–13; R. Wilson: 119–123; Hallo: 231–242; Heintz: 71–87).

4.11   Although Daniel 7–12 contains "wisdom" motifs and vocabulary, these chapters also reflect prophetic motifs, symbols, and language. For example, Dan 8:2 and 10:2–9, 10–14 seem to reflect motifs in Ezekiel, while Dan 9:2 refers to Jeremiah's prophecies of the end of the exile. Dan 10:15–17 may invoke the dumbness motif in Ezekiel, and the various series of animals mentioned in Daniel 7 seem to be drawn from prophetic sources (Isa 11:6–7; Hos 13:7–8; Jer 5:6; cf. Jer 4:7; 15:3; 51:38; Hab 1:6–10; Joel 1:6). In addition, in contrast to the first part of the book, in Daniel 7–12 Daniel is not longer portrayed as a wise, self-sufficient dream interpreter but as a confused and disturbed visionary who, like the prophet Zechariah, must have all of his visions interpreted for him by a divine intermediary.

4.12   The reasons for the sudden appearance of these prophetic elements are difficult to determine, but at least two factors may be involved. First, the sudden resort to the prophetic tradition may indicate a change in the composition of the group. While in its early history the Daniel group may have been composed primarily of upper-class bureaucrats and former government officials, by the time Daniel 7–12 was produced the group may have included people with closer links to Israelite prophecy. The change in the composition of the group would have then caused a shift in the language and imagery used to express the group's apocalyptic program. Second, the appearance of prophetic imagery and vocabulary may indicate that the Daniel group at some point moved more firmly back into the biblical tradition and rejected some of the foreign influences that helped to shape earlier chapters of the book. Shifts of this sort sometimes occur when apocalyptic groups are persecuted and driven even farther onto the periphery of society. In such cases the group may become isolated and begin to think of itself as the "true community of the faithful," the "saints" who are opposed by the unbelievers in the rest of the society. Under these conditions the group may seek to revive elements of its earlier religious history that clearly identify it as the true community of believers. The Daniel community clearly came to think of itself as the "true Israel," the "people of the holy ones" who were opposed by the rest of the world and perhaps by the rest of Israel (Collins: 167–175). As the "true Israel," the group may have sought closer identification with the prophetic tradition of the Bible and may even have begun to imitate the style of the prophetic literature. Also like earlier members of the true Israelite community, the group may have begun to write its literature in Hebrew. This may explain why the group wrote the visions of Daniel in 7–12 largely in Hebrew rather than in the vernacular Aramaic used earlier to compose Daniel 2–6.

5.   This analysis of Daniel suggests that it is impossible to trace a direct line from a single tradition or movement in Israel to later apocalyptic. Rather, it appears, as the anthropological evidence indicates, that apocalyptic groups may develop whenever the required social conditions are presnt and that the *shape* of a particular group's religion and literature will depend on the group's social and religious background. The group that produced Daniel seems to have had both wisdom and prophetic roots, and it is likely that other groups in Israel exhibited similarly complex structures. For example, the group that produced Ezekiel 38–39 and 40–48 may have come from a mixture of priestly and prophetic backgrounds, while the much later Qumran community may provide an example of predominantly priestly apocalyptic. However, each apocalyptic group in Israel must be examined individually before any safe conclusions can be reached. Ultimately the shape of apocalyptic religion and literature in Israel depended on the unique characteristics of each apocalyptic group.

WORKS CONSULTED

Aberle, D.
1970   "A Note on Relative Deprivation Theory as Applied to Millenarian and Other Cult Movements." Pp. 209–214 in *Millennial Dreams in Action*. Ed. S. L. Thrupp. New York: Schocken.

Barber, B.
1941   "Acculturation and Messianic Movements." *American Sociological Review* 6: 663–669.

Baumgartner, W.
1926   *Das Buch Daniel*. Giessen: Alfred Töpelmann.

Burridge, Kenelm O. L.
1969   *New Heaven, New Earth*. New York: Schocken.

Cohn, N.
1970   *The Pursuit of the Millennium.* Rev. ed. New York: Oxford.

Collins, J. J.
1977   *The Apocalyptic Vision of the Book of Daniel.* Missoula: Scholars Press.

Flusser, D.
1972   "The Four Empires in the Fourth Sibyl and in the Book of Daniel." *Israel Oriental Studies* 2: 148-175.

Hallo, W. W.
1966   "Akkadian Apocalypses." *IEJ* 16: 231-242.

Hanson, P. D.
1975   *The Dawn of Apocalyptic.* Philadelphia: Fortress.
1976   "Apocalypticism." *IBDSup*: 28-34.

Heintz, J.-G.
1977   "Note sur les origines de l'apocalyptique judaïque à lumière des 'prophéties akkadiennes.'" Pp. 71-87 in *L'apocalyptique.* Ed. F. Raphaël et al. Paris: Paul Geuthner.

Jarvie, I. C.
1969   *The Revolution in Anthropology.* Chicago: Henry Regnery.

La Barre, Weston
1971   "Materials for a History of Studies of Crisis Cults: A Bibliographic Essay." *Current Anthropology* 12: 3-44.
1972   *The Ghost Dance.* New York: Dell.

Lambert, W. G.
1978   *The Background of Jewish Apocalyptic.* London: Athlone.

Lanternari, Vittorio
1965   *The Religions of the Oppressed.* New York: Mentor.

Lawrence, Peter
1964   *Road Belong Cargo: A Study of the Cargo Movement in the Southern Mandang District, New Guinea.* Manchester: Manchester University.

Lewis, I. M.
1966   "Spirit Possession and Deprivation Cults." *Man* n.s. 1: 322-329.

Linton, Ralph
1943   "Nativistic Movements." *American Anthropologist* 45: 230-240.

Lofland, J.
1966   *Doomsday Cult.* Englewood Cliffs, N.J.: Prentice-Hall.

Nicholson, E. W.
1979   "Apocalyptic." Pp. 189-213 in *Tradition and Interpretation.* Ed. G. W. Anderson. Oxford: Clarendon.

Plöger, O.
1968   *Theocracy and Eschatology.* Richmond: John Knox.

Rad, Gerhard von
1965   *Old Testament Theology.* Vol. 2. New York: Harper & Row.
1972   *Wisdom in Israel.* Nashville: Abingdon.

Russell, D. S.
1964 *The Method and Message of Jewish Apocalyptic.* Philadelphia: Westminster.

Smith, M.
1971 *Palestinian Parties and Politics that Shaped the Old Testament.* New York: Columbia University.

Spier, L., Suttles, W., Herskovits, M. J.
1959 "Comments on Arberle's Thesis of Deprivation." *Southwestern Journal of Anthropology* 15: 84–88.

Steck, O. H.
1977 "Theological Streams of Tradition." Pp. 183–214 in *Tradition and Theology in the Old Testament.* Ed. D. A. Knight. Philadelphia: Fortress.

Talmon, Y.
1962 "Pursuit of the Millennium: The Relation Between Religion and Social Change." *Archives européennes de sociologie* 3: 149–164.

Wallace, A. F. C.
1956 "Revitalization Movements." *American Anthropologist* 58: 264–281.

Wilson, B. R.
1963 "Millennialism in Comparative Perspective." *Comparative Studies in Society and History.* 6: 93–114.
1973 *Magic and the Millennium.* New York: Harper & Row.

Wilson, Robert R.
1980 *Prophecy and Society in Ancient Israel.* Philadelphia: Fortress.

Worsley, P.
1968 *The Trumpet Shall Sound.* 2d ed. New York: Schocken.

Zygmunt, J. F.
1972 "When Prophecies Fail: A Theoretical Perspective on the Comparative Evidence." *American Behavioral Scientist* 16: 245–268.

RESPONSES TO ARTICLES

REFLECTIONS ON PROPHECY AND PROPHETIC GROUPS

Kenelm O. L. Burridge
University of British Columbia

0. Time and circumstances in relation to the deadline for receipt of copy require that this commentary be shorter and less measured and detailed than it might have been. It is confined, therefore, to the four broad problems raised by the essays under review: the nature of the anthropological approach (Buss); apocalyptic messages and their associated groups (Wilson); conflict and prophetic rivalry (Long); and the prophetic process (Overholt).

1. Anthropologists differ considerably in their conceptions of the subject, in their "theoretical" approaches, and in what the finished product of their researches is supposed to do. But there is a general agreement that data should be obtained systematically, that analysis should be logically consistent, systematic, and match the data. Most importantly perhaps, anthropology is a "mode of thinking about" both data and analyses. This "thinking about" is not easy to explain in a few words. It becomes explicit in the process of making field investigations—in continually asking who, what, where, when, why, in what circumstances—and speaks largely to the constraints present in total social situations in relation to the ways in which participants in these situations are placed in relation to each other. Though these concerns usually entail a present or quasi-present tense in analysis, out of them comes the too often muted question, as significant to anthropology as to other disciplines dealing with human or social relations, whether what happened was inevitable, whether there were any possible options or alternatives, whether the situation might not as easily have developed in some other way. . . . Much depends on the answer, especially in relation to charismatic or apocalyptic movements. Is it inevitable that what seems to have happened in history should have happened thus?

2. When, after an admirable summary of anthropological work on the matter, Wilson (3.1) writes that the "anthropological evidence suggests that apocalyptic religion can arise at any time when the necessary sociological conditions are present," the immediate question is precisely what are those *necessary* conditions. The fact is that the conditions outlined by

Wilson can often occur without an apocalyptic message, and, unless an apocalyptic message is defined by the conditions which supposedly produce them, apocalyptic events also occur in quite different conditions. Those crucial negative instances are never studied because, one supposes, they are intrinsically without interest or points of entry. The pedestrian lying dead or injured in the road has an imediate interest. And accounts of what seems to have happened grow in number with the telling and in relation to the positions of particular observers. But the accounts of the latter would make little sense if there were not implicit some understanding of how it is that thousands of pedestrians manage to cross a road without getting injured or killed. Just as, without the awareness of negative instances, one might easily conclude that the injured person in the road must have been mad, or in some way rendered less sensible than he or she might have been, so have many anthropologists tended to view apocalyptic groups as varieties of social pathology. Hence the vocabulary of relatively deprived, frustrated, and so on: a view to be expected of scholars securely ensconced in an established station. The notion that apocalyptic messages may be natural to human groups, culturally prescribed, or an intrinsic part of the evolutionary process, is not, at the moment, generally accepted. But it bears thinking about. In nineteenth and late eighteenth century Britain (as in North America today) such occurrences were common, and nobody batted an eyelid.

3.1   The same sort of argument applies to Overholt's argument that the message of a prophet or charismatic leader should "make sense." Such "sense" as has been made has been usually made *post hoc*, the result of much painful research and analysis directed precisely towards making some sort of sense. If, for example, participants in a Melanesian cargo cult were asked before the event whether in such and such circumstances they would do what after the event all know they did, I am confident the answer would be a heartfelt and resounding negative. And there is plenty of evidence to show that, after the event, participants wonder why they did what they did. Or again, why is it that so many would-be charismatic leaders who do "make sense"—according to an observer—obtain no response? Nor does "responsibility" (Buss) have much to do with the matter so far as such utterances are concerned. Indeed, the reverse would seem to be more true. The "responsible" man is not normally apocalyptic or prophetic. If he should become so, he is generally consigned to a limbo of the insane. Rather is it that the irresponsible or insane person who, in saying something that strikes an intelligible spark, commands attention. To push the point a little further, in what way did the Jonestown tragedy "make sense"—except by taking effects as their causes and saying that the participants must have been possessed of some sort of death-wish? The truth is that we do not know what causes people in the nowness of the moment to do things they would not otherwise have done. There seems to be no kind of inevitability to it. Indeed, given the sorts of conditions that are supposed to produce apocalyptic or charismatic activity, there are so many negative instances that one may well wonder why so little has in fact been done to unravel what is specific to the positive instance and not present in the negative.

3.2 The answer to this is simple enough. We do not know what to look for. Nor is it an easy task to choose what might seem to be a likely situation, whether in the field or in the documentary record, and ask why it is or was that something did *not* happen. Yet that is precisely the question that must be answered.

4. Still, there is no doubt that, for one who is not used to biblical studies, a reading of the four essays seems to add enormously to one's understanding of the Old Testament. Things seem to fit together much more than they did. What was apparently stark and, to some, inexplicable, is given context and meaning. Even if what is actually happening is that the unknown is being squeezed into the familiar, so that what is in fact unknown can seem to be known, there is a very real sense of avenues of understanding opening up. Precisely this—too often forgotten in the attempt to be scientific, consistent, and systematic, is the essence of anthropology. Dependent as it is (as Overholt points out) on data that happens to be collected at a particular moment or phase in history, anthropology is necessarily rough, refining itself in its concepts perhaps, but always dependent on the coarse and adventitious materials of its data. Common sense might have, but in fact surely did not, open one's eyes to the nature of the conflicts and rivalries in which Jeremiah was involved (Long). At the same time, one has to bear in mind that the reduction of the particular to the general case—and it is a reduction—can often do less than justice to the former. If Jeremiah instances the general nature of shamanistic rivalry and conflict, it was his particularity that caused him to be remembered as a prophet. It is at this point that anthropology, like the other social sciences, begins to founder and take refuge in notions of inevitability.

5. ' There is no need here to follow the Azande and resort to witchcraft as an explanation of why a particular thing happened at a particular time. Nor do the vicissitudes of history necessarily require a theory of divine intervention. We have to be satisfied with explications rather than explanations. The Hebrews had a niche for shamans or quasi-shamans (often called prophets) as well as a quite separate niche or tradition for prophets proper which a shaman—or anyone else—might occupy. The Plains Indians had shamans but, so far as we know, no tradition of prophets. Neither Wovoka nor Handsome Lake behaved like shamans, yet they commanded attention. The Melanesians had neither shamans nor prophets, but when prophets manifested themselves they were listened to, and they commanded action. The Nuer had no shamans, and their prophets, quite different from the

Leopard-skin chiefs of tradition, commanded respect—they were possessed by God—but not necessarily action. In Melanesia old crones and young boys with dreams or visions—those with least authority and responsibility—were certainly heard out, laughed at, or treated seriously. And in some areas, over the course, now, of nearly a century of European and Christian influence, a succession of prophets begins to assume the form of something like a tradition. But the longest lasting cargo cult, the Jon Frum of Tanna in the New Hebrides, now some 40 years in existence, had no precedents. As Overholt points out, Yali had no charismatic ambitions. He was in fact an administrator's man to start with—a fink or collaborator if you like—who reversed his role and became one of the more famous and revered of cargo cult leaders. If Jeremiah could also be said to have been some sort of fink or, more ignominiously, collaborator, his theme seems to have remained constant. There was that in what he said (but precisely what?) and did which required remembering. For we may be sure of one thing: no set of editors could have kept in remembrance that which was trivial or merely incidental to a particular time and place.

6.   "Prophetic authority" is a much more chancey business than both Long and Buss would seem to imply. The Californian proving grounds reveal the sincere, the silly, charlatans, confidence tricksters, and the purely evil as more or less equally authoritative. Yet Californians are not more gullible than the ancient Hebrews, the Melanesians, the North American Indians, and/or many others. By and large, the participants in Californian apocalyptic, charismatic, and prophetic movements do not reveal those relative deprivations, frustrations, etc. so beloved by so many of the students of the phenomena—unless of course we have arrived at the point where all those adjectives are defined by unorthodox cults. Rather than strive for uniformities (which probably only exists in relation to those in secure, established, and orthodox positions) it would surely be more fruitful to look for pertinent differences. In one situation, for example, factors a, b, c, d, e, f, might seem to be present; in another situation factors c, e, g, h, f, might seem to be present, in a third situation we might find factors a, f, h, i, to be present. . . . Carrying on with such a procedure, looking for differences, specific relations—of which, as yet, we really have small knowledge—might be adduced.

7.   Even then there is a long way to go. The point of this commentary is not a plea to look for what is not in the situation. On the contrary, bamboozled as one generally is by what authorities say should exist, it is a plea to look for those aspects of the situation which are there but have been missed. So, by way of conclusion let me say that I enjoyed reading the essays. I was most stimulated by them, and have grown in understanding. In playing the devil's advocate I have been moved not by the trite conviction that we do not know nearly as much as we think we know or need to know, but in the sincere belief that if we really looked we would see much more than we do.

PROBLEMS AND PROMISES IN THE COMPARATIVE ANALYSIS OF RELIGIOUS PHENOMENA

Norman K. Gottwald
New York Theological Seminary

0.1   The articles above make laudable disciplined attempts to appropriate anthropological method and theory for an understanding of biblical prophecy and apocalyptic. The basic rationale is that religious phenomena in ancient Israel were sufficiently similar to religious phenomena in recent and contemporary societies studied by anthropology that the fuller data afforded by anthropology help us to understand the less documented or less adequately contextualized biblical data. Provided that the data from ancient Israel and other societies are properly examined in their own contexts and compared on relevant points (Wilson: 349–351), the enterprise is entirely justified. It is well at the outset, however, to be aware of the different ways that continental, British, and American anthropologists have conceptualized the discipline and have sub-divided its tasks (Rogerson: 9–10; Penniman: chapter 1), so that a monolithic view of anthropology is avoided. It is equally instructive to note how biblical scholars have misconstrued or unknowingly adopted anthropological theories, or have advocated positions long outdated in the discipline (Rogerson).

0.2   The contributors to this issue seem to know their way through the thicket of anthropological inquiry. Indeed, their essays serve the admirable function of bibliographical surveys that acquaint the reader with at least one major sector of anthropological literature pertinent to biblical prophecy. Rather than to temper their work with excessive caveats, however, they have attempted to theorize constructively, sometimes even to speculate beyond evidence in hand, by mining the anthropology of "prophecy," i.e., studies of shamanism, spirit possession, and nativist or millenarian movements. The results offer fruitful possibilities which call for further research and reflection to establish them more securely, with necessary correction and refinement.

1.1   Overholt. This comparative study of Jeremiah and Handsome Lake is felicitous because we happily possess more documentary evidence of the

Iroquois prophet's developing career than is frequently the case for such figures studied by anthropology. What is most significant, however, is Overholt's attempt to find a heuristic device for comparing prophets within and between traditions that is not vitiated by culture-specific idiosyncrasies of form or content. Since biblical scholars focus mainly on the historical and theological distinctiveness of prophets and anthropologists concentrate chiefly on the general culture or the specific cults in which prophets function, Overholt observes that little attention has been given to "the prophetic process" for which he hopes to supply an operational model that is relatively content-free.

1.2   The model of three actors (god/prophet/people) who interrelate in four modes (revelation/proclamation/feedback/expectation of confirmation) appears to be a useful one which nontheless invites careful scrutiny. That the feedback of prophet to God, in contrast with the feedback of people to prophet, is not taken by Overholt to be a necessary feature of the model seems to hypothesize a single revelation and proclamation and a single response from the people. That many, if not most, prophets have several revelations and give many proclamations, raises the issue of how the model can encompass the career of a prophet rather than a single typical moment of prophesying. Also, the factors shaping the people's feedback (their cultural and religious traditions/their reading of the sociopolitical situation) are in fact greatly informed by deposits of revelation from past religious figures, prophets among them, so that the people relate each new prophetic revelation to a fund of revelations. These complications do not invalidate Overholt's model but they do suggest need for further refinement and discrimination in the model. What he calls popular "expectations of confirmation" of the prophet's proclamation appear much more like "signs/evidences of confirmation," and it might well be claimed that prophets too are questing for these signs and evidences and that, when they do not eventuate, the shock of "cognitive dissonance" gives rise to the prophets' protesting feedback to the deity (Gager: 37–49; Carroll).

1.3   This analysis of actors and functions in the prophetic process (analogous to V. Propp's formal treatment of roles and functions in folktales) yields an elegant outline of prophecy as a feedback system. It serves to underline prophetic authority as a process of social assessment. The perceived effectiveness of the prophet in a shifting socioreligious field underscores "charisma as a function of recognition" and emphasizes the relative freedom of every audience to choose the prophet it will accredit. It accords well with the re-examination of charisma in the Weberian tradition (Eisenstadt: Introduction), which should be a timely antidote to biblical scholars who have imbibed a simplistic form of Weber's notion of charisma which makes it into a virtual ahistorical and asocial force.

1.4   What Overholt's model does for me is to suggest the importance of re-examining the cultural and religious traditions actually operative for a prophet's audience, going beneath and behind the way the traditions now appear as a result of the canonical process in the Bible or in the immediate observer/participant report in anthropology. Likewise, a strenuous effort must be made to grasp the various options perceived by the prophetic audience for responding to the current sociopolitical situation, and in doing so not simply to take as the last word what the texts or reports choose to highlight. This latter inquiry is taken up in one way in Long's study of prophetic conflict. Moreover, we need to inquire about the feedback of the spectrum of effective cultural/religious traditions and sociopolitical assessments/options on the very genesis of a prophet's revelation. After all, we only begin with the revelation as "the original moment" because we have to begin somewhere, but the revelation does not appear in a void. The filter or grid which guides the people in discerning prophets also operates as a benchmark or indicator for the kinds of revelation that a prophet is likely to receive. While Overholt is correct to eliminate from the model every detail of form or content in the revelation, it is necessary for the model in some way to represent the socially shaped predispositions of persons who become prophets toward revelations and proclamations of a particular form and with a particular content (Gottwald: 627–631).

2.1   Buss. Buss organizes his analysis of prophetic call visions around rubrics drawn from social psychology and communication theory (more fully developed in Buss: 3–44). Fundamental is his contention that a call is typical of most specialized religious roles taken up by "personal diviners," even in cultures lacking warrants for preserving call traditions. Many of the supposed exclusionary opposites that have vexed interpreters of biblical prophecy (*either* prophecy as a life-time activity *or* as a single special task; *either* recompensed service *or* unrecompensed service; *either* full-time activity *or* part-time activity) are shown to be of dubious applicability in the light of the many permutations of role performance exhibited in the large body of data on such specialists.

2.2   In his section on communication, Buss offers the judgement that the prophet is supremely suited to grasp complexity and uncertainty as an opportunity for receptivity toward new ways of organizing experience and meaning. His view has certain resonance with von Rad's stress upon the eschatological novelty of prophetic theology in fundamental discontinuity with earlier Israelite theology. One might, however, just as readily perceive the Israelite prophets at least to have been highly goal-directed and selective in cutting through the complexity of their times, and, in fact, severely reducing complexity and ambiguity both in tradition and in contemporary sociopolitical experience. Yet again, prophets might be seen as persons who absorb the new complexity around them, sifting or balancing it, so as to emerge with an incisive line of action/thought that looks much simpler than it actually is, or whose "simplicity" or "parsimoniousness" is on a new synthetic level that transcends any of the exclusive opposites perceived in the old view of things. The prophet, in short, offers a different reading of the contradictory elements in a supposedly familiar situation (see my remarks on Long below.) Examination of the relative order/looseness of the prophetic mind, its way of factoring contradictions, could have important implications for assessing the judgement/salvation dialectic in a prophet like Isaiah, not to mention implications for understanding the history of the formation of prophetic books so largely organized around that dialectic.

2.3   Buss's contention that anthropological analysis can help in dating the content of literary materials points to a much neglected tool in biblical research. Anthropological clarifications of tribalism and peasant movements, combined with literary and historical evidence, have assisted me in identifying a solid core of pre-monarchic materials in biblical traditions that received their present form only in monarchic times (Gottwald: 25-44). Buss is also on target in cautioning that ancient Israel's social organization was neither so simple as many nonliterate peoples studied by anthropology nor so complex as statist societies that surrounded Israel, which suggests that anthropological data on tribalism and prophecy may be used with profit in biblical studies, but only with the accompanying recognition that ancient Israel was well within the orbit of statist social organization that exerted a strong pull toward differentiation of labor and role specialization.

2.4   The call reports of prophets are not so much a way of convincing people who are undecided about the prophet's claim to truth as they are an attribution that grounds truth already accepted in an ultimate "cause" and "responsibility." On the surface this seems congruent with the view that the biblical call accounts had their primary setting and function among the prophet's successors and followers who were making particular interpretations of the prophetic words as claims upon their own situations (Long: 6-13). It is not clear, however, whether Buss sees the call as an attribution of ultimacy that the prophet or a successor/follower is more likely to make. Actually an attribution of ultimacy seems already to be made by the prophet, at least implicitly, in proclaiming a *revelation*, and not merely an opinion. Thus, what additional force did the call report offer either an immediate hearer of the prophet or someone in the later prophetic tradition?

2.5   Finally, Buss argues that anthropological analyses cannot in themselves establish a theological perspective, but they can contribute to one by shedding light on the process of faith. I have argued from the side of a sociohistorical analysis of premonarchic Israel that a valid theology for our epoch must incorporate or mediate a cultural, historical material understanding of ancient Israel, a kind of socioeconomic demythologization, but my remarks constitute only a propaedeutic for such a theology (Gottwald: chapters 55 and 56). From the side of theology proper, some forms of political theology are contending that social scientific analysis, and especially Marxist methodology, can supply the medium of discourse for a full-fledged theology of the sort provided in the past by more abstruse philosophical systems such as those of Plato, Aristotle, Kant, or Heidegger (Fierro: chapters 7 and 8). In particular, Fierro propounds the outlines of a fundamental, (as contrasted with a dogmatic) historical material theology which has to do with "the genesis of faith . . . to reproduce on the level of discourse the movement that takes place in life when one comes to believe" (Fierro: 329–330).

3.1   Long. Adopting an anthropological view of the prophet as dependent on public opinion and support, Long shows that conflict among prophets to establish authority by enlisting a following is a built-in feature of many societies, resulting in "a network of client and peer relationships" (quoting P. Fry). In most cases this conflict system strengthens rather than weakens the society over-all, but Long does not deal centrally with cases of societies in decline or collapse, which is of course typical of anthropology's bias in preferring stasis and equilibrium notions of society. Historical sociology will have to help provide the longitudinal developmental view that few nonliterate societies are able to give. The agonistic, or zero-sum game, dynamics of ancient Greek society held public life together for a long time by its very maximization of competition; however, when this agonistic drive later combined with pressing economic need for large numbers of slaves, it fueled fratricidal wars from which Greece never recovered (Gouldner).

3.2   Long is convincing in showing that conflict among religious specialists claiming divine revelation is often functional in societies. By using the book of Jeremiah with its considerable sociopolitical information, he is able to show that alignments of prophets, priests, and princes crystallized around antagonistic political programs of "autonomy" from Babylon and "co-existence" with (or submission to?) Babylon. These conflicting alignments have been much studied by biblical scholars. What Long adds is the perspective of the "normalcy," or at least the high frequency, of ideological conflict among prophets when major rifts have opened in the body politic and when factors of personal status and prestige are entailed (although he is not sure how to assess the latter reliably). The analysis of the structures of the respective ideologies, and particularly the relative weights given to the factors in the heated sociopolitical situation, is aided by a dialectical model of dominant and secondary contradictions (Mottu).

> What then is the actual dominant contradiction in the situation? It is, I think according to Jeremiah *the overdetermination of the conflict Babylon-Judah by another conflict*, a conflict altogether ignored by Hananiah—namely, by *the conflict*

> between the subjective interests of the ruling class in Jerusalem and the objective interests of the people of Israel/Judah as a whole. . . . This internal conflict, because of its socioeconomic roots, is much more basic to the situation than the more easily observed inter-state conflict between Babylon and Judah . . . Jeremiah sees not only the religious aspect of the antagonism between pseudo- and authentic prophecy [these terms applied of course from Jeremiah's judgmental perspective] but also its concrete and practical social effects. . . . What is at stake in the last analysis is not the correct religion or doctrine but rather the *survival*, "the good" of people of flesh and blood. . . . For Jeremiah the secondary aspect of the contradiction is set into a social context in which the prophetic debate about truth and falsehood is merely a part. . . . Thus, far better than his opponent, Jeremiah has seen the wholeness of the situation, a situation in which the religious secondary contradiction is never "pure and simple" but always overdetermined by the conflicts and power relationships among the social groups with their respective interests. (Mottu: 63–64; italics his)

It is probable that Long's "autonomist" coalition equated survival with the continued independence of Judah under present leadership, whereas the "co-existence" coalition equated survival with the socioeconomic and religiocultural preservation of the Judean populace. The autonomists saw the ruling class as a perfect, or at least fully adequate, representative of the people's interests and therefore its overthrow would mean the downfall of the people. The co-existers, by contrast, viewed the domestic policies of the ruling class as decisively antagonistic to the interests of the people and regarded any strengthening of that ruling class against Babylon as precisely a promotion of policies that would further harm the people, whereas submission to or cooperation with Babylon would more likely foster a viable life for the Judean people.

3.3 If Mottu's depiction of the antagonistic alignments is correct, then the probability that both parties were headed by socially prominent and powerful persons (and in this I think Long is right) is not the sole or decisive factor in assessing the social class dynamics of the confrontation. His analysis signals a division within the ruling class, one segment seeing domestic socioeconomic and cultural deprivation as central to the determination of foreign policy, whereas the other segment either does not recognize major deprivation within Judah or does not think it determinative of foreign policy. Long's dismissal of the applicability of Wilson's peripheral/central prophecy to Jeremiah and his prophetic rivals seems unduly abrupt (Wilson: 241–251). Jeremiah and his allies were not simply "outsiders" ideologically according to Deuteronomic retrospection; they were "outsiders" sociopolitically in the sense that the public policies they fought for lost out. Autonomists and co-existers could not both win; their policies were mutually exclusive. The validity of Long's emphasis is that the co-existence program was represented "inside" the ruling establishment before it was vanquished and its advocates neutralized.

3.4 Of course what is not clear is how far the split reflected in ruling circles extended into the general populace. We do not know the extent to which the disputing coalitions were fed by a base in the general populace, either through attempts of the disputants to mobilize the people behind their positions or through sectors of the populace pressing the leaders to adopt one or another state policy. It would be instructive to explore analogous situations from anthropological and historical sociological studies (e.g., peasant movements; Wolf), in order to see how divided ruling classes (or leaders of rank in non-statist societies) fight out their conflicts and appeal to or mobilize the populace on their behalf in relation to the ideological, and specifically prophetic articulation of conflict. To do this properly, we need to take account of Long's observation (his note 2) that prophetic conflict appears in some societies and is absent in others. A study with control societies (samples of societies with and without prophetic conflict in relation to other variables) might throw some light on the types and mechanisms of sociopolitical conflict that tend to occur in conjunction with prophetic conflicts. Yet to do this there seems to be a need to be clearer about what we mean by "prophet," how narrowly or widely the term is used for the purpose of gathering presumably comparable cases of religious conflict. For example, in drawing on the Mexican and Algerian peasant uprisings, would differences among the Catholic clergy and among the Islamic clergy and story-tellers be counted as cases of "prophetic conflict?"

4.1   Wilson. After exposing the weaknesses in attempts to root apocalyptic literature and thought primarily or exclusively in one or another tradition type (van Rad in wisdom and Hanson in prophecy), Wilson proposes that the key to apocalyptic is the alchemy of social deprivation which prompts groups to literary expression in any one of a number of traditional rhetorical/conceptual modes, either singly or in combination. Without spelling it out, Wilson urges that post-exilic Israel offered a matrix for groups to experience deprivation in a manner that was not true of pre-exilic Israel. However, his tersely expressed indicators such as increased "factionalism" in "well-formed groups articulating divergent views" and "a deteriorating political situation" are broadly applicable to pre-exilic conditions as well. How did post-exilic factionalism differ *in concreto* from pre-exilic factionalism? Were "the fringes of society" more sharply circumscribed in post-exilic times so that to be pushed there was to suffer much harsher consequences than previously? Were post-exilic times marked by greater "scarcity" in available power and wealth, with fewer leadership roles, reduced resources, and less room for autonomous communal maneuvering?

4.2   Wilson proposes that a block of apocalyptic tradition may in fact not be homogeneous, but may be a compound of sub-units that reflect changes in sociopolitical location and possibly changes in the types of adherents composing the apocalyptic group, especially in terms of the prophetic, priestly, or wisdom rhetoric and thought that its members may have been accustomed to use. In illustrating how this would apply to the book of Daniel, Wilson posits three temporally successive moments in the trajectory of the Daniel community that reflect different sociopolitical settings and find expression in different literary deposits in the book.

4.3   The first moment, in chaps. 3 and 6, reflects highly placed Jewish officials who remain in Babylon after the exile and are able to keep their Jewish identity within a tolerant or benign Persian government. In the second moment, in chaps. 2, 4, and 5, reflects Jewish bureaucrats under Greek rule when the government is less tolerant and it is expected that the foreign kingdom will be destroyed and power will be transferred to the apocalyptic group. The third moment, in chaps. 7–12, reflects later Greek (Maccabean) times when government repression has grown and there is intense Jewish factionalism which are to be remedied by a divine cosmic intervention to destroy all foreign powers and to institute the apocalyptic group as the ruling elite of a new world order.

4.4   This reconstruction depends on many prior critical judgments about the book that Wilson does not directly rehearse, so that it is not always possible to know how he has come to his conclusions. If we grant for purposes of discussion that there are three recognizably different deposits in Daniel as Wilson presents them, there remain many questions which the briefly argued proposal does not answer. If the tradents of the first group of texts are Jewish officials in the Persian administration, does it necessarily follow that they are actually in Babylon? Or in Persia? May they not as well have been Persian administrators in restored Palestine? If the tradents of the third group of texts are continuous with those of the first two groups, are members of the apocalyptic group still high officials in Seleucid Palestine? If not, is the sharpening of a sense of deprivation expressed in the texts precisely their expulsion from office? Is it really evident that the first group of texts shows a more benign foreign government than the second group? The deliverance of the Jews in the stories of chaps. 3 and 6 owes nothing to the good will of the rulers but solely to miraculous divine intervention. On the other hand, the resemblance of chaps. 2, 4, and 5 to the Egyptian prophetic texts implies a government open enough to allow, or even to invite, high officials to make critical statements about social and political conditions. On the surface this suggests that the government in the second group of texts may be experienced as more benign than the government in the first group of texts. Finally, it may be asked: are the peculiarities of literary form (edifying legends in the first two groups and visions in the third group) skewing factors of such magnitude in filtering sociopolitical realities that it becomes problematic to arrange such text families on a sociohistorical continuum? Within the stories themselves, the difference between a legend type that focuses on narrowly averted martyrdom and a legend type that features the wise interpreter of dreams may also be no certain indicator of the over-all mix or balance of policies in the actual governments experienced by the tradents in contrast to the legendary stylized governments of the stories.

4.5   If there are weaknesses in working from apocalyptic rhetoric to presumed wisdom or prophetic origins, there are also problems in reading off complex sociopolitical situations from ambiguous literary traditions when our sociopolitical information is so sketchy. Wilson has provocatively argued for apocalyptic as a particular amalgam of diverse religious traditions oriented around a group experience of sociopolitical deprivation, whereas his attempt to elucidate Daniel on this model shows how enormously conjectural the enterprise may become. For this model to be more than suggestive we will need to know much more about apocalyptic groups, how they employ and transform traditional materials, the composition of their memberships, the kinds of sociopolitical stress they either articulate or are known to have experienced, where independent information is available.

As with prophetic conflict in Long's study, so with Wilson's apocalyptic groups, we need control group studies of many such groups in terms of a range of variables. Immediately this poses, as with "prophets," the task of formulating what we mean by "apocalyptic group," so that we will know which nativist of millenarian movements we are studying for cross-cultural comparison with Israelite apocalyptic groups and the grounds on which we are making the comparisons. For instance, at one point Overholt refers to an apocalyptic period in the career of Handsome Lake. Are there criteria for judging whether the Handsome Lake cult, at least at some period in its history, ought to be studied as an apocalyptic group? In short, the issue here is not a petty quibbling over terms but rather the question of *criteria by which we selectively group some religious phenomena for comparison while excluding others*. The essays in this collection go some distance in pushing us toward greater clarity in method, not so that we can be satisfied "purists" but so that we can give a reasonable account of what we have compared and why, and thereby acquire a consistent and coherent way of judging how the religious phenomena and processes under study are similar and different.

WORKS CONSULTED

Buss, Martin J.
    1979   "Understanding Communication." Pp. 3–44 in *Encounter with the Text*. Ed. M. J. Buss. Philadelphia: Fortress and Missoula: Scholars Press.

Carroll, Robert P.
    1979   *When Prophecy Failed: Cognitive Dissonance in the Prophetic Traditions of the Old Testament*. New York: Seabury.

Eisenstadt, S. N., ed.
1968   *Max Weber: On Charisma and Institution Building.* Chicago: University Press.

Fierro, Alfredo
1977   *The Militant Gospel: A Critical Introduction to Political Theologies.* Maryknoll: Orbis.

Gager, John G.
1975   *Kingdom and Community: The Social World of Early Christianity.* Englewood Cliffs: Prentice-Hall.

Gottwald, Norman K.
1979   *The Tribes of Yahweh: A Sociology of the Religion of Liberated Israel, 1250–1050 B.C.E.* Maryknoll: Orbis.

Gouldner, Alvin W.
1969   *The Hellenic World: A Sociological Analysis.* New York: Harper.

Long, Burke O.
1977   "Prophetic Authority as Social Reality." Pp. 3–20 in *Canon and Authority.* Eds. G. W. Coats and B. O. Long. Philadelphia: Fortress.

Mottu, Henri
1976   "Jeremiah vs. Hananiah: Ideology and Truth in Old Testament Prophecy." Pp. 58–67 in *The Bible and Liberation. Political and Social Hermeneutics.* A Radical Religion Reader. Eds. N. K. Gottwald and A. C. Wire. Berkeley: Community for Religious Research and Education.

Penniman, T. K.
1965   *A Hundred Years of Anthropology.* 3rd ed. New York: William Morrow.

Propp, V.
1968   *Morphology of the Folktale.* 2nd ed. Austin: University of Texas.

Rogerson, J. W.
1978   *Anthropology and the Old Testament.* Atlanta: John Knox.

Wilson, Robert R.
1977   "Prophecy and Society in Ancient Israel: The Present State of the Inquiry." Pp. 341–358 in *Society of Biblical Literature 1977 Seminar Papers.* Ed. Paul J. Achtemeier. Missoula: Scholars Press.
1980   *Prophecy and Society in Ancient Israel.* Philadelphia: Fortress.

Wolf, Eric R.
1969   *Peasant Wars of the Twentieth Century.* New York: Harper.

PROPHETS AND THEIR PUBLICS

Ioan M. Lewis
The London School of Economics and Political Science

0. While Lévi-Strauss himself baulked at applying his Structuralist style of analysis to biblical material because it was part of a literate, 'hot' cultural tradition, others have not hesitated to take up the challenge. On the anthropological side, the structuralist assault here is led by Edmund Leach whose assimilation of written biblical source material to oral mythology has been trenchantly criticised by Julian Pitt-Rivers who rightly insists on the need to distinguish between history and myth in treating these sources. Leach's failure to do this and insistence on treating the Old Testament as a single myth raises very serious problems. This method of decoding arcane messages sometimes produces fascinating results. The trouble, however, is that one usually does not really know what the results mean. Do the dazzling patterns and contrasts that this structuralist approach discloses exist for anyone else, other than the analyst? More particularly, what is their bearing on what the biblical texts meant to their original compilers, and how, in turn, do they relate to the actual, historical events and settings from which the compilers got their material? Ultimately, one feels, Leach would have to defend his misapplication of Lévi-Strauss (as Pitt-Rivers sees it) in terms of the master's famous justification of this analysis of 'cold' American Indian myth. In this view ". . . it is immaterial whether the thought processes of the South American Indians take shape through the medium of my thought or whether mine take place through the medium of theirs" (Lévi-Strauss, 13).

1.1 This is obviously not the position taken by Professors Long, Overholt and Wilson who have shunned the seductions of Structuralism in favor of a perhaps more old-fashioned but I think less problematic approach. With becoming scholarly caution, they employ ethnographic parallels in order to elucidate the social and political conditions associated with prophecy (especially apocalyptic prophecy) in the Old Testament. As Long phrases it, the aim here is to get behind the *ideology* in which discussion of the status of prophets is customarily couched, to the actual social setting, thus rendering prophetic utterance as a product rather than producer of social transformation. While emphasizing the cultural conditioning and specificity of different prophetic traditions, all three authors insist that, in principle, any cultural tradition can produce apocalyptic prophetic movements. I think the evidence for comparative religion, particularly on messianic and ecstatic cults, makes this abundantly clear, although not all anthropologists would agree. Some anthropologists insist, just as obdurately as the Old Testament scholars berated here, on the alienness of messianism or ecstasy to the particular cultures they study. Such foreign phenomena, were they to occur, would thus inevitably be ascribed to foreign influence and explained in the same diffusionist terms as those criticised by Wilson.

1.2   The comparative evidence does not support such ethnographic opinions and as Long, Overholt and Wilson point out, the problem becomes that of identifying the precipitating factors which encourage prophetic and messianic currents *within an existing religious tradition*. This, of course, does not exclude susceptibility to foreign cultural influence, or the borrowing of new cultural elements and ideology. For, after all, however much their adherants may protest the pristine purity of their faith, *all* religions are in some sense syncretic. What we must try to do, however, is to investigate the social conditions which would be likely to promote receptivity to such foreign elements. As Buss rightly reminds us: "a cultural trait will not spread easily if the receiving society is not open to it." Thus, for instance, to take what is for many people perhaps the quintessence of prophecy—"speaking-in-tongues"—here we see at once, and very dramatically, foreign influence. But the crucial question is not so much the mere provenance of the exotic language itself. Of much greater significance is the meaning it carries for the prophet and his public. If the language employed is spoken by a group of higher status than those in the prophet's culture or sub-culture, this suggests a desire for upward mobility, or even a change of ethnic identity. Archaic language may similarly be called upon to recall and assert the original identity of a group in its purest, pristine form. In this context, Wilson's remark that the visions recounted in Daniel 7–12 are almost all recorded in Hebrew rather than the vernacular Aramaic, is suggestive of the kind of syncretic nativistic strand that Overholt detects in the movement of the Seneca Indian prophet, Handsome Lake.

1.3   Thus, while I understand and sympathize with the desire to get beyond ideology, I think much may still be gained from considering the character of the language of prophecy. For while it is true, as Overholt says, that the content of prophecy is culturally conditioned, in cross-cultural perspective there are often striking similarities in the idiom and metaphor prophets characteristically employ, as well as much stereotyping in the way in which the prophetic role is assumed and exercised. I am particularly struck, for instance, by the "wisdom" idiom which is used here to contrast priests and prophets. On anthropological grounds, Long, Overholt and Wilson are right to question the absoluteness of this postulated dichotomy and to emphasize the collaboration of prophets and priests in the same religious context. Since the comparativist anthropological literature on inspired prophets and shamans abounds in descriptions of visionaries discovering "wisdom," "truth," etc., I wonder whether there might not be greater movement between these two poles in the Israelite tradition than the literature contrasting them suggest. Is there evidence in the Old Testament texts, for instance, of priests becoming prophets, or vice versa? In the contexts discussed here, as elsewhere, their roles seem complimentary and one would like to know more about their patterns of recruitment and career profiles. In considering the specificity and uniqueness of the "Covenant" theme in Judaism, I wonder whether it is relevant to recall how frequently inspired prophets and shamans in other religious traditions (including Haitian Voodoo) describe their relationship to the deity in terms of a contract or even marriage (cf. Lewis, 63).

2.1   Returning now to the behavioural aspects of prophecy which are stressed by all contributors, Long is obviously right to insist on the "normality" of conflict between prophets and to see this in terms of recurrent competition between rival claimants for prophetic leadership. Long's analysis can, I think, be pushed further since trauma and conflict are stereotypically associated with the assumption of the ecstatic vocation. Overholt notes, for instance, how Jeremiah protests against the role he is being called upon to assume. This is very interesting, since all over the world, the *sine qua non* of authentic calling is precisely this protest by the future prophet of his unworthiness to accept divine election. Prophets do not come running. They have to be coerced into assuming the heavy burdens that the gods thrust upon them. Very frequently, this is expressed in the form of a searing illness, trauma or some other calamity as with St. Paul on the Road to Damascus, whose conversion was literally blinding. These and other experiences which announce the assumption of the prophetic role are (*pace* Overholt) thus far from being entirely private. The comparative evidence indeed indicates that the insistence with which the gods summon their chosen vessels (or spokesmen) is directly related to the personal circumstances of the future prophet and the general social situation. The less well-qualified the novice is and the wider the range of his potential appeal, the more florid will be the phenomena which are interpreted as announcing his divine election. This is well illustrated in the Shona material to which Long refers and is interestingly discussed in Buss's contribution.

2.2   Bearing in mind that protestations of the unworthiness of the human representative of the gods are most emphatically not to be taken at face value, Overholt's tripartite model for the interaction between the supernatural, prophets and their publics seems attractive and useful. Indeed this might be seen as integrating Long's focus on the role of the prophet with Wilson's stress on the ambient social setting (i.e., the prophet's public). The emphasis this schema places on feedback in the interaction between prophet and public is clearly important and, in my view, should be extended to include *recognition* as a prior event to confirmation (cf. Buss). The model might also be extended to explicitly include disconfirmation and rejection, leading to the redefinition of a failed (false) prophet, possibly as a witch or other purveyor of mystical malevolence.

3.1   Turning now to the effectiveness of prophets, or of candidates for the role, it seems to me that the question of their background ground and provenance merits more attention, particularly in the light of the familiar idea that *outsiders* are particularly well-qualified to assume the mantle of prophecy. Like the foreign expert sent to solve the problems of a Third World country, such prophetic intervention is detached, neutral, objective and authoritative in large measure because *it comes from outside*. Where prophecy is also couched in alien tongues, this, of course, compounds the prophet's exotic character, in certain circumstances adding authority to his pronouncements. The paradox here is that linguistic unintelligibility enhances the authority of prophecy. Persian or other foreign influences should perhaps also be considered from this point of view.

3.2   While Long's focus on competition between individual prophets or aspirants for such recognition highlights the context in which we should expect florid displays of mantic acrobatics, Wilson indicates the wider cultic setting which could similarly be expected to promote ecstatic flurries. Professor Wilson's optimism about the abilities of anthropologists is flattering; but I am inclined to doubt whether we shall really succeed in discovering "the precise nature of apocalyptic groups." If apocalyptic and ecstatic flamboyance are, as he, Overholt and Long agree, all to be expected in times of crisis, it is also important to recognize how such dramatic religiosity may also mark the rise or decline of religions. The Bible narrative appears to stress continuity, for obvious reasons. This seems likely to obscure fluctuations in relative centrality over time of the cult of Yahwe which might be expected to have assumed a subsidiary position within the Persian and Babylonian empires—as indeed Wilson argues.

WORKS CONSULTED

Leach, Edmund
    1969   *Genesis as Myth and Other Essays*. London: Jonathan Cape.

Lévi-Strauss, Claude
    1970   *The Raw and the Cooked*. London: Jonathan Cape.

Lewis, I. M.
 1971   *Ecstatic Religion*. Baltimore: Penguin.

Pitt-Rivers, Julian
 1977   "The Fate of Shechem or the Politics of Sex." Pp. 126–171 in *The Fate of Shechem or the Politics of Sex: Essays in the Anthropology of the Mediterranean*. Cambridge: Cambridge University.

REPLIES TO THE COMMENTATORS

ON SOCIAL AND INDIVIDUAL ASPECTS OF PROPHECY

Martin J. Buss
Emory University

1.1   Anthropology exhibits no established orthodoxy, either in method or in content. Thus I am greatful for Professor Burridge's response and for his expression of caution in regard to what the discipline can accomplish.

1.2   At two or three points Burridge differs, at least on the surface, from notions developed in my paper. It is not entirely clear to what extent these differences are substantive. For instance, Burridge states that one has to be "satisfied with explication rather than explanations." If this statement implies that the procedure of anthropology is to be contrasted sharply with that of the natural sciences, it expresses a view opposed to mine. Yet Burridge earlier offered some "explanatory models" (1969a:164) and suggested that in certain "situations and oppositions" the role of a prophet "may be necessary" (1969a:154).

1.3   On the topic of social responsibility, Burridge counters the claim that reference to a spiritual world embodies a sense of responsibility anchored in a larger-than-private perspective. In his study of the Australian Tangus he applied the term "responsibility" to a system of reciprocal relations. He found that in the view of this group God, children, and certain marginal persons stand outside such an order; according to one story, deity punishes by death a group of "responsible" persons who exclude an orphan (1969b:205). The moral claim of a prophet indeed goes beyond that of reciprocity. Further, one can agree with Burridge's observation that many prophecies are unrealistic and even a danger to the welfare of human communities (similarly, Buss: 138). Yet (as Burridge, 1979:157–164, 198–204, 251–253 has pointed out) relative disorder can provide seeds for a new significant order.

2.1   In his detailed assessment of my paper, Gottwald suggests that prophets may very well reduce complexity and ambiguity. I fully agree with that judgment. Indeed, it is normally the aim of a guide to provide a meaningful vision within the welter of events and circumstances. Yet an insightful prophet does not oversimplify matters. Quite likely, the greatness of prophecies by Amos and Jeremiah—expressed in rich poetic form—lies in large part in the fact that they saw divine election as not simply equivalent to protection or exclusivity (Amos 3:2; 9:7; Jer 25:9). Gottwald appropriately points to the judgment/salvation dialectic in Isaiah as an example of complexity.

2.2   Gottwald asks for clarification in regard to the function of call reports, in view of Long's thesis that call narratives have their predominant setting in the tradition of a prophet's disciples. Long is correct in pointing out that "accounts of a call are rarely cited by charismatic specialists to counter criticism" (10), but he does not consider the positive features of the comparative data of call narratives. Most of the reports of a prophetic call in the Bible and elsewhere are autobiographical in style (including Amos 7:14–15); third-person form appears primarily in accounts concerning nonprophetic or relatively distant figures. One should thus search for a function which is associated with the life of a prophet, although not one of establishing (as distinct from expressing) legitimacy; it is probably that of relating the individual to the prophetic task. In particular, a self-report may be given to justify one's activity to relatives, friends, and others or as part of the retrospective reflection of an older person (as among the Blackfoot Indians [Eastman: 9]). The latter process may give a partial hint about how collections of prophecies came to be formed, although disciples undoubtedly played major roles in gathering and editing.

2.3   In some strands of biblical scholarship, the person of the prophet—and the sense of a call—has been relegated to the background, in part because of a theology reluctant to treat faith in a psychological or, in general, anthropological perspective. (So, e.g., E. March; differently, G. Lindblom and A. Heschel, cited in my paper). Yet as has already been emphasized self-awareness is closely connected with self-transcendence. This paradox shows itself in the frequent appearance of both first-person pronouns and negatives ("not," etc.) in many call narratives (Exod 3:11, 4:10; 6:30; Judg 6:15; 1 Sam 9:21; 1 Kgs 3:17; Amos 7:14; Isa 6:5; Jer 1:6). The personal and the social should thus be viewed together within the dynamics of faith.

WORKS CONSULTED

Burridge, Kenelm O. L.
    1969a   *New Heaven New Earth.* New York: Schocken.
    1969b   *Tangu Traditions.* Oxford: Clarendon.
    1979   *Someone, No One: An Essay on Individuality.* Princeton: Princeton University.

Buss, Martin J.
    1969   *The Prophetic Word of Hosea.* Berlin: Töpelmann.

Eastman, Charles Alexander
1911 *The Soul of the Indian.* Boston: Houghton Mifflin.

Long, Burke O.
1977 "Prophetic Authority as Social Reality." Pp. 3–20 in *Canon and Authority*. Eds. G. W. Coats and B. O. Long. Philadelphia: Fortress.

March, W. Eugene
1970 "Jeremiah 1: Commission and Assurance." *Austin Seminary Bulletin* 86: 5–38.

PERILS GENERAL AND PARTICULAR

Burke O. Long
Bowdoin College

1.1   Burridge quite rightly warns against our too quickly seeking generalization and explanation at the expense of particularity in our studies of the social settings of prophets. In his words, he enters a plea for us "to look for those aspects of the situation which are there but have been missed." Or, as he puts it elsewhere, the "reduction of the particular to the general case—and it is a reduction—can often do less than justice to the former." And again, "we have to be satisfied with explications rather than explanations." I am very taken by the sense of wonder and surprise, chance and unpredictability, which he maintains in observing social phenomena.

1.2   Burridge takes aim at an important target. In one sense his comments seem directed to the quick move that scholars may take toward causal explanation of social phenomena. I wonder if he also implies that it is too soon or somehow inappropriate to attempt sensible and responsible comparative statements across cultural boundaries. If reduction of the particular to the general is a danger, so is its opposite: losing the general in the particular. The one may be a refuge in theories of cause and effect, or explanation, and the other may take refuge in atomistic, ethnographic studies, unrelated to context beyond the particular culture.

1.3   The issue I raise is not a new one, and certainly not new to modern anthropologists. I want to agree that we need to give particularity its due, but also say that I feel something of a responsibility to provide broader frameworks of interpretation or explication. The aim is to see particular cultural phenomena with their own integrity, but also as related to broader categories of understanding. This volume in its own way illustrates both the problem and the promise of such a goal.

2.1   Lewis may invoke causal explanation more easily than Burridge thinks advisable. It is the strength of Burridge that he gives us pause for considering method. But the strength of Lewis is that he pushes us by example to see more particularity than we might have otherwise seen in Israelite materials.

2.2   For instance, Lewis suggests the importance of our considering the social implications of the *use* of language. In his words:

> ... the crucial question is not so much the mere provenance of the exotic language itself. Of much greater significance is the meaning it carries for the prophet and his public.

Biblical scholars will know that a good many studies of the prophets during this century have emphasized the *forms* of prophetic discourse and their relation to social context. The latter has usually meant provenance. Often the enterprise led to hypotheses about the nature of prophetic "office" and the work of prophets. Rarely if at all was the prophetic language examined as indicator of social class, mobility, aspiration, and identity. To contemplate these possibilities is to extend the range of Biblical form criticism, and to take more seriously the insights from sociolinguistics (see Samarin). Even if evidence is obscure and difficult to find, it strikes me that the new range of questions is so important as to demand exploration.

2.3   Another example of Lewis's fruitful suggestions: extend the theme of conflict to include the trauma associated with the assumption of prophetic vocation. The language of selection is surely stereotypical, and as Lewis says, is "directly related to the personal circumstances of the future prophet and the general social situation." With Burridge's comments lingering in our ear, we might draw back from Lewis's causal explanation when he writes:

> The less well-qualified the novice is and the wider the range of his potential appeal, the more florid will be the phenomena which are interpreted as announcing his divine election.

2.4   Nevertheless, Lewis looks in the right direction. We ought to investigate with seriousness the social meaning and implication of this aspect of a prophetic conflict. What does the initiatory struggle with the gods and the language used to describe these occasions have to do with a prophet's social position? What social facts correlate with this ideological claim of being marked by the gods? In this regard, it is interesting to note an apparent case of ritual reinforcement of initiatory conflict. While calling the spirits, the Copper Eskimo shaman repeats like an incantation formula the language of conflict: "It is a hard thing to speak the truth. It is difficult to make hidden forces appear." Helping women crowd around and reassure him of his position and capabilities, shouting things about his power and strength. The whole scene strikes me as possibly an extension into regular ritual contexts of the shaman's initiatory trauma and the society's stake in that conflict (Rasmussen: 56–61). Certainly the matter needs further investigation.

2.5   Taken together, Burridge and Lewis caution and stimulate at the same time. For what better or more natural expression of the investigative spirit could one wish?

3.1   Like Burridge and Lewis, Gottwald is a spoiler. I mean that as a compliment, for he seeks to complicate rather than simplify our analyses of prophecy. Thus, for example, Overholt's model of the prophetic process has to be rebuilt so as to give adequate place for "socially shaped predispositions" of participants in the process, and for the changes that are an inevitable part of any historical phenomenon. Wilson begs a number of questions and too easily aligns Biblical text with the ideology and program of a particular socio-political group. And so on.

3.2   Yet, for all his "complicating" of the analysis, Gottwald still seems to look for something like generalizing sociological "laws." He mentions twice the necessity for establishing "control groups" in order to gain a firmer grip on typical socio-political factors involved in (and giving rise to?) the phenomena which we study. It is well to remember Burridge's interesting counterpoint: things are more "chancey" than analysts are wont to allow. While we are justified in looking for controls, then, we may not be able to find them, or overlook the limitations inherent in the search (see comments on Burridge).

3.3   Gottwald goes beyond the role of question-asking complicator in pushing my analysis of prophetic conflict one step further. Taking his cue from Mottu's Marxist-like analysis of ideological and class conflicts, Gottwald seems to make Jeremiah into a hero of sorts. He writes as though Jeremiah were the champion of a deprived, or about to be deprived, populace— the true advocate of the peoples' good over against that segment of the ruling class which saw itself as being necessary to Judah's (and the peoples') survival. Thus,

> It is probable that Long's 'autonomist' coalition equated survival with the continued independence of Judah under present leadership, whereas the 'co-existence' coalition equated survival with the socio-economic and religio-cultural preservation of the Judean populace.
>
> The autonomists saw the ruling class as a perfect, or at least fully adequate, representative of the peoples' interests. Therefore its overthrow would mean the downfall of the people. The coexisters by contrast, viewed the domestic policies of the ruling class as decisively antagonistic to the interests of the people and regarded any strengthening of that ruling class against Babylon as precisely a promotion of policies that would further harm the people, whereas submission to or cooperation with Babylon, would most likely foster a viable life for the Judean people.

3.4   If I understand Gottwald correctly, I believe he has made an implicit value judgement, aligning Jeremiah and the "co-existers" with the good things of cultural survival, and the "autonomists" with the bad things of cultural suicide. Allowing the analysis for the moment, it seems likely that both groups in the situation would have identified their own self-interest with the survival interests of the wider population. For Gottwald (and Mottu also) to favor one group over the other, even implicitly, is to transpose a sixth century B.C. ideological conflict with its inherent value choices onto the level of twentieth century historical reconstruction. Surely, Mottu and

Gottwald are right in directing our attention to a level of socio-economic conflict beneath the more overt struggles over inter-state and religious matters. Yet to direct attention is one thing, to make assertions another. One may fairly ask for the evidence in the literary materials. Considering how little and slim are the data for reconstructing political ideologies and allegiances, I wonder how much further one may go?

WORKS CONSULTED

Rasmussen, Knud
    1932   *The Intellectual Culture of the Copper Eskimos.* Report of the Fifth Thule Expedition, 9. Copenhagen. Nordisk Forlag.

Samarin, W. J.
    1976   *Language in Religious Practice.* Rowley, Massachusetts: Newbury House.

MODEL, MEANING, AND NECESSITY

Thomas W. Overholt
University of Wisconsin-Stevens Point

1.1   With respect to Prof. Burridge's comments on the prophet's message, it occurs to me that there must be several stages in the process of "making sense" out of what one hears, and that "making sense" of an utterance on the spot is a somewhat different matter than interpreting the same utterance after the fact. To subsequently repudiate an earlier decision to follow a prophet is probably not so much an indication that the message was not really convincing in the first place, as a later revaluation in the light of spoiled hopes. I would imagine that, if the ancestors had arrived bearing "cargo," the participants' answer to the question of whether they would do it again would be different. Jer 44:15–19 comes to mind, along with the proverb about hindsight being better than foresight. It has long been my opinion that discussions of the problem of "false prophecy" by OT scholars have too often failed to do justice to the "existential" situation of the hearers, who were called upon to make a response, but did not have the luxury of sufficient time to see whether the prophecy would "come true" before doing so. In responding to such a leader one is always taking a chance; the agony of decision is implicit in the prophetic process.

1.2   The crux of the matter is the problem of defining the "*necessary* conditions" for a given instance of prophecy (in the full sense of utterance-plus-acceptance). As Burridge puts it, there seems to be "no kind of inevitability" about the process by which in the immediacy of a situation people choose "to do things they would not otherwise have done." One measure of the difficulty of this problem is the fact that in his now-famous survey of studies of "crisis cults" La Barre devotes over half the text to a discussion of "theories of causality." His general conclusion is that no one theory taken alone is sufficient, that (to use his words) "in the study of crisis cults, the word 'and' serves better than the contentious word 'only'" (1971:26).

1.3   While I acknowledge the complexity of this problem and would not want to be party to the kind of "reductionism" La Barre finds to be "rampant in crisis cult studies" (1971:26), I find myself wondering whether the presence of a prophetic-type leader is not the critical element in the emergence of a "crisis cult" (the terminology presents its own problems) within a given socio-historical situation. La Barre is critical of "the 'great man' theory" of the origin of such movements, largely it seems on the basis of instances of "failed" messiahs and a well-founded objection against using the notion of "charisma" in the sense of some "mysterious belief-compelling *authority* of the 'supernatural'" (1971:20). I take this not so much as undermining the contention that the leader is a centrally important causative factor as a warning against misconstruing his power and role. Thus, he warns that "so far as 'true' and 'false' messiahs are concerned, the religious 'genius' is a psychosocial phenomenon only if and when he is psychodynamically relevant to others and is functioning in his proper sociocultural context, for otherwise he is likely to be adjudged as psychotic, given his discrepancy with reality and regnant 'common sense'" (1971:20). I take it that my comments on the nature of a prophet's "authority" are compatible with this caution. The whole problem is exacerbated by the fact that each instance of prophecy is a particular case, and, as Burridge points out, "the reduction of the particular to the general case . . . can often do less than justice to the former."

1.4   Finally, Burridge's plea that we "look for those aspects of the situation which are there but have been missed" prompts an observation. I suspect that one of the major practical differences between field anthropology and biblical studies is that in the former there is potentially a wealth of observed or observable data, while in the latter one is largely stuck with a text, which, because of the particular biases of the transmitters, conceals much. He has correctly seen that precisely because "common sense" has failed to open our eyes to certain presumed aspects of the social situation, we are in fact squeezing what is unknown "into the familiar, so that what is in fact unknown can seem to be known." The transmitters of the text have to a large extent hung a "theological veil" before our eyes (cf. Overholt), but I for one am confident that the insights of anthropologists like Prof. Burridge can help us to find (or make) holes in that barrier, the better to understand the social reality which in the nature of the case must lie on the other side.

2.1   Prof. Gottwald calls attention to places where my model of the prophetic process would benefit from some refinement. I think his "signs/evidences of confirmation" is in fact a better rubric than my "expectations of confirmation," a somewhat infelicitious phrase that occurred to me when I was working on the Ghost Dance materials and has remained more out of neglect than commitment. But more importantly he points out something I have neglected altogether, viz., that the prophets themselves quest for these signs and are affected by their presence or absence. It appears that some redesigning of Figure 1 with respect to the place of this element is necessary.

2.2   Several of Gottwald's comments relate to the cultural context in which a specific instance of prophecy occurs. I understand my general statement about the people's response to a prophet (1.4) to be in harmony with his more specific suggestion "that the people relate each specific prophetic revelation to a fund of revelations." Further, he suggests the need to have the model represent the "socially shaped predispositions" of prophets "toward revelations and proclamations of a particular form and . . . content," since otherwise we might be tempted to view prophets as "mysterious sources" of religious ideas "which are later adopted into a social routine" (to quote from Gottwald's discussion of Weber's "idealist 'escape hatch'" to which his citation refers). The problem is whether the relationship of both prophet and people to their broader social context can be represented in the model itself. I will have to give it some thought.

2.3   Finally, it does seem to me that the model is applicable to prophetic careers of any length. To conceive of prophecy as a dialectical process implies the possibility of a duration beyond a single encounter between prophet and people.

3.1   Prof. Lewis's remarks on "the character of the language of prophecy" suggest a matter which my model for a cross-cultural description of the prophetic process simply ignores, viz., whether there are in fact "striking similarities in the idiom and metaphor" employed by prophets of differing cultures. He mentions two clusters of concepts (wisdom-truth; covenant-contract-marriage) that might prove to be examples of such metaphors. At the broadest level of content I think I would still be surprised to find much similarity among prophets (Jeremiah and Handsome Lake spoke to audiences that were literally worlds apart). Still, it would be worth inquiring into the presence of similarities both in important themes (like those suggested) and also in specific formulae related to the way in which a prophet exercises his role in society (what, for example, is the equivalent in other cultures of the OT prophet's, "Thus says Yahweh"?).

3.2   I am also inclined to take seriously Lewis's suggestion that the experience by which the prophet felt himself to have been designated to perform that role need not be quite so private as I have claimed. Handsome Lake's "death" and "resurrection" were in fact witnessed by a number of other persons, though they and we remain dependent upon his account for our knowledge of important aspects of that experience. Stereotypical possession behavior may be one sort of observable phenomenon attending a prophet's call. Such manifestations would be examples of what I have termed "expectations of confirmation," and that aspect of the model may require more emphasis than I have given it (and perhaps a new rubric!).

3.3   Lewis suggests some modifications of the model, among them extending the notion of feedback between prophet and public "to include *recognition* as a prior event to confirmation." The whole process by which papers for this volume were circulated and responded to has been rather fluid, and I must confess that in response to some comments from Burke Long the section of my paper that deals most specifically with this matter (4.2) was strengthened after the completion of the draft that Prof. Lewis had at his disposal. Insofar as his "recognition" can be taken to mean "acceptance" or "acknowledgment," this is now explicitly stated. On another point, the model does describe only what might be called "confirmed" instances of prophetic activity. What happens in cases of failure must be implied: absence or total disruption of either of the two major sequences (3.1, 3.2) would by definition mean that the occurrence under investigation was not an instance of *prophecy*. But there is a certain ambiguity here. To speak of acceptance or rejection always implies the question, "By whom?" Perhaps most prophets experience both, since occasions on which audience and support groups are coterminous must indeed be rare.

3.4 Finally, I find myself wondering about Lewis's point that "*outsiders* are particularly well-qualified to assume the mantle of prophecy," because their message is likely to be perceived as "detached, neutral, objective and authoritative." These are all somewhat problematic terms when applied to prophets. Jeremiah and Handsome Lake were both "insiders." They thumped a party line, so to speak, and were hardly detached and neutral. Perhaps both they and their supporters would have said that their analyses of their respective situations were "objective," but then opponents might well have made the same claim for quite different views (cf. Jer 44:15-19!). Amos, on the other hand, *was* an "outsider," who came from Judah to prophesy in Israel, but the same points seem to hold true for him. His confrontation with the priest at Bethel (7:10-17) reveals that some significant members of his audience perceived his activity as anything but detached, neutral, and objective.

WORKS CONSULTED

LaBarre, Weston
    1971   "Materials for a History of Studies of Crisis Cults: A Bibliographic Essay." *Current Anthropology* 12:3-44.

Overholt, Thomas W.
    1979   "Commanding the Prophets: Amos and The Problem of Prophetic Authority." *CBQ* 41:517-532.

THE PROBLEMS OF DESCRIBING AND DEFINING APOCALYPTIC DISCOURSE

Robert R. Wilson
Yale University

1.1   Professors Burridge, Lewis, and Gottwald have all pointed in various ways to one of the crucial unsolved problems raised by the study of ancient and modern prophecy and apocalyptic. Although modern anthropological studies have demonstrated a correlation between the existence of certain types of social conditions and the appearance of prophecy and apocalyptic, the fact remains that these conditions sometimes exist in societies where prophets and apocalyptic groups do not emerge. This state of affairs can be illustrated in modern societies and probably also in ancient Israel. The appearance of apocalyptic literature in Israel seems to correspond roughly with the deterioration of political, religious, and social conditions during the post-exilic period, and it is therefore fair to assume that some Israelites responded to the conditions of this period by creating or joining apocalyptic communities. However, not all Israelites responded in this way. Some apparently sought to restore equilibrium to their lives by living within the guidelines set out by Israel's wisdom traditions, while others looked to the interpretation of the Torah as a way of regulating daily life. Apocalyptic religion was not the only form of post-exilic Israelite religion, and there is no evidence that it was even the predominant form. Rather, apocalyptic, the scholarly study of the Torah, a concern with the development of wisdom literature, the elaboration of the cult, and an interest in the interpretation of earlier prophetic literature all seem to be features of Israel's post-exilic religious life. This religious diversity suggests that apocalyptic was not the inevitable result of certain social conditions. In the same way, as Gottwald has pointed out, various sorts of cultural upheaval and relative deprivation existed in the *pre-exilic* period; yet the biblical literature provides no clear indication that the formation of apocalyptic groups was a major feature of religion in pre-exilic Israel. Although it is theoretically possible that some of the so-called proto-apocalyptic passages in the prophets are pre-exilic rather than post-exilic, it is generally assumed, firm evidence on this point is lacking.

1.2   In both the ancient and modern situations, then, more work needs to be done on the question of the non-appearance of prophecy and apocalyptic in societies where social conditions might normally be expected to encourage the development of these phenomena. It may be that the willingness of societies to tolerate the phenomena plays a role, but the problem must be explored thoroughly in modern societies where more data are available. Without additional comparative evidence the ancient sources can be of little help.

2.1   In the same way, additional anthropological and biblical research needs to be done in order to shed some light on Gottwald's question concerning the criteria on the basis of which ancient and modern groups are defined as "apocalyptic." Anthropologists are in general agreement that certain specific groups or movements clearly fall into the category that biblical scholars would call "apocalyptic," but there is disagreement about the status of other groups because they do not share all of the features usually associated with apocalyptic groups or because they share these features only to a limited degree. This difficulty in categorizing groups suggests that apocalyptic groups may exhibit a good bit of individuality and that the category "apocalyptic" must be allowed to remain somewhat flexible. However, the limits of this flexibility still need to be determined, and this is a task that might be fruitfully undertaken both by anthropologists and by biblical scholars.

2.2   It is the individualistic characteristics of apocalyptic groups that cause the greatest difficulties in applying contemporary anthropological research to the study of Israelite religion. My reading of the anthropological literature suggests that although contemporary apocalyptic groups share certain general features, these groups also differ markedly from each other because they are composed of individuals with differing social, political, cultural, and religious backgrounds. These differing backgrounds are reflected in the ways in which various groups perceive themselves and render an account of their self-identity to themselves and to the outside world. This means that in some sense each apocalyptic group is unique and must be studied in its particularity as well as viewed in the larger context of apocalyptic groups in general. My application of the anthropological material to Daniel was designed simply to show that the group that produced this particular piece of apocalyptic writing did not come from pure "wisdom" or prophetic roots but was a unique group that blended earlier Israelite traditions in its own distinctive way. To carry the exploration further, it would be necessary to examine each piece of apocalyptic literature to try to uncover evidence of the unique characteristics of the writers.

2.3   However, it is precisely at this point that the student of Israelite religion runs into difficulty, for except in the case of the Qumran community, Israelite apocalyptic groups are known to us only through the literature that they produced. To date, external evidence on these groups is nonexistent, and we have no choice but to reconstruct each individual group as best we can on the basis of its literature. In some cases we can, as Gottwald suggests, try to discover more about the sociopolitical situation in the time the literature was created, but in the end this information is unlikely to tell us much about the specific group that produced the literature. We are therefore left with the problem which Gottwald rightly highlights, the problem of how to analyze the literature of a group in order to reconstruct its social, political, and religious background. This problem is essentially a form-critical problem, and since the time of Gunkel form-critics have found it a difficult one to solve, for literary forms are not always tied to a single social setting, and as a result it is difficult to reconstruct the setting on the basis of the form alone. This problem is particularly difficult in the case of Daniel, for most modern form- and tradition-critics agree that the book is the product of a complex editorial process. This means that the question of social matrix must be asked at each point in the history of the text. When we attempt to deal with such complexity, certainty is never possible, and even the most sensitive form-critical analysis is unlikely to be able to uncover more than the bare outline of the social matrix. Given our present extra-biblical information, a reconstruction of the "complex sociopolitical situations" which must have existed at the time each layer was composed is a virtual impossibility.

2.4   It is for this reason that my analysis of the Daniel group was brief and schematic, and I am unwilling to claim for it the degree of historical specificity which Gottwald attributes to my reconstruction. Following several recent critics and on the basis of my own form-critical analysis of the book—an analysis which unfortunately cannot be included in a brief article—I suggested that the earliest layers of the book were written in the Persian Period, while the last chapters reached their final form in Maccabean times. In between these two points is a period of slow growth which can be traced through form-critical analysis. For the sake of brevity I spoke of three major phases in this literary history, but in fact many more layers seem to be present in the text. This complexity means that it is difficult to pinpoint the historical and social location of the writers and tradents with any certainty. It seems reasonable to accept the book's own statement that the chief characters were exiled Jews who were working in a foreign bureaucracy, and in fact the text deals with the issues that would have been of particular concern to such people. However, even if one assumes that the book originally dealt with the problems of a particular class of Jews during the Persian Period, it is difficult to say more than this, and it is particularly hard to reconstruct the group's subsequent history with any specificity. An increase in the severity of outside opposition can be inferred from the writers' increasingly negative view of foreign rulers, from the group's increasingly radical views on the degree to which society must change in order for injustices to be rectified, and from explicit references in the latter chapters to persecution, but details cannot be reconstructed because of uncertainties about the historical location of the group. Similarly, the latter chapters of the book seem to reflect some sort of religious dispute within the Jewish community, but the details are unclear. The most that can be said, then, is that the group became increasingly apocalyptic in its orientation over the course of its existence and that, like all apocalyptic groups, it was unique, reflecting in its outlook and literature the background of its members. Although we would like to know more about the group and although we might plausibly guess why it developed in the way it did, we cannot go further without moving too far away from the text. Many questions are unanswered, and for the moment they must remain unanswered.

www.ingramcontent.com/pod-product-compliance
Lightning Source LLC
Chambersburg PA
CBHW032300150426
43195CB00008BA/527

Connecting with the Expert Within

Connecting with the Expert Within

Re-Awakening to Your Strength and Competence

Richard D. Parsons, Ph.D.

 PRESS

Copyright © 2022 by Cognella, Inc. All rights reserved. No part of this publication may be reprinted, reproduced, transmitted, or utilized in any form or by any electronic, mechanical, or other means, now known or hereafter invented, including photocopying, microfilming, and recording, or in any information retrieval system without the written permission of Cognella, Inc.

Trademark Notice: Product or corporate names may be trademarks or registered trademarks, and are used only for identification and explanation without intent to infringe.

Cover image: Copyright © 2010 iStockphoto LP/apomares.
Copyright © 2020 iStockphoto LP/koto_feja.

Printed in the United States of America.

Contents

1. IN NEED? CALL AN EXPERT — 1
2. POSITIONING FOR GROWTH — 15
3. MOVING FROM "I THINK I CAN" TO "I WILL!" — 29
4. START WITH A VISION—MOVE TO A GOAL — 45
5. PATHFINDING: GETTING TO YOUR GOAL — 63
6. FROM PLAN TO ACTION — 79
7. RESILIENCY—ESSENTIAL FOR SUCCESS — 97
8. MORE THAN SURVIVING … THRIVING AND FLOURISHING — 111

EPILOGUE: WHO NEEDS 120 MILLION EXPERTS WHEN YOU HAVE YOU? — 127

ENDNOTES — 129

chapter one

In Need? Call an Expert

> *We do not need to be shoemakers to know if our shoes fit ...*
>
> —Georg Wilhelm Friedrich Hegel[1]

If you asked my wife—actually, if you asked anyone who knows me—they would attest that I am NOT mechanically inclined. Now, don't get me wrong—my first strategy for dealing with a broken pipe, a lawn mower that won't start, or a heater making an unusual noise is to grab my toolbox and confront the demons.

Suppose history is a good predictor of the future. In that case, you can almost assuredly predict that my tinkering will not only fail to produce a positive outcome but will most likely result in a more expensive repair.

I guess a sign of maturity, or at least my maturing, is that I am much more apt—following prompts and pleads from my wife—to call an expert!

A Time to Seek Assistance

The title of this book, *Connecting with the Expert Within*, may lead you to conclude that we should never rely on others' knowledge, skills, or expertise. Clearly, that is not the case. Many things in life require unique knowledge and skill sets if they are to be "fixed."

This can even be true at those times when that which needs to be "fixed" is ourselves.

While I am more than likely willing to grab a screwdriver and dismantle a lawn mower's carburetor, I will surrender my scalpel to a well-trained surgeon when surgery is needed, or my drill to the dentist for my root canal, and even my scissors to my local barber. The same is true when I am seeking self-improvement. I will invite the wisdom and feedback of a golf pro to help me with my slice. I will engage a professional trainer to assist me with my workout. And I will—and have—turned to a professional psychologist when I have found myself somewhat burdened by a series of personal losses.

Having the availability of others with unique talents is a gift in times of need. However, we need to understand what exactly is our time of need—and whether or not an expert is required.

Knowing When and Who

Don't you just love it when you are hard at work on a project, perhaps something for school, or a home renovation or car repair, and your friend—the "expert"—swoops in to point out how it should have been done? Me neither!

That doesn't mean that my friend isn't an expert, nor that her suggestions are not really good. It merely means that I wasn't ready to take advice and was preferring to claw my way through the project on my own.

Knowing when to seek and accept expert advice is just as important as knowing who to seek that advice from.

When?

Perhaps the most immediate answer to the question "When should I seek out an expert?" is ... anytime you want to. There is no one right time or set of conditions that should dictate when you seek advice or another's expertise. The bottom line is to seek another's opinion or expert advice anytime you are uncomfortable going it alone.

A more prescriptive answer would be that it makes sense to seek assistance anytime that going it alone is riskier, or potentially more costly, than engaging another. It is one thing to attempt to fix a faulty lamp on your own, even when you fail to have experience or expertise working with electricity. It is quite another thing to try to run a 200-amp electrical service line from a power source to your house.

It is also helpful to turn for assistance anytime you find yourself stuck and need a different perspective. In my 40 years of practice as a clinical psychologist, I have encountered many individuals who possessed the knowledge, skills, and self-competence to resolve the issues they were confronting. Their challenge was not finding or developing new knowledge or skills. Their challenge was to regain a sense of objectivity and clarity about their competency and the nature of the challenge.

When you are overwhelmed by stress or feeling down, it may be hard to get an accurate perspective on the magnitude of a problem being encountered or your own ability to cope. Under these conditions, finding a supportive friend or a helpful professional might be an effective way to regain clarity and perspective.

Who?

If you decide to turn to another for some assistance, the next challenge is to determine how to choose the expert who may be of value.

We live at a time when we do not lack for "experts." If you can post a video or create a blog, you, too, can enter the world of the "expert." So, in times of need, it is crucial to weed out those self-acclaimed experts from those who indeed *are* the experts.

So where do you turn for expert assistance?

It would seem that your best option is to find an individual who can give evidence of (a) having the knowledge needed, (b) being able to perform the task desired, and (c) having a history of successful experience that increases their probability of being successful once again.

When I was diagnosed with cancer and opted for robotic surgery, I was able to find six physicians in my area who were all knowledgeable and trained in the procedure. Of the six, one had successfully operated 20 times over the past year. Another surgeon had completed the surgery 20 times each month for the past year.

Hmmm? Same training. Same degree. The same procedure, and even the same hospital.

You can guess which I selected—and thankfully, that was 12 years ago, and I'm still good to go.

Let's Not Make It a Habit

Turning to others for guidance, assistance, and expertise is a wise decision in many situations. Yes, it is essential and reasonable to turn to an expert when that expertise is genuinely out of our reach. The potential pitfall is that the process of turning to the expert can become a habit. It is possible that we can rely so often on others that we surrender our belief in our own competency.

Perhaps you know someone who is continuously seeking advice and affirmation, fearing that they will make a mistake or look stupid or be inadequate. Or perhaps you know of individuals who are told repeatedly that they can't do this or that or that they are major screwups. With this barrage of input, it would not be unexpected for that individual to repeatedly turn to others for the "answer" or the "direction."

Seeking the guidance of others can be helpful; however, seeking direction from others can also be less than helpful, even detrimental, if the direction received is simply not that which we need or will work for us. Perhaps a little personal story might help illuminate what I mean.

Throughout my formative school years, I was a less-than-stellar student. I was the type of student who couldn't sit still in class, would often impulsively call out answers (without much reflection), and in general was truly disorganized (or so I thought). Upon my entry into college, I decided to turn the page, turn over a new leaf, and become the "model" student.

Given my history and school performance habits, I decided to ask others—others I saw as successful students—how they approached schooling. I was curious about how they took notes, studied for tests, and even organized their schedules and learning spaces. The "experts" I turned to provided me with a template or profile of "the successful student."

The picture depicted was of a student who was extremely organized, often employing color-coded notes and file folders. This "model" student would not only read and highlight material before coming to class but would go to the library or a study carrel and reorganize the notes following class. When studying for a test, the directive was to eliminate all distractions—no noise (certainly no music)—and employ bright lights, a warm temperature, and a desk cleared of extraneous material like a cup of coffee or snacks.

This all sounded reasonable.

Perhaps this is in line with how you would approach this issue of becoming a successful student. So I tried it. I really did. It was a miserable failure.

The behavior and the conditions suggested by these "experts" not only failed to help me focus and concentrate, but they were actually additional distractions.

Bright lights make me uncomfortable. When I work, even now as I write, I prefer a cool temperature and a relaxed social setting, one in which I can have something to drink or eat while writing. And, perhaps most surprisingly—I can concentrate so much better when there is background noise. That may or may not be strange to you, but it reflects the elements of a learning style—my learning style.

While I didn't understand the neurological basis for these learning preferences (until much later in my education), I knew on the level of my gut that my attention, retention, and ability to produce increased when I moved my studying from the library to the student union. Here was a place where I could eat, drink, move about, and be immersed in an informal social setting. Not what the "experts" ordered.

Well, actually, it was precisely what THIS expert ordered!

Given my learning style and how I am wired, the advice to retreat to the quiet, bright, warm, and formal setting of the university library study carrel was precisely what I did not need. It indeed was a case where I didn't need a shoemaker to know whether my shoes fit. What I needed to do was to listen to the expert within.

When confronted with a life challenge or a block to goal achievement, it is not unusual for any one of us to look to an "expert" for guidance. As noted, there are plenty available. Like me, you may have turned to family, friends, colleagues, or even those identified as professional helpers—doctors, therapists, and spiritual leaders. Tapping others' expertise is undoubtedly a valuable practice, but then so is tapping the expert within.

The Expert Within

The ability to take time out to simply look inside and begin to increase our awareness of and familiarity with our own strengths and resources is a gift and an essential step to becoming more self-reliant. There are areas of knowledge and skill that are so far beyond my understanding and competency that I wouldn't know what to ask, look for, or even expect. Perhaps you can say the same.

In the same light, there are areas where—through training and education, trial-and-error experience, or perhaps even the magic of my constitution—I do have some understanding and skill. For lack of a better word, these are areas in which I do have the *competency*, if not expertise.

The same is true for you.

It can be said of you, me, and everyone we know that we are less than perfect. How do I know? Simple. We are humans, and as humans, we are works in progress. But being less than perfect also means that we are less than entirely, or perfectly, incompetent.

No matter how you feel about yourself at this moment, there is a truth, one that we discuss in detail in the next chapter. The truth is that you have successfully navigated many of life's challenges to arrive at this place and time. This is not to suggest that your current circumstances are all that is desired. You may even be facing some significant life challenges at this very moment. But, even if that is the case, it is essential to realize that you have employed your resources, talents, and personal strengths to survive (and hopefully thrive) up to this point. These same personal resources may be of use if called to service at present.

We are works in progress, and as such, if we so choose, we can progress. We can grow, develop, and more successfully navigate our lives. To do so requires that we start by taking stock of who we are and what we currently bring to the table.

Gaining Knowledge of Self: Authentic and Accurate

If you are like most people, you probably haven't taken much time to ponder the question of *"Who am I?"*

You can likely identify the activities or hobbies that you enjoy. You may be able to describe the type of people and social settings and interactions that you prefer to avoid. You may be able to articulate many of your beliefs, your values, those things you hold as a priority in life. All of this is evidence of self-knowledge. It is a beginning. But is there more to discover?

The idea of engaging in an honest—thorough—self-assessment may seem daunting or, perhaps for you, unnecessary.

You may be a person who has a clear, accurate sense of your strengths, weaknesses, and areas for growth and thus see little value in further assessment. That may be true—however, engaging in self-assessment can help increase your awareness and confidence in your abilities and help you to discern those areas of growth that you value and wish to pursue. Knowing your strengths and weaknesses will also set the stage for knowing when it will serve you well to seek another's expertise or when you can and should rely on the expert within.

Taking Stock of Strengths and Areas for Growth

As you begin to take stock, to develop an awareness of your strengths and areas for growth, it is crucial not to ignore the more "common" characteristics that are strengths but may be easily overlooked or taken for granted. While it may be easy to identify a specific area of weakness, such as *"I'm not good at math,"* it is also easy to ignore a strength, such as *"I am open to suggestions and guidance."*

Too often, we simply dismiss some of our assets as something taken for granted and, thus, somewhat devalued. Perhaps you have been in a situation where somebody compliments you on your sense of humor or your act of kindness. At these times, do you find yourself smiling and saying, "Thank you," while internally devaluing the trait identified as no big deal?

Being able to find healthy humor in a moment is a gift. Don't believe me? Ask an individual who is depressed. The ability to offer a kind word or act in a caring fashion is also special. These simple acts of kindness can be lifesaving for an individual who feels ignored, isolated, or abused.

Sometimes that which feels so natural to you or comes easily can be dismissed as no big deal. For your self-assessment to be of value, you need to consider all of those characteristics, those traits, those special skills or areas of knowledge that make you unique among those you know.

Several strategies can help you in this process of taking stock and increasing your authentic understanding of self, techniques such as employing introspection, seeking feedback, or utilizing structured assessments.

Introspection

The first and perhaps best strategy for gaining self-knowledge and a better understanding of the strengths and challenges you bring to your life experiences is to engage in self-reflection, or introspection.

The idea of taking time to sit and simply reflect on oneself may seem like an act of frivolous self-indulgence. Such time out for self-reflection may also appear quite impossible given the daily demands placed on your time and energy. The world is coming at us too fast, and we are too harried to find time for self-reflection. Taking time out to review where you are and where you wish to go is essential to your ongoing development. Exercise 1.1 invites you to take a moment—a moment for reflection, for introspection. It is a moment to increase your genuine self-knowledge.

As you engage with the exercise, pencil in hand, reflect on those personal strengths (remember, that includes knowledge, skills, attitudes, and dispositions) that have served you well in navigating your life and relationships to this point. Remember, don't overlook those softer, intrinsic strengths, such as *"I am kind,"* and don't be humble.

Exercise 1.1. Self-Reflection on Personal Strengths and Assets

Directions:
Part A: Review each of the following descriptors and circle those you feel reflect "you" and your strengths and personal resources.

Part B: revisit the list and place an X next to those characteristics you feel you would like to adjust, either by reducing or by increasing their presence in your profile.

Remember, you are not trying to pick things that are good or things that are bad—the truth is that most of what is listed can be of service in some circumstances. The goal is to gain an accurate accounting of your characteristics.

(Continued)

Curious	Energetic	Caring	Motivated	Outgoing
Value others' perspectives	Empathic	Self-sufficient	Enjoy alone time	Enjoy others
Compassionate	Logical	Intuitive	Enthusiastic	Spontaneous
Tactful	Practical	Considerate	Self-assured	Trustworthy
Persuasive	Serious	Lively	Tolerant	Idealistic
Forceful	Observant	Practical	Generous	Open
Warm	Humorous	Determined	Flexible	Versatile
Logical	Honest	Appreciative	Creative	Brave
Impatient	Independent	Aggressive	Leadership	Logical
Controlling	Supportive	Orderly	Disciplined	Impulsive
Naïve	Dedicated	Impatient	Ambitious	Talented
Intelligent	Shy	Straightforward	Moody	Persistent
Knowledgeable	Skilled with my hands	Precise	Responsible	Hardworking
Inspiring	Positive (attitude and perspective)	Self-regulating (behavior and emotions)	Humble	Withdrawn
Coordinated/Athletic	Influential	Helpful	Funny	

While it may be true that you are the most knowledgeable source of information about yourself, you may not be the most accurate source. A big challenge with attempting to gain self-knowledge through reflection is that we serve both in the observer's role (i.e., assessor) and as the subject of the assessment. Playing both roles can distort our perceptions and affect the accuracy of the information we gather.

The tendency to give ourselves higher grades than deserved or minimize that which is less than desirable is a natural consequence of our self-bias. It is also true that we have blind spots when it comes to profiling all our strengths and limitations (think bad breath!).

Accurately uncovering blind spots, increasing your awareness of those personal characteristics that are less than desirable, and gaining clarity over those personal traits and characteristics that are out of your immediate awareness will help round out the picture of your self-assessment.

As you are reading, you perhaps see the dilemma. If these are blinds spots, then how does one become aware of them? That is where a little help from our friends can be of great value.

Feedback: A Little Help from My Friends

Fortunately, you have friends, family, or colleagues who have witnessed your behaviors and experienced your attitudes, values, beliefs, and overall style. Inviting their feedback can be a beneficial and valuable way of gaining personal insight and understanding. Knowing you as they do, this person (or persons) can serve as a sounding board, a source of validation for your view of self, as well as providing a different perspective on the "you" that they experience.

Exercise 1.2 invites you to share your self-assessment with someone who has had the opportunity to observe your behavior and character in various situations and who you feel will be up-front and honest with you.

This is not a time to surrender your self-evaluation to the assessment of others. It is also not a time to defend yourself against alternative assessments offered by those who know you. The idea is to gather data from various perspectives—perhaps looking for areas of overlap, areas you feel are valid but failed to notice, and areas where maybe more thought and consideration could be applied.

Exercise 1.2. An Alternate View

Directions: Invite a friend, family, or coworker to serve as coassessor. Share your responses to Exercise 1.1. Invite your coassessor to review those items you identified as reflective of your characteristics (both those circled and those with Xs).

1. Are there descriptors of your strengths and areas for growth that they feel are applicable and you failed to identify?
2. Do they have questions about something you identified as a personal strength or resource?

Structured Measures

Introspection and feedback are two beneficial strategies for gaining a greater awareness of your strengths and weaknesses. A limitation to such an approach is that all aspects, all domains, may not be reviewed or may simply not be considered. An additional challenge to introspection and feedback is that both methods are vulnerable to personal bias.

After all, it is hard for a person or a friend to be completely objective and to identify less-than-desirable characteristics.

Expanding the domains to be assessed and increasing the assessment's objectivity and validity may be achieved by employing a structured technique. A quick internet search will reveal numerous self-administered scales, questionnaires, and surveys developed to assist in the pursuit of self-understanding.

You can find a self-administered test assessing a wide variety of personal traits, characteristics, styles, interests, and aptitudes. For example, *Psychology Today* offers self-tests assessing mental health levels, happiness levels, career personality and aptitudes, and even your relationship attachment style, just to name a few (https://www.psychologytoday.com/us/tests).

While any measure may be interesting and even "fun" to employ, the quality that contributes to validity and objectivity should always be considered. The more valid the measure, the more useful the information provided. And yet, even for the most "valid" assessment instrument, it is essential to realize that none of these are perfect nor absolute in their findings. Each is simply one more data point for you to consider in your search for self-knowledge and understanding.

Several self-assessment measures, often employed by counselors in their work with clients, are available and may be useful to your own process of increasing self-understanding (see Table 1.1).

TABLE 1.1 Self-Assessment Measures

MEASURE	FOCUS	MORE INFORMATION
Myers-Briggs Type Indicator	Describes a person's preferred style of interacting with the world. This measure provides four dimensions (Extraversion or Introversion; Sensing or Intuition; Thinking or Feeling; Judging or Perceiving), which in combination reveal 16 possible psychological types.	https://www.myersbriggs.org/my-mbti-personality-type/mbti-basics/home.htm?bhcp=1
Keirsey Temperament Sorter	Based on the Keirsey Temperament Theory, the test assesses an individual's temperament as either guardian, artisan, rational, or idealist. The data are further divided into four character types for each (for a total of 16 character types).	Free assessment available at: https://profile.keirsey.com/#/b2c/assessment/start

(Continued)

TABLE 1.1 *(Continued)*

MEASURE	FOCUS	MORE INFORMATION
Big Five Personality Assessment	The Big Five personality traits, also known as the five-factor model (FFM), is based on the common language descriptors of personality. The Big Five Personality Assessment evaluates people according to five personality traits: openness, conscientiousness, extraversion, agreeableness, and neuroticism. It can help you identify your particular learning styles and working preferences.	Free assessment available on the Open Source Psychometrics Project website: https://openpsychometrics.org/tests/IPIP-BFFM/
Life Values Assessment Test	The Life Values Assessment Test (LVAT) examines your priorities in life. With this test, you will notice which core values matter the most to you at this point in your life.	The test is accessible at https://www.whatsnext.com/life-values-self-assessment-test/
16 Personalities Assessment	The 16 personalities assessment describes how people belonging to a specific personality type are likely to behave, outlining indicators and tendencies. The information on this website is meant to inspire personal growth and an improved understanding of yourself and your relationships.	Access at https://www.16personalities.com

So Now What?

Hopefully, your engagement with introspection, self-administered tests, and feedback from others has helped you increase your internal self-awareness (i.e., how you see and understand yourself) and your external self-awareness (i.e., understanding how others see you). Research has found that such self-awareness is the "single most important and yet least examined determinant of success or failure."[2] Self-reflection and the resulting increased understanding of self can help you in the following ways:

1. Make you more proactive, boost acceptance, and encourage positive self-development.[3]
2. Increase your ability to see things from others' perspectives, practice self-control, and increase self-esteem.[4]

3. Lead to better decision-making.[5]
4. Enhance your self-confidence.

In addition to the above benefits, my hope in inviting you to engage in such self-assessment is to provide you with at least a little "peek" at the expert within.

As we move forward in our journey together, we will return to this "expert," and we will tap this valuable resource to help you achieve your goals and experience a happier, more fulfilled life.

chapter two

Positioning for Growth

Don't push your weaknesses; play with your strengths.

—Jennifer Lopez[1]

S tepping on the scale, looking at the checkbook balance, or even feeling unsure of where the next phase of life will take you can be, and often is, an invitation to beat up on yourself. Perhaps, after multiple attempts at the latest and greatest weight-loss programs, you've surrendered. Or, upon receiving one more job application rejection, you've concluded—"I just don't have it."

Most of the time, we strive to be the best version of ourselves. We work to make the right decisions, engage in behaviors that we value, and feel in ways that support our sense of personal worth. However, sometimes when we fall short, we become our own worst critics—and our criticism does anything but position us for growth.

Positioning for Growth: Constructive Self-Criticism

I find it interesting (I'm sure there are better words) that if I am engaged in a project or activity and someone, being "helpful," points out a mistake I made, no matter how polite I try to sound in responding, I know there is often a slight edge to my "*Thank you.*" Yet, if I am on the golf course and one of my sons offers an observation that may explain why I just sliced a shot, I often welcome the feedback and request more detail. Both of these times are times of receiving critical feedback, feedback that could prove useful. Yet my openness to such feedback can vary dramatically. Perhaps you have had similar experiences?

Acknowledging a mistake, a failure, or some personal limitation, regardless of whether the initial recognition was yours alone or offered by another, can position you for positive change. When critical feedback is embraced and leads to a new perspective on self or the issues being confronted, it is genuinely constructive. This is also very true for the assessment of and the feedback we give to ourselves.

When being constructive, our self-criticism often takes the form of thoughts such as the following:

- "I need to check my work. I'm making too many errors in my calculations."
- "Slow down—I am way over the speed limit."
- "I was a bit harsh on my coworker; I want to work on my empathy."
- "Boy, I'm grumpy—I wonder what's going on?"

Each of the above reflections seems to highlight some action or behavior in which the person was engaged, one they feel is undesirable or at least not in service of their goal achievement. In each case, if the person can take the criticism to heart and adjust what they are doing, the criticism will have proven constructive.

Too often, however, our criticism is anything but constructive.

Often our self-criticism is precisely that. It is a criticizing of *self*. It is a negative evaluation of ourselves as a person, and not a commentary on what we did or failed to do. At these times, the message sounds more like this:

- "I'm such a loser."
- "I can't do anything right."

- "Face it; I'm not good enough."
- "I'm a mess."

This form of self-criticism is an all-encompassing negative assessment of one's self. There is nothing "constructive" about it. This type of evaluation doesn't highlight that which can be improved. It does the exact opposite. This form of criticism invites us to throw up our hands and simply surrender. After all, if I'm a loser who can't do anything right and is not good enough ... why bother?

Sweeping critical generalization about our entire selves based on a limited number of experiences, events, or outcomes is not only destructive to our well-being and happiness but flies in the face of reality. To be a loser means I could never, or have never experienced winning. If you were a person who "can't do anything right," I would have to wonder—how did you make it this far?

For an individual to be so excessively self-critical, they must use unrealistic, perfectionistic standards of evaluation. The individual must also employ a personal filter that allows them to see their mistakes, shortcomings, and missteps without similar attention to all that is positive about them. In other words, such excessive self-criticism requires that an individual distort reality—the reality of who and what they are—and overly generalize from one data point.

I can remember an adolescent client I saw in my clinical practice who had a complete meltdown during one of our sessions. As I helped her share her dismay and began to identify the source of the upset, the story that emerged focused on her upcoming prom and the recent appearance of facial acne.

It appeared that that morning when she woke, she discovered a very red, pus-filled "zit" on the side of her forehead. As she pointed out this blemish to me, her tearful commentary revealed the real source of her upset. *"This is disgusting. I look horrible—I hate the way I look, I'm so ugly!"*

Without going into details on the case or the session, what is clear is that she was not processing all the data. Her view of self was that she *was* a zit, not that she *had* a zit.

Yes, the pimple was not attractive, but it was not a reflection of her attractiveness as a person. She was not, in any sense of the word, ugly, though the pimple may have been.

Her distortion of equating "it" with "her" made it impossible to solve. After all, I'm good (as a therapist), but I can't take an ugly human being (whatever that means) and make them beautiful as a person.

What I could do—and so can you—was to help her generate ways to "hide" this pimple. To help her resolve the issue, she first needed to identify the real problem accurately, which was the pimple. Adjusting her assessment and criticism from "I am ugly" to "I have a terrible-looking zit" was the first step in an accurate self-assessment that would lead to problem-solving.

It amazes me that most of us can see this distinction and the value of making such a distinction when it comes to others, and yet still can fall prey to periodically thinking, "Boy, I'm a mess."

Before continuing, take a moment for a little self-reflection (see Exercise 2.1).

Exercise 2.1. OMG

Directions: When we screw up or make a mistake or fall short of some goal, there is what actually happened, and then there is our view of what happened. Sometimes these don't match. Sometimes our view is hypercritical and not only fails to address the actual event or provide insight on how to proceed but simply makes matters worse.

Think about a time when you messed up. Now think about how you assessed the "you" in this event. Was it an accurate self-assessment, or were you a harsher self-critic than necessary?

THE EVENT	THE CRITICISM	THE ACTUAL, REAL LONG-TERM CONSEQUENCE	A MORE OBJECTIVE EVALUATION
(Example) I forgot to get the car inspection, then got stopped and ticketed.	What an idiot—I can't believe I did this. This is so stupid!	It cost 45 dollars more than if I had gotten the inspection on time.	Damn. I probably should slow down. I have a few too many things going on. It may help if I got back to using my "things to do" pad. Oh well, live and learn.

Hopefully, engaging in Exercise 2.1 made you aware of a couple of things. First, it is hoped that you recognized that there are times when you have messed up or failed to achieve a goal. Secondly, as you reviewed these times of shortcoming, hopefully you understood that this event or experience was not the totality of your life experience, nor was it evidence of your total inadequacy.

This self-assessment and self-criticism can be a healthy way to increase self-awareness and identify areas for personal development. However, for self-criticism to be constructive, it needs to be an accurate assessment of mistakes or failures and not an unfounded attack on yourself. Constructive self-criticism has to be an assessment in the context of the whole person, placing shortcomings *next to* strengths and successes.

Positioning for Growth: Self-Assessment

Engaging in self-assessment can unearth several areas that you may want to consider for growth and development. If the list of growth areas is hefty, you might begin to feel like, "Wow, I need a lot of work."

That may be true.

However, don't forget—you have done a lot of work. You have made significant development and progress in life. This is not merely a nice thing to say. It is a truism.

You have come a long way since the day you announced your arrival in this world. You have faced multiple challenges and have survived. It is easy to dismiss the determination reflected in you as an infant learning to stand, walk, and self-feed. You may want to negate the difficulty and the eventual benefits of learning to read. You may even feel that your developed social skills were just things that happened, no big deal. The truth is we have all faced adversity and encountered obstacles to our goal achievement, and amazingly, we have succeeded.

Take a moment and reflect on your strengths and talents, the skills that you can demonstrate, and the knowledge you have acquired up to this point. Now, contrast where you are today with where you were five years ago. I bet it is safe to assume you can see growth, right?

Okay, so I can hear your inner voice saying, "Yes, but ..."

You and I still have room to grow. Areas are waiting to be developed. But it is crucial to remember that regardless of your room for growth, the truth is that you have been successful in navigating your life and have made it this far. That counts for something.

It doesn't mean you have arrived. It doesn't mean that it is and will be smooth sailing. It does reflect that you have competently dealt with life and its adversity, big and small, and that bodes well for your future.

It is important not to let a setback or adversity blind you to your competency and the resources you can bring to the challenge. You are an expert, and the expertise that has guided you this far is a resource to value and employ moving forward.

I once had a client who was depressed and feeling quite hopeless. In our session, she was very "resourceful" in identifying all her failures and shortcomings, while at the same time blind to the resources that she brought to the situation. She used her listing of personal missteps to support her conclusion that "I can't do anything right; it is hopeless. I am such a loser."

Sadly, for this person, these were not empty words.

Her assessment reflected firmly entrenched beliefs. These perspectives colored her view of herself as a person who was worthless as a human being; her world, which was joyless and purposeless; and her future, which was hopeless. The impact of her assessment was genuinely devastating and, sadly, so wildly inaccurate and untrue.

There was abundant evidence that she did many things right. Others could attest to her gifts, her value, but these eluded her. Even the very fact that she could decide to come to therapy, navigate directions, and schedule to arrive at the appropriate time and, once in a session, even with the pain of depression, present as reflective, articulate, and engaging was evidence of her competency.

I know that she discounted these positives, but nonetheless, they were positives. They reflected some of her abilities, her resources. They were traits that could be called upon to help her move from the darkness of what was to the light that she sought.

A significant step to achieving her goal was to gain an accurate sense of the issues confronting her and the gifts, talents, and resources that she brought to the process of resolving those issues. This is also true for you as you attempt to address the challenges in your life.

Our tendency to ignore our successes or diminish them as of little note or value must be challenged. Regardless of the challenges you may face or the disappointments you may have experienced, there is much to celebrate about you and much to be valued and employed as a resource.

Even when we mess up, the truth is, we can and most likely will have the opportunity to mess up again. (I guess that didn't sound encouraging?)

Really—we do mess up. You have most likely messed up on several occasions throughout your life. Messing up, or falling short, is simply one side of the coin.

The other side, the side we often ignore, is that we have rebounded from these episodes—to not only be able to mess up again but to succeed and enjoy life in the interim. The truth is, there is something to celebrate about making it this far, even if where we are is less than perfect.

A Valid Assessment

The following exercise (Exercise 2.2) invites you to review some of your previous life challenges AND successes. The goal here isn't to simply revel in past accomplishments but rather to highlight the talents, resources (knowledge and skills), attitudes, and dispositions you called up to be successful. These are valuable resources reflecting the expert within. These are resources that we can call upon as we continue to move forward.

Exercise 2.2. Checking on Resources

Directions: While we have all experienced failure, it is also true that we have experienced success. This exercise invites you to identify specific times and contexts in which you have experienced success. You will be asked to specify how you did that: What skills did you have and employ? What knowledge was needed and possessed? What personal traits—characteristics, attitudes, or dispositions—did you tap? Remembering that we have these resources—these "tools" in our toolbox—will prove valuable as we continue to move forward.

(Continued)

A TIME ...	SPECIFICS	KNOWLEDGE	SKILL	PERSONAL TRAIT, CHARACTER, ATTITUDE, DISPOSITION	TAKEAWAY IN TERMS OF RESOURCES I HAVE
(Example) Learning a new skill	Learning to drive a car	1. Familiarity with fundamental car parts (i.e., steering wheel, breaks, gas pedal, etc.) 2. Previously watched parents drive (and learned some of the steps involved) 3. Had a driver's education class with book and field instruction	1. Strength to navigate pedals and steering wheel 2. General coordination (eye-hands-feet) 3. Ability to maintain speed and direction 4. Ability to observe and maintain a safe distance 5. Ability to start, stop, and park	1. Appropriately cautious 2. Strong desire to get a license (motivation) 3. Perseverance (kept trying to parallel park) 4. Believed I could do it	1. Ability to learn through various modes, including observation 2. Possess necessary coordination skills 3. Motivated and persistent when the goal is important 4. Able to persevere when you have positive expectations
A time when you learned something new or developed a unique skill					
A time when you solved a "significant" problem					
A time when you set and achieved a "long-term" goal					
A time when you bounced back from a disappointment or defeat (failure)					
A time when you asked for help that proved successful					
A time when you decided to bail from a project or a relationship or an event ... and it was the right thing to do					

If you are like many of us, you may have failed to push yourself to identify the resources you bring to navigating through life. It would not be unusual to find that you shortchanged yourself and didn't recognize the talents, the resources, that you possess.

I'm not sure if it is an outgrowth of our "Puritan" heritage—but many of us have embraced the belief that it is acceptable to identify personal limitations, but when speaking of our successes or valued qualities, we need to be humble. Of course, humility can be a virtue. Humility can be a useful grounding tool if employed with a sense of "objectivity." But it is essential to gain clarity about all the valuable resources we hold, as they can be called forth to help us address adversity and achieve goals. Exercise 2.3 invites you to assess your strengths and challenges from another perspective, one that will hopefully allow you to create a more accurate list.

Exercise 2.3. Strengths Versus Challenges

Directions:

Step 1: Think about a person in your life whom you admire. This is someone you see as being of value. Now write a list of the personal strengths that you believe that person possesses.

Having completed that list, now write a list of their challenges, their weaknesses. (Again, this is all from your very subjective perspective.)

Step 2: Repeat this task, but this time, the focus of your assessment is you. On the paper, list those personal qualities, characteristics, and traits that you feel are your strengths. Next, identify those areas of your personal "weakness."

Step 3: Look at both lists. Is it possible that the positives found in Step 1—thinking about the individual you admire—outweigh the lists of weaknesses you listed for that person? Is the same true for you? If not—are you sure you are accurate in your self-evaluation? Perhaps you should invite your friend to do the same activity, but with you as the target in Step 1.

Positioned for Growth: A Changed Perspective

Hopefully, the previous exercises have helped you see that you have talents, resources, abilities, and strengths that have served you well in your adaption to life challenges. At a fundamental level, there is plenty of evidence to support the fact that you have demonstrated competence and the ability to succeed.

When our life is less than what we hope for or when we are challenged by adversity, we may find that the problem colors our sense of self or our world. It is crucial not to allow this adversity to be the only element in your reality. Rather than being absorbed in the "problem" and the fact that your "now" is less than desired, it is helpful to shift your focus from the problem currently confronted and search for a time when you experienced less of this problem, or better yet, when you experienced more of what you desired. In identifying these exceptions to the current situation, we will be reminded that we are survivors, that we have succeeded, and that we possess the resources called for at this moment.

I can remember working with a person who was court-ordered to come to therapy because of a road rage incident. As we talked, he made it very clear that he has "always had a short fuse" and just "couldn't control [his] anger." He noted that this has "been a problem throughout [his] early school years and even now as an adult." Given this long-standing issue of a short fuse, he questioned the value of coming to therapy.

It just so happened that this individual was a professional athlete. We discussed his professional role and experience, and in the process, we identified numerous occasions in which he was "taunted" or in some way "invited" to lose his cool and aggressively freak out. But—he didn't. Somehow, he'd had the resources needed to restrain himself and curb his reaction in these situations. He did not exhibit a short fuse nor explosive rage.

In discussing these situations, it became clear that if we could identify just how he could control himself under these conditions, perhaps he could call forth those capabilities and strategies at times of frustration and control his response to events outside of his professional world. We did ... and it worked.

The value and process of employing exceptions as a guide to reconnecting with your expert problem-solver will be elaborated on in Chapter 5. In the meantime, Exercise 2.4 provides a brief illustration of this search for exceptions and invites you to engage in the process.

Exercise 2.4. Finding Exceptions

Directions: This exercise invites you to think about an issue of concern or a challenge you are attempting to navigate, but this time, use a lens from a previous success.

1. What one thing are you currently experiencing that presents a problem or a challenge? Is it something you would like to experience differently? *(For example: "I seem to be eating a lot of junk food and sweets. I am even drinking alcohol more than I should. I wish I could make healthier choices in my diet.")*

Your problem—the issue or challenge (i.e., something you wish to experience differently):

2. When was there a time that you experienced less or none of this problem? Or, alternatively, when you experienced more of your desired goal? *(Example: When I was pregnant, even though I was putting on some weight, my food choices were healthy. I stayed completely away from alcohol consumption.)*

Your time of exception (i.e., either experiencing less of this issue or experiencing more of the goal):

3. When considering this exception, what factors do you think contributed to reducing the problem or achieving the goal? Specifically:
    a. What environmental factors may have contributed to this exception? *(Example: We were building a house and were temporarily living with my parents.)*
    b. What social factors may have contributed to this exception? *(Example: While living with my parents, I took on the role of cook, and they both have health issues (Dad is diabetic). Thus, I was conscientious about what I prepared.)*
    c. What thoughts/beliefs may have contributed to this exception? *(Example: I read a lot about pregnancy and fetal development, and both my husband and I committed to doing everything we could to ensure a healthy pregnancy.)*
    d. What activities or behaviors may have contributed to this exception? *(Example: Each evening after dinner, my husband*

and I would take a mile walk—to be able to spend some alone time and as a way of helping me keep the pregnancy under control.)

Your response:
_____
_____
_____

4. Look at the elements that contributed to your exception. How might you create or experience similar factors to address your present situation and bring it more in line with the exception? *(Example: Well, we are in our new home in a beautiful neighborhood, and our "baby" is now three, so I know we all could take a walk each evening after dinner. My husband has just been diagnosed with high cholesterol and prediabetes. I think remembering that could help guide me in preparing healthier foods and clearing out the pantry's unnecessary sweets.)*

Your response:
_____
_____
_____

The Power of Coping

It is possible that your search for exceptions to your current situation was unproductive. Perhaps the challenge is somewhat unique, and therefore, there are no exceptions with which you succeeded in similar encounters. If this is what you are experiencing, you may find it helpful to consider your ability to cope.

We can and do encounter unique challenges at different points in our lives. We may find that we cannot readily pull up the resources or enact a solution to address the challenge and thus are stuck (temporarily) in the experience. Under these conditions, we are called to endure, to cope.

I had an adolescent client who was going through treatment for cancer. The nature of her cancer and the toxicity of her treatment was having devastating effects on her body. She knew that the treatment was needed, and she was hopeful about the possibility of a good outcome. But her physical reaction to the treatment had her questioning her ability to continue with the protocol.

In our discussions, it was clear that she had never encountered anything like this treatment protocol and found it challenging to locate an exception for analysis. However, she did remember times as a child when a thunderstorm resulted in such anxiety that she would experience extreme palpitations, gasping for breath, and nausea. She recalled that her mother would sit on her bedside and have her close her eyes and listen to a story.

The stories her mother created varied in character and tale but always incorporated "loud, sudden sounds." But in the story, these sounds always were connected with something good. For example, in one of the tales, there was loud and continual cannon fire. These booms (all of which my client's mother would act out) were fired in celebration of grand events, such as the prince and princess's marriage. In another tale, the rumble and roar heard in the distance, one that would grow louder as the story progressed, announced the arrival of the princess's playful dragon. These stories and the images that were created helped my client reframe the thunder of the storm outside her bedroom into something that, while still arousing, was not threatening. The stories helped her cope.

In our sessions, she was able to identify the specific bodily reactions that were so disheartening, and she began to incorporate them into her own mental story and imagery. She reframed the pain, nausea, and even the rapid and unsettling heart rate encountered during treatment as her "defenders." She weaved a tale of these defenders successfully battling with the "disfigured knight of doom" (cancer). Focusing on the story did not substantially reduce the physical impact of the treatment. It did, however, divert her attention and focus and did allow her to cope more effectively.

You have coped with adversity. If you can identify all of the elements that went into your successful coping with adversity, those resources can be called forth to assist you at this moment.

Exercise 2.5 invites you to review and analyze a time of your ability to endure and cope with adversity. Analyzing your success at coping can help you unearth your talents and resources and highlight that perhaps these same resources can be brought forward to help you resolve the current challenge or difficulty. Your expert within can and has positioned you for growth.

Exercise 2.5. Coping

Directions: There are times when the best we can hope for, at the moment, is to be able to cope with the adversity encountered. Identify a time when you were in a situation that you could not escape or modify and simply had to endure. It may have been sitting at a boring meeting or being stuck in the dentist chair ... or perhaps something more significant and life-impacting. As you reflect on the experience, consider each of the following "coping questions":

1. What actions or behaviors did you employ to help you endure the discomfort, the upset, and/or the distress during this experience?
2. What thoughts or mental images might you have employed to help you cope with this experience?
3. What social elements (e.g., presence of loved ones) may have contributed to your ability to cope with this undesirable encounter?
4. What other factors came into play to see you through this moment of adversity?
5. Given your response to each of the above, identify your internal strengths and resources that can be called forth to support your coping in times of adversity.
   a. _____
   b. _____
   c. _____
   d. _____
   e. _____

Connecting with the Expert Within

Let's do a quick fact check.

Life is not always easy. You will experience and maybe currently are experiencing adversity. You may have goals that seem difficult, if not absolutely unachievable.

The facts don't stop there.

You have evidence that you have succeeded. You have proof that you have and can endure and cope. You have proof of your knowledge, skills, and personal qualities that position you to succeed.

Let's reconnect with the expert within and arouse your sense of self-efficacy.

chapter three

Moving from "I Think I Can" to "I Will!"

I think I can; I think I can ...

—Watty Piper[1]

The story of the *The Little Engine That Could*, written by "Watty Piper,"[2] a pen name for Arnold Munk (1888–1957), is one of the more familiar iterations of a children's story of overcoming seemingly unimaginable obstacles and achieving a significant goal.

As you sit reviewing the ever-growing list of "things to do" or attempt to find a path forward when confronted with a significant life hurdle, you may sense that your hope and expectation of success are faltering. You may have tried and tried and are simply running out of options or even the desire to continue pushing on toward that goal.

There are times when our goals seem unachievable or the challenges unsolvable. It can be disheartening.

During these times, our *"think I can"* attitude can up and leave us. During these times, we need to connect with the expert within, not only to reignite that attitude but to move from simply *"I think I can"* to "*I know I can and will.*"

Awaken Your Self-Efficacy

Experiencing defeat or the frustration of being blocked in your goal achievement can result in a lot of self-doubt about your ability to be successful. The greater the self-doubt, the less the motivation to try and the lower the expectation that trying will succeed. Falling short of your goals can erode the "think I can" attitude.

The belief in your ability to complete a task successfully is called self-efficacy. Belief of self-efficacy regulates motivational processes in a variety of ways.

Confidence in your competence determines the level of effort that you will put into any activity. Self-efficacy beliefs enhance your ability to persevere in problem-solving. Self-efficacy beliefs contribute to your ability to be resilient when facing adverse situations and confronting obstacles.

Your self-efficacy level is a significant contributor in your ability to achieve your goals, and thus a characteristic worth understanding and developing.

A Belief—Not a Personality Trait

Self-efficacy is a belief and not a characteristic or trait of some individuals. As a belief, it is not a fixed, stable characteristic of any one person. It is not something some people have and others do not.

We all have areas in which we see ourselves as self-efficacious. But having a sense of self-efficacy in one area, such as resolving a problem with a car, does not automatically mean that a person will feel self-efficacious when confronted with a math or tax problem. Self-efficacy is domain-specific and, as a belief, can change over time.

The strength of your self-efficacy, your belief in your ability to be successful at any one moment, is affected by several factors—most importantly, your previous experience.

The most influential source of self-efficacy belief is the degree to which a person has encountered success in a particular achievement area. Thus, if you have a history of success in sales, mathematics, telling jokes, renovating houses, or fixing cars, these successes will contribute to your positive attitude and approach to similar tasks in the future. Your past success will set you up for an expectation that this time will also prove successful. While actual success nurtures self-efficacy, a series of setbacks or failures can undermine confidence and self-efficacy beliefs.

Therefore, the question is, what should you do if your "can do" belief has been undermined? While it may be difficult, there are steps to take to pick yourself up and structure for success. Nothing nurtures a "will do" attitude like success.

"I Think I Can" Requires a Realistic Perspective

Have you ever felt like this or that was hopeless? Perhaps you have heard yourself say, "This is impossible; it can't be done." Such a thought is undoubtedly useful when that which you are facing is, in fact, impossible. Under these conditions, the healthiest directive may be to cease and desist in trying.

Amazingly, too often we take something challenging yet doable and distort its importance and/or its difficulty, to the point where we believe it is insurmountable. Whether it is an accurate perspective or not, this belief can dash any of our "can do" spirit.

I can remember one junior faculty member who approached me with a mixed set of emotions—elated and yet dismayed. He had been invited to write a professional textbook.

This faculty member had previously written papers for professional journals and papers for conferences on topics covered in such a book. However, as he talked about the task and his thoughts of writing an entire book, he noted, "I can't do this. I have no clue what to do. I've never written a book. This is going to be a monumental failure."

From his viewpoint, the task was non-doable, and all efforts would result in MONUMENTAL FAILURE! Wow, if that were true, then he would have to be a fool or a masochist to take up the task. Under these conditions, his loss of motivation made sense. But were the conditions reflective of reality or self-imposed distortions of that reality?

Now, I don't have a crystal ball that would show me whether his efforts would prove successful, but there were a few obvious facts that suggested, at least to me, that this task was not as insurmountable as he was perceiving and feeling. Perhaps as you reflect on the situation, you, too, can identify elements that conflict with his conclusion of being unable to do this. One conspicuous detail of his life that he overlooked is that he had successfully written, published, and presented smaller versions of what could be a book. If this "fact" were included in his perception of his reality and the task presented, he may have a more "can do" attitude. Until he could see the task the way you do, or I did, with a more realistic lens, the possibility of his successful and enjoyable engagement with book writing was not likely.

The Power of Perspective

The power of our perspective, or the way we see and interpret a situation, is truly amazing. While the importance of our beliefs was discussed in Chapter 2, the power of perspective and the role it plays in the creation of our feelings and the direction of our actions can be clearly seen in a child's experience with "monsters" (see Case Illustration 3.1).

**CASE ILLUSTRATION 3.1:
MONSTERS—BELIEVING MAKES IT SO**

The scream coming from his room was bloodcurdling. I don't remember how I got up the stairs, but it felt like I transitioned from Clark Kent to Superman and made the leap to our second story in a signal bound. Entering his room, I saw my son, age 3, sitting up in bed, shaking and hysterically crying. I immediately ran to his side, placed my arms about him, and began to gently rock him and use a calm voice to try to get him to relax. It was not easy—but it was successful.

Once somewhat calm, he told me that there was a monster in the room. He'd heard it. It was a noise coming from the closet.

As I sat for a moment asking for more details, I also heard the noise. It was a noise in the closet. Turning on the light, I gently opened the closet door, and what we both discovered was our dog, Bud, who not only had built a bed in the closet but was wrapped in my son's winter coat—hat and all. The sight brought both of us to laughter and helped rescue the night for sleep.

What wasn't lost on me at the time was the power of his belief that the noise was evidence of a monster. In the absence of the contrary information, information that would point to Bud as the source of the noise, his belief alone shaped a sound of stirring in a closet and made it an unthinkable threat and danger, resulting in an unbearable feeling of panic. Believing it ... made it so.

Case 3.1 provides a simple yet powerful illustration of the power of our "meaning-making." The child, believing there was a monster in the room, experienced real, intense, painful anxiety. As a result of his belief, he was frozen in fear, unable to move and certainly unable to sleep. The world he'd created through his interpretation of a real-life event (i.e., noise in the closet) resulted in real fear. However, it was not the real-world event—that is, it was not the noise in the closet—creating this very upsetting experience. While the example referenced a child's faulty belief, his distortion of reality, and with that distortion, the devastating impact on his feelings, the power of our thoughts is not limited to children.

Consider one of the clients with whom I worked. The client was a 52-year-old man, a successful small business owner who came to the therapy at his family doctor's recommendation. The client shared that his wife of 30 years had just presented him with divorce papers, something that from his perspective was unexpected and "out of the blue." He found himself frozen in anxiety about his future and presented as an individual thrust into the grips of depression.

While it is a fact that divorce will change the conditions of a person's life, and that divorce will have real-world consequences, the question that can be asked is, does getting a divorce **cause** "depression"? The answer is no.

This client's experience of depression was real. It was experienced as devastating, but just like the child responding with intense anxiety to their life experience, this depression was not a direct and automatic response to the actual conditions surrounding divorce but rather the result of his beliefs, his perception, his interpretation about what divorce meant about his life—his future—and his value as a person.

When experiencing life challenges, we must see them as they are—no better, nor worse. The accuracy of our perception and the meaning we give to these challenges will significantly determine our ability to overcome them and achieve the goals we desire.

Keep It Real

So, what do we do to keep our perspective real? Dare I say, turn to the "expert inside"? There are many occasions on which you have approached an event with the objectivity of a "scientist-researcher" and tested reality before responding or jumping to conclusions. This may be something as commonplace as sitting down at dinner and testing a bowl of soup's temperature. The soup appears very inviting, and yet you notice some steam coming from the bowl. Perhaps you simply ignore the steam and swallow a large spoonful. Or maybe you sit back and wait for the steam to cease, assuming it is too hot to eat. I bet that in most cases, you do neither. Rather than believing that the soup is drinkable or undrinkable, I bet that you develop a testable perspective. You may bring a little soup to your lips and literally "test the temperature" before deciding to drink the entire bowl.

This testing of your interpretation of an experience is something you do quite often, most likely so often you fail to take notice. Seeing an icy patch on your sidewalk invites interpretation and, most likely, testing of that interpretation by taking a small yet cautious step. Similarly, hearing that the boss wants to speak with you might give you pause. You may stop to gather your thoughts about the various possibilities, but hopefully you choose to test the options by talking to the boss rather than jumping to the conclusion you are fired and so pack up the desk.

When confronted with an event, it is essential to understand that our interpretation, the meaning we give to that event, is NOT automatically accurate and factual. Remembering that the meaning we give to an experience is a hypothesis, not an automatic fact, will help us to take pause and gather more information before buying into our initial conclusion.

Writing a book requires a level of knowledge and skill and, indeed, time and energy. But contrary to what my junior faculty believed, it is not an insurmountable task? Moreover, since he had yet to begin writing—what was the evidence that it would be a monumental failure? Believing these things does not make it so. Believing these things would make him feel as if it were so—and direct him to act as if it were true.

Whether it is testing the assumption that the soup is too hot to drink or testing the conclusion that "I am unlovable," gathering data and testing the hypothesis is vital to resolving challenges and reaching our goals. It is a process that you, as an expert, have used on multiple occasions.

The Value of Testing Reality

This process of engaging a reality check and testing our perspective has value, especially when we are confronted with significant life challenges, and often it is at these times when we fail to engage the expert within. Consider the situation of a person just receiving a diagnosis of cancer. Could we imagine that person being distraught—perhaps even devastated? Now, while this may sound insensitive, let me ask, "Why?" The person has been diagnosed with a potentially fatal disease. "So what?"

Now, I am not suggesting that this statement of "so what" is meant to be a flippant, insensitive response. No—it is a legitimate and valuable question to ask.

As presented here, my "so what" is seeking to identify what, precisely the diagnosis means. Even in this situation, the individual receiving such a diagnosis needs to manage the meaning assigned to that diagnosis. Jumping to the conclusion that this is a death sentence will undoubtedly elevate the stress experienced. And while this conclusion may be a possibility, it is just that—a possibility and not an absolute fact.

Recognizing that our interpretations, especially those that are elevating our stress, are hypotheses needing to be tested will direct us to tone down our stress response and turn our attention to gaining the data—the facts we need to develop a more accurate view of what is and what needs to be done. Hearing the diagnosis and assigning the meaning that "this **could be** life-ending" rather than "this **IS** life-ending" positions the individual to believe there are alternative outcomes possible. This belief would serve as a motivation for gathering data that supports one or the other predictions. In either case, when we know the facts, the truth will better position us to deal with that reality.

It is the engagement of this process of testing our interpretations of life events—a process that we use in so many other areas of our life—that needs to be called forth in times of our biggest challenges. We cannot resolve an issue if we don't have an accurate understanding of that issue.

De-Catastrophize

When confronted with some disappointing news or an unexpected challenge, we must learn to fight the tendency to catastrophize, or exaggerate the meaning and consequences of the situation. This is not to suggest we should take on a rosy view of all things ugly. It is not helpful to blanketly convince ourselves that everything is or will be fine when, in fact, it will not. While not underestimating the challenge, we must fight the tendency to *overestimate* the challenge. We need to see it as it is. Not worse, not better ... just as it is!

Now, granted, there are occasions when what we are confronting is serious—very serious. Even under these conditions, we need to identify precisely how serious it is and, if you will, what is the realistic (possible) worst case? Pushing yourself to identify realistic possibilities, even when these are dangerous and undoubtedly undesirable, will help you determine the real issues that might have to be addressed and position you to begin to see possible solutions.

Let's imagine that here it is, Christmas Eve, and a person, a father and husband with a family of five children, has just received notification of being let go from his job of 14 years. Wow. What do you think? How would you feel? Bad? Really bad? Time to panic?

Hold on.

Before we respond, how can we identify the degree to which this firing is a bad event? Don't we need to know much more information? What are the real, immediate consequences? What are the realistic, probable consequences? Are there financial implications? Do we know if there is a significant severance package? What do we know about his savings? How about the possibility of a new job? Was he thinking about moving on anyway? Was he ready to quit to spend time with his family? These are just a few of the data points we need to have before responding to the question.

It is hard to slow down when confronted with a situation that is significant and may be disruptive to our lives. But even in these situations, we must control the tendency to jump to catastrophic conclusions. When our mind starts spinning apocalyptic outcomes, the impact not only increases our distress level but blocks our ability to problem-solve. We must try to slow down and ask the "so what" question.

As we face life's challenges, it is vital that we see them as they are, no bigger, no smaller . . . just as they are. Exercise 3.1 invites you to practice keeping perspective as applied to life challenges and the particular task(s) you may face.

Exercise 3.1. It Is What It Is

Directions: Below are listed several inconveniences of life, some of which you may have experienced. As you read each scenario, write down the OMG view of the situation, one that dramatically over-catastrophizes the anticipated outcome. Next—challenge the OMG scenario by analyzing the facts, from the data presented within the brief description,

Chapter Three Moving from "I Think I Can" to "I Will!" | **37**

and then write a realistic, evidence-based, possible worst-case scenario. The goal is to awaken the expert within and strengthen your ability to challenge and de-catastrophize.

SCENARIO	CATASTROPHIC INTERPRETATION	REALISTIC (DATA-BASED) INTERPRETATION
(Example) After encountering difficulty going to the bathroom, you notice a little blood on the toilet paper.	OMG—I have colon cancer.	I'll have to keep my eye on this. I really strained. I wonder if I popped a blood vessel or maybe a hemorrhoid?
The mortgage check for this month was returned, and the bank just sent notice of a charge for insufficient funds.		
I've been working up the courage for a month to ask her out. Now I do, and she says … no, thank you.		
I just bought a new car—I can't believe it, my first. As I drive out of the dealer's lot, a driver who is busy texting T-bones my car and totals it.		
I have made well over 20 job applications—and nothing.		
(A challenge you are facing.)		
(A challenge you are facing.)		

Your Expert Within—A Reality Tester

It can be tough to keep a reality-based view of life. When experiencing something undesirable, it almost appears that we are wired to go from "this is bad" to "this is a catastrophe." Yet, amazingly, our expert within is good at seeing things as they are—especially when it is another person that needs grounding.

Think about it. How would you react to a friend who is experiencing a real moment of self-doubt? There she stands, upset, stating that she just screwed up at work. Referring to what occurred, she concludes that she will get fired, that she is incompetent, and that this will result in being a total embarrassment to her family.

It is very likely that as you listen to her description of all of the event's details, you begin to question her interpretation of what it all means. As you listen to what she has done and her interpretation of these data, you find yourself having difficulty coming to the same conclusions.

The reason?

You have other data points, such as memories that highlight her competence. After all, she was voted Employee of the Month twice. You process her description of the "screw up," and from your vantage point, it appears fixable. You know her family and how much they love her and that, even under the worst conditions, they would never see her as an embarrassment.

With all of the contradictory data points you possess, you may find that your inner expert recognizes her reasoning errors, and you attempt to debate her conclusions. If only she could see the event through the totality of evidence that you possess. With all of the information engaged, her catastrophic conclusion would be toned down to realistic concerns, which she most likely has strategies to address.

Our expert inside processes data and can analyze and reflect on the data to provide us with valid conclusions. We tap that expert to test the soup, the danger of an icy path, or the temperature of a pool. We also call upon the expert to understand the distortions in the reality often experienced and presented by others. So how might we learn to tap that expert when it is our perceptions, our interpretation, that are out of sync with reality?

A strategy employed in cognitive therapy, one that can help ground us in reality, is the use of a "thought journal."[3]

We know that it is easier to recognize the distortions and misinterpretations of another person's conclusions about an experience because, in listening to their presentation, we process the information they relate through all of the information we already possess, knowledge that may be contradictory. This process of filtering our interpretation through all of the information and objectively analyzing it before drawing a conclusion can be facilitated by the process of writing our thoughts down. As we write down how we are interpreting an event, the very process of putting it on paper and rereading invites our expert within to engage some reality-checking.

Thought-journaling is a strategy that helps us identify our beliefs about an experience and then test the validity of those beliefs and conclusions. When we find that we are way off in our reality-checking, the adjustment we make to our interpretation can lead to both adjusted feelings and actions that help us resolve the issue at hand. Exercise 3.2 provides an example of such a thought journal and invites you to employ one in your daily life.

Exercise 3.2. Practice with Thought-Journaling

Direction: The process starts with you writing down a feeling and an action that concerns you (do this in Column C—consequence). Next, go to Column A (activating event) and describe what transpired that you think is causing this reaction in C. These steps are relatively straightforward. The next step may take a little patience. Return to the event that you listed in A. As you read your description or think about the event, listen to that voice in your head that is interpreting that event. How do you see it? What are you saying about it? Write your thoughts down in Column B.

Now here is a caution ... don't edit. What you write down might immediately be obvious as something exaggerated or untrue. But leave it. Remember, you didn't think it was excessive or erroneous until you wrote it down. Column D is where you should offer evidence that contradicts your interpretations. It may help to imagine that a friend is drawing these conclusions about the event. What evidence might you provide that challenges that interpretation? Finally, the last column, E, is where you should write out a new, reformulated and more reality-based interpretation of the event. Can you imagine how that new interpretation may have resulted in different feelings and actions? If so, list those in the last column.

(Continued)

A (Activating event)	B (Belief—the way I am interpreting the event)	C (Consequences—how I am feeling and acting)	D (Debate—evidence that contradicts my original interpretations)	E (My reformulated, reality-based interpretation of the event)	Result (Impact of the new interpretation)
(Example) On the way to a job interview, I am stuck in traffic at a toll-booth accident.	This is so unfair. I never get a break. These jerks around me need to get the hell out of the way. Why can't people learn to drive?	Really pissed off ... honking my horn, trying to sneak between cars to advance. Really angry.	Okay ... hold it; they are all stuck as well. It looks like it will be some time until the damaged cars are removed and the lanes open. This is not unfair ... it is an accident. As for believing I never get a break—that's not true. I mean, I got an interview, when others did not.	I am definitely not going to make the meeting on time. I hope I can reschedule. I'll call and let Mr. Elkinson know about the accident.	Anxious, not angry. But now I am calling the office to try to reschedule and plead my case. Sitting back now, listening to music, waiting for a call back and the lane to reopen.

From "Can" to "Will"

I remember working with a client who had an intense fear of heights. If he attempted to step up onto a two-step kitchen ladder, he would begin to hyperventilate, feel dizzy, and show the signs of an anxiety attack. Presenting this client with the goal of climbing a fourteen-foot extension ladder would not only be cruel, but it would also be ridiculous. The reality of his previous experience and his current self-efficacy beliefs about climbing that ladder would make even the possibility of approaching the task totally out of the question.

Climbing the 14 steps of that ladder was a mountain he could not, at this point, conquer. But what about the first prong of the ladder?

While even stepping on the first prong was a challenge, it was one of molehill proportion compared to moving from the floor to the top rung. Reframing the goal, from conquering the 14 steps to climbing the first step, reduced the severity of failure and presented a challenge within the realm of the achievable.

The change in perspective and the focus on one small step helped renew his "can do" attitude. As you might imagine, doing the one step successfully and calmly helped set the stage for a belief that conquering two steps was now doable.

A primary source of a person's level of self-efficacy is their experience of success. Having succeeded at a task sets the stage for having an expectation of succeeding at that task or one very similar the next time it is encountered. Having success nurtures our perspective that not only "I can" but "I can and will."

The following steps are those that contribute to both success and self-efficacy when addressing a challenge.

Goal Setting

Setting unrealistic and, thus, unachievable goals is the worst way to foster self-efficacy. My client (the one fearing heights) would be setting himself up for failure and further eroding his self-efficacy beliefs if he set as his goal climbing the entire length of the 14-step ladder. While such a goal may be desirable and even achievable (at some point), it is unrealistic at this juncture in his quest.

Goals that contribute to the development of our self-efficacy beliefs are those which are specific, measurable, realistic, and achievable (see Chapter 4). Also, for the experience of achieving our goal to contribute to our self-efficacy belief, it must be one that requires effort. It is the "goldilocks" principle in action. Goals can't be too hard or too easy ... but just right. Our goals have to require a reach while at the same time being with our grasp.

Monitor Progress

Moving from the point of "here" to a place of where you wish to be often takes time and lots of effort. Seeing signs of progress is important in maintaining our motivation and expectation of success.

While the payoff for all of your efforts may be realized once the final goal is achieved, it is vital to provide payoffs and evidence of success all along the way. It is valuable to set mini goals or markers that, once completed, will remind you of the value of your efforts AND the real possibility of ultimate success.

Not Just Outcome—Effort Counts

There are situations in which an immediate outcome is hard to identify and thus hard to reward. For example, perhaps you have decided to begin a weight-loss program, including going to the gym and exercising. A day of sweat (and tears) at the gym will not immediately translate into a toned body, increased stamina, or a reduction in your pants size.

The sweat and fatigue—and the muscles that will be sore in the morning—all signal your effort and hard work. Taking note of the signs of your effort can go a long way toward helping you maintain a belief that your goal is achievable. Even though the terminal goal may take time to achieve, the work you are doing to move toward the goal should be recognized and affirmed.

Reward Yourself

Perhaps you, like me, have developed a work ethic that diminishes the value of rewarding oneself for the work done. Whether it is solving a significant work issue or planting a garden, many people fail to step back and not only review the fruits of their efforts but provide a well-deserved reward for the effort and the outcome.

Rewarding evidence of successful efforts—to achieve each of the markers that monitor progress—contributes to the belief that this task will ultimately prove successful.

The reward need not be something dramatic.

I remember riding home on a train with a colleague, a person with whom I had written several books. As we sat on the train, after meeting with a publisher and signing a book contract, he said, "Let's have a drink in celebration of our success!" I responded somewhat quizzically, "What are we celebrating? We haven't even begun to write." His response was perfect. He noted, "Why wait until the end? We should celebrate each step along the way. Let's celebrate the contract, then the draft of the chapters, our revisions, and a big one once we are finished. These are all signs of accomplishment, and they deserve a celebration."

I got the point—and a drink.

It is useful to simply take a moment to step back and consciously recognize all that you have done and the positive impact of all your efforts. It may be as simple as giving yourself a pat on the back, a word of praise, or a dramatic crossing off of the subgoals from your "things to do" list. Remember, success breeds success.

Exercise 3.3 invites you to apply these principles to a challenge you may be experiencing.

Exercise 3.3. Organizing for Success and Self-Efficacy

Directions: Identify a challenge you are facing. Let's organize the attack in a way that will increase the likelihood of success and contribute to your self-efficacy. Respond to each of the following prompts.

Challenge: Describe the challenge you are attempting to resolve.
_____

Identify the Goal: If you can overcome the challenge, how will this look? This is the goal. Remember to be sure that the goal is both realistic and will require effort (reasonable effort) on your part. Now write it down with as much specificity and detail as possible.
_____
_____

(Continued)

Progress: Review your goal and identify three mini goals or markers that would indicate that you are on the right path and making progress toward your goal.

1. _____
2. _____
3. _____

Affirm: Plan for celebration. List some form of reward or affirmation that you will provide yourself upon reaching each of the markers.

Marker	Reward
#1	_____
#2	_____
#3	_____

Can What?

One of the underlying themes of this chapter is the value of an *"I think I can, I think I can"* attitude. The discussion of perspective and self-efficacy highlighted these principles as essential ingredients in the development and maintenance of such a positive attitude.

But thinking you can is only part of the equation. "Thinking you can" finds value once it is connected to the "what" you seek to do.

Giving yourself permission to dream, to experience a vision of your preferred future, and then translating that vision into effective goals turns *"I think I can"* into a meaningful perspective. It is this identification of dreams, vision, and goals that is addressed in the next chapter.

chapter four

Start with a Vision—Move to a Goal

Always remember, your focus determines your reality.

—George Lucas[1]

When in a jam, most of us are very adept at describing, in great detail, the problem or problems we are encountering. It is not unusual to give voice to all that we don't like or that we feel is missing. Knowing what we don't like or identifying that which is missing in our lives seems to come easy.

As discussed in Chapter 2, and as highlighted by the Lucas quote cited above, we create our reality. As such, being absorbed by our problems can set the stage for believing and feeling as if our life is one massive problem. Navigating such a "life as problem" reality can result in feeling overly burdened, frustrated, and perhaps even stuck and hopeless. This "created reality" and the feelings that follow are counterproductive in helping us move to a more desirable state.

Let's do a little mind experiment. Imagine that you've sat down and listed ten goals that you would like to achieve. Maybe these include taking a vacation, buying a house, learning to play a musical instrument, or even finishing a book you started. There are ten goals occupying space on your paper.

Now, imagine that you wrote down ten problems that you are experiencing. These can be big problems or more common day-to-day issues. They could include anything from having a bad hair day to facing a severe decision regarding a medical condition.

If you sat and reviewed these two lists of ten items each, would reviewing each list result in the experiencing of different feelings and thoughts? Would reviewing the problem list ignite your motivation, your enthusiasm, even your vision of what to do, as much as viewing the goal list? Probably not.

We typically think about making changes in ourselves or our lives when something is just not right. That certainly makes sense. After all, why think about changing something if it is not broken?

But feeling a need for change is just the beginning.

To be of value, identifying our concerns and problems needs to be a springboard to identifying that which is desired. Having a vision of the desired future (big or small) and translating that vision into meaningful goals is a powerful tool possessed by your expert. It is a resource, a device that you have used to move you from experiencing that which "is" to that which "is desired." It is a tool of expertise that can be brought to bear anytime you choose.

Can't Get There Without Knowing Where "There" Is

Perhaps you are very aware that you are unhappy or dissatisfied with something about yourself or your life. Without knowing where you wish to go, you will not know what is needed, nor which path to follow.

I can remember being in high school when I got my driver's license. I was fortunate to have the use of our family car once in a while on the weekend. At these times, a couple of friends and I would hop in, all excited and ready to go. On more than one occasion, however, the night and our gas money were spent on aimlessly driving around, asking the same question over and over: "Where do you want to go?" On these occasions, the answers coming from within the car were always, "I don't know, where do you want to go?"

An excellent exercise in aimlessness. It is also an illustration of the value of goals or, if you will, the cost of failing to have goals.

The Value of Goals

It is easy to dismiss the process of goal setting as something that can be done on the fly or only needs to be done for those big things in life. Extensive research demonstrates that goal setting is necessary for any problem-solving or task completion.[2] Having goals can excite your motivation, set your wheels of planning in motion, and provide you with road signs to lead the way to your destination.

Goals Stimulate Motivation

Take a moment and think about a goal that you set and achieved. Perhaps you decided to take a vacation. This process may have started with a comment such as "I need a break," but this recognition of a need or a problem soon took form as a goal: a vacation. Or maybe the old clunker in the driveway was on its last legs, and you decided, "I need a new car." Again—a problem served as a springboard for the creation of a goal. But these were just the beginning.

As you considered the vacation options or the cars available, you may have visited websites, read brochures, or visited showrooms in the case of the car. Did you notice something? The feeling that you needed to escape on vacation or replace that death trap no longer took up primary space in your experience. The focus now was on the future—a desirable endpoint.

Having this desired future state beginning to take form most likely increased your motivation and your positive expectations. Looking at the sunny beach pictures or sitting in the various new car models very likely made you eager to continue your quest with an expectation that it could be done. That is the value of a goal focus versus a problem focus. Goals, excite, motivate, and stimulate hope (of a better tomorrow).

Goals Map Direction and Mark Progress

There is much to do between thinking about a vacation or a new car and having an umbrella-adorned drink on the beach or experiencing that "new car" smell in the driveway. Knowing what you are hoping to achieve sets in motion the process of aligning the steps necessary to get from here to there. Each step completed not only signifies that you are heading in the right direction but serves as an indication that your goal is getting closer. This awareness increases your excitement and inflames your motivation.

I can remember the occasion of taking my family to the beach for summer vacation. The preliminaries were exhausting: packing our bags and then the house, gathering snacks for the 90-minute drive, and intervening when the brothers fought for window seats. But once we were on the road, the mood changed. The excitement grew as we crossed the bridge, entered the turnpike, exited onto the seashore drive, saw the "welcome" sign, and pulled up to the house.

Knowing where we were going—with all of the identified markers highlighting our progress—made the 90 minutes an enjoyable, exciting experience.

That is one of the benefits of a goal: it allows us to mark progress.

Challenges to Useful Goal Setting

Goal setting is not always easy. Several factors can interfere with or at least challenge your ability to set useful goals. Fortunately, once you recognize the nature of these challenges, your expert within will be able to overcome them. In fact—I am sure—you and your expert have successfully navigated these obstacles multiple times throughout your life, helping you achieve your goals.

Limiting Possibilities

One of the biggest challenges to goal setting is that we often discount the possibilities even before we begin. Perhaps you know someone, and that someone could be you, who quite often thinks of a goal and immediately undermines the possibility with a variety of negative thoughts. Often, even before we speak of our goal out loud, the inner critic begins the undermining attacks with thoughts such as *"It will cost too much,"* *"I am not smart enough,"* or the ever-faithful, *"Why bother? It won't work anyway."*

Each of these negative thoughts is a self-imposed challenge that undermines your goal setting. Yes, there are real constraints to what we can achieve, but let's dream—and dream big. At a later time, you can take the dream and reshape it to a size that the reality of your circumstances will allow for. For now, the dream—the vision—is what we need.

Remember when you were a child? Did you only have small goals, or were you filled with the excitement of big dreams and aspirations? Granted, many of those goals might have been unrealistic. But making them remained exciting and inspired hope. You, as a dreamer, did not cease to exist with childhood. You both know how to dream big AND see the value of doing so.

Yes, when setting your sights high—very high—you run the risk of falling short. However, as Michelangelo, the Italian sculptor, painter, architect, and poet of the High Renaissance, observed: "The greater danger for most of us lies not in setting our aim too high and falling short; but in setting our aim too low and achieving our mark."[3]

So, let's start our goal setting by thinking out of the box and thinking BIG!

Escaping the "Box"

One strategy that can be used to free you up to identify your goals is to respond to the "miracle question."[4] While the term "miracle" may lead you to conclude that the question is designed to encourage you to place your faith in the occurrence of magic or miracles, this is not the case.

The miracle question is simply a future-oriented question that invites you to envision a time when you and your world are precisely as you wish them to be. In its generic form, the "miracle question" would look like the following:

> Suppose that one night, while you are asleep, there is a miracle, but because you are asleep, you don't know that the miracle has already happened. When you wake up in the morning, what will be different that will tell you that the miracle has taken place and that your goals were achieved through this miracle?

In this form, the question is very broad and purposely vague. The miracle question can also be framed to lend itself to a more specific response. When a more targeted response is desired, the miracle question may look like the following.

> So, you are wondering about your career. Imagine that tonight, as you were asleep, a miracle occurred and resolved all of your career concerns. When you wake,

what would you notice or experience that would tell you
a miracle had occurred?

The use of a "miracle" focus invites your inner dreamer to think out of the box. It is an invitation to access your creative capacities, which are most adaptive when not constricted by the realities of life. The miracle question permits you to think broadly and invites you to think about goals in ways that do not trigger thoughts that nullify the hope and belief in the possibility of achieving those goals.

Now, don't dismiss your response as unrealistic. Accept it as the "ideal" future. Allow yourself to dream.

Sadly, the ability to dream without constraint is all too often left in childhood. Envisioning a future that is genuinely desired will position you to begin to take steps, even small ones, that will move you closer to that ideal. So—dream, and dream big.

Exercise 4.1 invites you to respond to the miracle question as a way of gaining an expanded view of what you would love to achieve.

Exercise 4.1. Goal Setting Without Constraint

Directions: Respond to the following question. Write down your response. You may want to reread the question a couple of times to see if other thoughts come to mind.

Suppose that while you are sleeping tonight, a miracle happens. However, because you are sleeping, you don't know that the miracle has happened. So when you wake up tomorrow morning, what will be different that will tell you that a miracle has happened and you and your life are more in line with how you wish them to be? What will you notice that is different? What, if anything, will others notice that is different?

_____
_____
_____
_____
_____
_____

Confusing a Strategy with a Goal

My 100-year-old father-in-law lived with me, and I would often ask him, "Bill, what can I get you?" His response was predictable. "How about a million bucks?"

Have you ever had a similar thought? "Yeah, I wish I had a million dollars"? If so, now ask yourself ... why?

Unless you are an individual who simply enjoys looking at lots of printed money or holding it, having a million dollars, in and of itself, really doesn't satisfy any actual need. The "value" of the million dollars comes in how you will use it. At first, it may appear that wanting a million dollars is a goal; it is only a means toward a goal.

What would this 100-year-old man do with a million dollars? Perhaps he wanted to leave his grandchildren an inheritance. Or maybe he wanted to use it for kindling. Now, you might wonder, why the big deal? A million is a million! I mean, who cares if we call it a goal or a strategy?

Knowing what you are seeking will allow you to consider numerous pathways or strategies to get there, should the initial approach be blocked. With multiple ways to achieve a goal, finding one path blocked will not prevent your eventual success.

While my father-in-law's goal might be to leave his granddaughters some inheritance, not having a million dollars does not eliminate the possibility of achieving that goal. In the absence of such wealth, he would still be able to leave his granddaughters an inheritance. The nature of that inheritance may change, but the intent of the goal could yet be achieved. Perhaps he could write each a personal letter or memoir or provide each with something he prized. It did not have to be money and certainly not the million dollars to achieve his goal. The million was only one strategy, one means, to achieve that goal, and if it did not exist, he could find alternatives.

Being able to discern your goal from a strategy opens up additional avenues for your success.

Imagine that your goal—your actual goal—was to eat dinner at *"La Fancy Place."* Upon your arrival, you see a sign saying "Closed for the Evening." That is certainly disappointing, and your goal will not be achieved. What if your goal was to spend an enjoyable evening out with a friend and you chose *"La Fancy Place"* as your dining destination? The sign on the door is the same, and the restaurant is closed, but now what? Do you surrender, or do you realize that you still can achieve your goal by merely going to an alternate restaurant, the *"Ain't So Bad Diner"*?

Exercise 4.2 invites you to review your goals and push to be sure they are goals and not merely one strategy toward achieving your actual goal.

Exercise 4.2. Goal or Strategy

Directions: Below, you are invited to write down a goal, perhaps drawing from your response to Exercise 4.1. After listing your goal, you are encouraged to answer the following question, "WHY?"

You are invited to continue to ask and answer this question of "why" until there is no additional answer. This is not an attack on what you are saying is a goal; it is merely a way of getting to the bottom line. If your initial statement is the goal, super. If your initial statement turns out to be a strategy to get to your actual goal, that is super as well. Knowing your actual goal will allow you to think of multiple strategies to help you achieve it.

Example 1: Goal: I want to retire
Why? To have more free time
Why? Then I could do things.
Why? I want to do things like play golf.
Why? I would be more relaxed, less stressed.
Why? What do you mean why? I would like to be less stressed.
(*BINGO* ... the real goal, to be less stressed)

Example 2: Goal: Lose weight.
Why? To be healthier
Why? Because I want to be healthy. (real goal)

My Goal: _____
Why? _____
Why? _____
Why? _____
Why? _____
Why? _____
Why? _____

Your Goals ... Not SMART

Creating goals that are impersonal, vague in presentation, overly generalized, or simply unrealistic will not only prove useless but may contribute to your experience of frustration and hopelessness.

Wait before you jump on me.

Yes, I know that the miracle question may have resulted in a very broad, overly generalized, and perhaps unrealistic goal. But remember? I said it was a beginning. We need to take it and transform it into a goal that is SMART.

Those who research the value of goal setting[5] assert that effective goals have the characteristics of specificity, measurability, attainability, result, and time (i.e., SMART.)

Specificity

Think about your morning routine. Many of the things you do may be so habitual that you don't even see them as goals. However, if, when you woke up, someone asked you what you were going to do, you may likely respond with something such as "I'm going to have my coffee ... then a little breakfast ... get a shower and get dressed. Probably I'll be out the door by 8:00 a.m." Each of the activities you cited is a clear, specific, and concrete goal. As you review your day, you will most likely find that you tend to be successful and feel like you have accomplished something when your goals are clear, specific, and concrete. You know that feeling of removing something from your "to do" list? Mission accomplished!

Specific goals have been found to produce higher levels of performance and success than ambiguous goals. Interestingly, even though you (or your inner expert) have navigated most of your life by setting goals that are clear and concrete, when we find ourselves in a jam or stuck, it is quite likely because we don't know where we are going, much less how to get there.

Stating that you are unhappy, or conversely that you wish to be happier or that you want to feel better about yourself, is not prescriptive nor directive. Identifying that you want to find another job, move on to a new relationship, or learn to relax and destress are goals that can be observed when achieved.

Having goals that are concrete and specific sets the stage for selecting and implementing the strategies necessary for their achievement. When your expert is engaged, your goals are specific. Exercise 4.3 invites you to begin to shape your goals into something specific—concrete and observable.

> ### Exercise 4.3. Making It Specific
>
> **Directions:** Return to Exercise 4.2 and select one of the goals that you identified for that exercise. Write the goal in the space below.
>
> As written, is the goal something that others could observe? If not, rewrite the goal so that it would be specific and observable to yourself and others. How would it look if you achieved this goal? What would be different, something that others may notice? Use your answers to these questions to rephrase the goal.
>
> *Example:*
> Original goal: I would be less stressed.
>
> Increased specificity: I would be able to fall and stay asleep. I would be able to concentrate at work, and my coworkers would tell me that I am less irritable and more pleasant to be around.
>
> Your goal (from Exercise 4.2):
> _____
>
> Increased specificity (is it observable?):
> _____

Measurable

When goals are specific, it is easy to see when they are achieved. But the value in creating goals that can be measured goes beyond knowing when you have arrived.

When goals are measurable—your progress will also be measurable. That can be a powerful motivation for continuing all your hard work.

As a child whose family celebrated Christmas, I can remember having a big calendar where each morning I was allowed to check off the day and reveal the number of days that remained until Christmas. This process gave me a sense of satisfaction and completion in removing one of the days, as well as a boost to my excitement and motivation, seeing December 25 approaching. The measuring of progress and the sense of satisfaction and increased motivation that resulted is something you have undoubtedly experienced.

Perhaps you, like I, measured progress to a holiday or your birthday. Maybe you noted the progress you were making in finishing a project or saving for a big purchase or even gaining the stamina needed to run a marathon. Documenting progress, or measuring movement toward goal achievement, is something of value, something that you (and your expert) know how to do.

Creating goals that are concrete makes measurement much easier. However, sometimes you may have a goal that is more subjective, internal, and not easily observed. Hoping to become more relaxed is a goal that could be restated in concrete terms that include blood pressure reading, muscle tension, and even levels of adrenaline. Typically, this is not how we "measure" relaxation. Most often, the goal of "being relaxed" is one of those things we "feel." So how can we gain the benefit of measuring such a goal?

Behavioral psychologists have used SUDS, or a Subjective Units of Distress Scale, to measure feelings of distress or nervousness. The concept of the scale has been used to measure other subjective goals, such as increasing a sense of pride or gaining self-confidence.

Remember, we are not going for a scientific absolute. We are trying to measure our progress to mark success and increase our motivation to continue. Both of these goals can be achieved with the development and use of a subjective measure of achievement.

Let's assume your goal is to feel more self-confident. You could start by identifying a specific time, place, or situation in which you experienced a great degree of self-confidence, the type you are hoping to once again experience. With this as a reference point, you could draw a horizontal line and place a brief description of this time and event at the far-right end of the line. This can serve as the goal, the experience that you are hoping to achieve. You could even assign a number to it, for example, 10 on a 10-point scale (your line).

With this experience as the reference point, you would now identify a time, place, or event during which your self-confidence was very low. If you placed a description of that time or event and how it felt on the line's left corner, you would have the other end of this continuum. You could identify this point as number 1 on your 10-point scale.

With these two subjective markers as your reference point, you can evaluate your current state of self-confidence and place it on this continuum. Revisiting your feelings of confidence will help you monitor progress across the scale as you move to 10 (and beyond).

Attainability

When you employed the miracle question as a start to your goal setting, you may have identified an extraordinary goal, one that exceeded your reach and grasp. While this is an excellent place to start, free of practical constraints, for the goal to be useful, it needs to be reformulated into something that is realistically achievable.

Perhaps you have set goals based on what you observe in others. I mean, if other people can do it, why not you?

Maybe other people can do it. Do they do it with your bad knees, work schedule, student loans, or the many family or life demands you are attempting to balance?

Useful goals need to be realistically attainable or achievable given your resources, capabilities, and other demands that you may be experiencing. This doesn't mean that you have to scrap the goal that emerged from your miracle question. It just means that you have to define it in a way that is respectful of your realities. Perhaps at another time, under different circumstances, the ideal goal could be within your grasp. For now, taking a small step in its direction is an excellent way to bring it closer to that reality.

One of my favorite "psychiatry" movies is the 1991 comedy *What About Bob*. The client in the film, played by Bill Murray, exhibits severe anxiety and numerous phobias. The therapeutic intervention most often repeated throughout the movie is *"baby steps."*

The idea of and term "baby steps" are not intended to be demeaning. It is a reference to the value of setting small, achievable goals. Goals need to be reasonably challenging and require you to stretch yourself. Still, they also need to be realistic and achievable. Remember my client attempting to challenge his fear of heights? One rung at a time, not 14.

When goals are too challenging or unrealistic, it is quite possible you will become extremely frustrated and may even begin to believe it hopeless.

Exercise 4.4 invites you to look at your goal and see if you may benefit from reframing that goal into smaller, more achievable subgoals. Remember, small steps can set the stage for bigger ones.

Exercise 4.4. Small Steps

Directions: Review the goal you identified in Exercise 4.3. Identify the possible real constraints you may be experiencing at this time in your life that make achieving that goal somewhat problematic. Given these other demands, break the goal down into smaller, achievable subgoals.

Example:
Goal: Get hired by a top-10 company within my profession.

Constraints:

1. Starting final exam week.
2. Organizing for graduation in a week.
3. Packing and getting ready to move from the dorm.
4. Needing a car or some form of transportation.

Subgoals:

1. Pick up examples of resume templates from the career center.
2. Develop resume.
3. Gather contact information for my top-five companies.
4. Draft a letter of introduction to go along with my resume.

Your goal (see Exercise 4.3):
_____

Constraints (time, energy, resources, other demands, etc.):
_____
_____
_____
_____

Subgoals:
_____
_____
_____

Results-Focused

It may seem obvious that if a person sets a goal, they understand the impact of achieving that goal, and these are outcomes or results that they desire. It may seem obvious, but it is often not the case.

Last night on my local news television show, there was an advertisement for the "mega-million" cash lottery. The jackpot flashing in big letters and numbers was cited to be $435 million. Now, I imagine that you may have at one time played the game of "What would I do with the million-dollar jackpot?" What would you do with your winnings? While you may have a very long list of goals that could be achieved with such a cash payout, have you considered the impact of achieving your goal?

Research has found that winning all of that money does not bring bliss. Sadly, there are numerous stories of lottery winners whose lives have been damaged, with some even committing suicide. These individuals purchased lottery tickets in hopes of one goal—winning lots of money. They failed to push beyond that immediate acquisition to consider the impact, the results of achieving that goal. Don McNay, the author of *Life Lessons from the Lottery*, noted that for many, winning the lottery throws the winner's life into upheaval, something they cannot handle. It actually results in making their lives worse, not better. This, for some, was the unanticipated result of achieving their goal.

When setting goals, it is essential to consider the impact of achieving the goals. It is crucial to ensure that goal attainment is associated with positive and valuable benefits. Indeed, the lottery winner envisioned the freedom and luxury that this money might provide. But did they also anticipate the number of demands on their time and their resources, coming from others knowing of their windfall? Did they consider how a radical change in their lifestyle might negatively affect their relationships?

It is not just a lottery win that can be upsetting to a person's life. Consider the previous stay-at-home parent who now pursues a degree with the intent of taking up professional employment. Have the added stress, the potential disruption to the house, even the added taxes that may result from moving into a new tax bracket all been considered?

Achieving our goals most often results in a change in our life circumstances or, in some cases, a change in ourselves. This may be very good and desirable. It also may come with some unanticipated and undesired consequences.

Chapter Four Start with a Vision—Move to a Goal | **59**

As you set your SMART goal(s), it is essential to consider the desired, positive outcomes should the goal be achieved, as well as the potential cost or unintended and undesired results of achieving your goal. Considering the possible downside or cost to goal achievement can position you to reduce these to keep the payoff-to-cost ratio favorable.

Let's return to your unfolding SMART goal to consider all of the pluses and minuses to goal achievement.

Exercise 4.5. Payoffs and Costs

Directions: Once again, return to your goal, as specified in Exercise 4.3. Now (and you may find it helpful to do this with a close friend), brainstorm as many possible positive outcomes (big and small) as you can imagine that could result from achieving this goal. The more, the better, since these can be posted and serve as motivational reminders. Next, consider any possible downsides or costs to you or others that you may want to eliminate or reduce.

Goal (from Exercise 4.3):

_____

Payoffs (big and small)

Payoffs to me (physical, psychological, social, financial, etc.)	Possible payoffs for others in my life.

Costs (for self or others) and strategies to reduce or eliminate

Cost to me (physical, psychological, social, financial, etc.)	Cost to others	Steps to eliminate or reduce costs.

Time

The final characteristic of an effective goal is that it is time-bound. That is, it has an identified target date/time.

Maybe you are one of those people who seem to "work better under pressure." Research would suggest we all do better or at least engage more actively in task completion or goal achievement when deadlines are set and are approaching.

Timelines serve as motivators and provide us with a means for gauging progress and adjusting strategies if need be. Timelines must be supportive and not merely something that is adding to your stress.

Your timeline should be one that allows for a sufficient amount of time to achieve your goal. On the other hand, it is important not to provide too much time. Lengthy time horizons, when unnecessary, can result in a loss of motivation.

Have you ever been assigned a task such as a school project assigned at the beginning of the semester or the year that was not due until the end of the course? Now, maybe you are one of those people who jumped right on it and kept your eye on the prize. If I had money to bet, I would bet that you, like many people, recorded the project and the due date and forgot about it until that date became a closer reality.

To maximize the motivational benefit of having a timeline, it needs to meet the goldilocks criteria—not too long and not too short, just enough to comfortably maintain motivation and progress toward goal achievement. Also, given the many uncontrollable factors that can impact your path toward goal achievement, your timelines need to be flexible, allowing for adjustment in the face of unexpected events or circumstances. Exercise 4.6 invites you to finish making your goal SMART by creating a timeline.

Exercise 4.6. Time!

Directions: In Exercise 4.4, you took a realistic view of your goal and considered reformulating it into subgoals. For each of the subgoals listed, complete the following steps:

a. Set a timeline for starting and completing.
b. Identify circumstances or factors that may interfere with the achievement of the subgoal within that time frame.
c. Adjust the time frame as needed.

SUBGOAL	START (TIME/DATE)	COMPLETE (TIME/DATE)	HOW MUCH FLEXIBILITY, IF ANY, EXITS? WHAT IS THE MUST-DUE TIME?	PLAN TO ADJUST SUB-GOAL OR GOAL (IF AND WHEN NEEDED)

From "Here" to "There"

So, you know where you want to be. You have identified your goal in concrete, measurable, and achievable terms. This is a great beginning. Now what?

Moving from your "here" to this desired "there" will now require action. The plan to be employed in helping you address your challenges and achieve your goals is the focus of the next chapter.

chapter five

Pathfinding

Getting to Your Goal

All roads lead to Rome.

—Alain de Lille[1]

The phrase or proverb that "all roads lead to Rome" has been attributed to a French theologian and poet, Alain de Lille, around 1175[1] Actually, his expression was *"mille vie ducunt hominin per secula Roman."* (I know—I was just trying to get your attention!)

The concept is straightforward. It posits that there are many ways to reach a conclusion or achieve a goal. Wouldn't it be nice if, no matter what your decision, which path you followed, it would always lead to your wished-for future?

Your life, unlike ancient Rome, has not been engineered for such an experience.

Some of your chosen paths will prove successful, others less so, and some may even fail. But even with the reality that some paths are dead ends, the truth is, there is usually more than one path that we can use to get from where we are to where we wish to be. Some may be more direct, while others may be less costly.

Identifying all of the strategies or pathways to move from where you are to where you wish to be provides you with the flexibility to address issues of time constraints, resources available, and the emergence of unexpected challenges or blocks to your journey. Options. This is a good thing.

However, when presented with options or choices, we need to do more than what was suggested by the great New York Yankees catcher Yogi Berra, who said, "When you come to the fork in the road, take it!" Take one path or another, but before you choose, engage your expert within to assist in identifying and evaluating each of the paths.

Finding a Path

In the introduction to this book, reference was made to the wide range of expert advice available to each of us. Each expert provides suggested pathways, strategies, or solutions that we can employ to achieve our goals. We have all been shaped, conditioned, to seek and follow the advice of others. Our childhood was shaped around such prescriptions. "Do this," "Don't do that," "Be like your brother (or sister)," "Do it this way," and "Watch me" should not be unfamiliar phrases. Each of these directives had a purpose, and at times each had a value.

We certainly do not lack resources that provide us knowledge, help us develop new skills, and assist us in resolving many of our day-to-day challenges. It is not just the millions of books on the market but also the equally vast number of internet links and videos. Have a leaky sink? Well, go to www.leakysink.com! Car making a funny noise? Check out "Click and Clack," your friendly mechanic's website. Planning on visiting Redonda Island? Then do I have a website for you!

When the steps needed to resolve the challenges you are confronting require you to gain additional knowledge, develop new skills, or receive guidance on applying your current knowledge and skill, turning to another is a great strategy. There are times when the expert outside of us is of value. But, as has been stated throughout the previous chapters, turning to an outside expert for assistance is not always needed (even if you feel a tad lost).

It is worthwhile to connect with the expert within to see if a plan, a pathway, and the resources required are well within your possession.

Your Expert Has Succeeded

The situation you are facing at present may appear unique. It may be the only time you have found yourself in this position. Even under these conditions, if you take a closer look, you may find that the approach you have previously used for problem-solving is of value in this current situation.

If you could deconstruct the problem, take it apart, look at all of the factors and how they seem to be going together, it is very likely that you would recognize elements that you have experienced and conquered in the past.

You may feel like disputing that statement. Perhaps this is the first time you have ever been fired from a job. Perhaps a series of events have eroded your self-confidence or feelings of self-esteem. Even with such unique specifics, it is very likely that you have seen this movie before.

There are consistent elements to these challenges, elements that you have experienced and have navigated. For example, it may be factual that you have never gotten fired before, but is the problem getting fired or the potential consequences of that experience?

With no job, you most likely have no income. Without a job, you may have lost your health insurance. Being fired may have stimulated feelings of self-doubt and self-putting down. These are all undesirable things and indeed can be concerning. But see if you can step back and think about each. Are they situations with which you have no experience? Even if the experience is minimal. Was there any other time when you were without income, or at least the amount of income you felt you needed? Was there a time when you were disappointed in your performance, where you wondered if you ever could get hired, pass the test, make the team? How about being somewhat down on yourself? Is this experience totally unique, a first-time occurrence? If these are experiences that you have encountered in some form and have successfully navigated, it would be valuable to take a moment to see what your expert within has to say (see Exercise 5.1).

> **Exercise 5.1. Experience with Navigating Life**
>
> **Directions:** You may be facing a significant life challenge. It may feel like this is something you are ill-equipped to handle. That may be true, but before you surrender, consider deconstructing the problem and

placing it against the context of other times of challenge. The example provided can be used as a scaffold to guide your deconstruction and problem-solving consideration.

Example Challenge: Diagnosed with Stage 4 Lymphoma		*Your Challenge:*	
Deconstructed elements	*Previous experience with problem-solving*	*Deconstruct (at least three elements or factors)*	*Previous experience with problem-solving*
Life-threatening diagnosis	With many problems of a personal nature and life issues, I have used data collecting to understand better and address the issues.		
Impact on my ability to work	With COVID-19, my courses have gone online. I have been able to employ technology to engage with my classes. If needed (because of fatigue or feeling ill after chemo), I could use the online material either while in class or if I have to stay out.		
Treatment regimen and aftereffects	I have been fortunate to have a high tolerance for pain and the ability to meditate. When addressing "minor" issues, for example, knee surgery or even a migraine, meditation has helped me; the same has value here.		

The point of all of this is not to debate the uniqueness or seriousness of the challenges you currently face. The point—and the hope—is that you realize you have experience in resolving difficulties. You can reconnect with those experiences of successful problem-solving to gain the perspective needed to resolve the issues you currently face.

A Better Time

Solution-focused therapy is an approach used in counseling.[2] One of the strategies employed in solution-focused therapy and briefly described in Chapter 2 is to find exceptions.

Exceptions are those times in your life when the current "problem," or its negative effects, was either nonexistent or only slightly experienced. From a more positive perspective, the exception would be finding a time when you experienced more of your desired end state, your goal, than you are currently experiencing.

The underlying belief is that there is always a time of exception. These times give evidence of your ability to resolve your conflicts and achieve your goals. Finding an exception and identifying the nature of the conditions that existed which gave form to the exception will provide the blueprint for creating a solution to the current dilemma.

Identifying an exception starts with a simple question: *Was there ever a time when you experienced more of your goal or, if you prefer, less of your problem than at this point?* Identifying all of the factors ... and I mean ALL of the factors ... that went into creating this exception can place you in a position to reengage those elements in the creation of a solution to your current challenge. Sound easy?

As is true for most things, what sounds easy requires quite a bit of effort. In this case, it also requires a real "explorer's quest" for detail.

Have you ever attempted to make something from another person's recipe? Okay, so all of the ingredients are listed, the oven's temperature is noted, and maybe you were even told the order in which the ingredients were supposed to be added. It appears that you have all that it takes to replicate the previously enjoyed dish. So what happened?

Perhaps in precisely following the recipe, your outcome was perfect. But if the dish fell short of your expectation, might it be that something was missing from the recipe? Ingredients, check. The temperature of the oven, perfect. Order of adding ingredients, also correct. The timing between adding ingredients—oops. How about the oven, was it on convection? Double oops. I think I have pretty much stretched this metaphor as far as it will go, but hopefully, you have the idea.

For the analysis of the exception to bear fruit (sorry, stuck in a food mode), all of the elements need to be accurately and precisely identified. The task requires that you really think about all of the details, not just the who, what, when, and where. It is essential to identify what you were feeling, what you were thinking, what your attitude and disposition were, and anything special about the conditions and time that contributed to this exception. You had one try at this process in Chapter 2 (Exercise 2.4). Let's have a go at it one more time.

Exercise 5.2 invites you to find and analyze an exception to your current experience, one that positioned you to experience more of your desired goal. It is hoped that your analysis of this exception will help you identify the resources you possess and bring those forth in service of your current plan for goal achievement.

Exercise 5.2. Using an Exception

Directions: Starting with identifying your current situation and a goal that you wish to achieve, use the following steps to help you find and analyze an exception.

Step 1: Current conditions. Identify the situation or condition you wish you could change and the goal you want to achieve.

Step 2: An exception. Describe a time when you experienced some or more of the goal or, if you prefer, less of the troublesome experience.

Step 3: Analyzing the exception. Try to answer each of the following questions in as much detail as possible (think of the analogy of the recipe).

1. What did you do to create the exception? (Describe all of the actions you took leading up to and during the creation of this exception.)
2. How did you do this? (How did you motivate yourself? What resources did you use? What steps did you take to organize yourself?)
3. What was the attitude or expectation that you had as you engaged in this exception?
4. What environmental conditions existed that may have supported you in the creation of this exception?
5. What social conditions existed (e.g., a friend was helping or encouraging) that may have supported you in creating this exception?

Step 4: Crafting a path forward. Look at the factors that you identified as contributing to the creation and experience of the exception. Which of these can be called upon to assist in the current situation? Develop a plan to gather and implement these resources, and describe that plan (or the steps to be taken).

Blazing New Trails

The goal you are hoping to achieve or the challenge you are attempting to overcome may be somewhat novel. The information you gleaned from reviewing others' suggestions, and even the reflection on your past strategies, may have been useful but inadequate. Sometimes you need to discover a new—uncharted—path to follow.

It is important to remember that there is not one and only one right path, nor should you shackle yourself to others' directives and approaches. Your path is unique. It is yours. Fortunately for you, your expert within knows how to blaze new trails and generate solutions to problems and pathways to goals. When blazing a new trail, or at least a new path for you, it is crucial to allow yourself to think out of the box and think in creative, novel ways.

Thinking Out of the Box

Often when you hear the call to think out of the box, it appears that the "box" is a bad thing. It isn't. The idea of a box is simply a reference to our tendency to employ the same rules, regulations, processes, and procedures when attempting to solve a problem or achieve a goal. Operating from within these standards is undoubtedly safe and somewhat comforting. After all, they worked in the past, or even when they failed ... we survived.

Approaching our life challenges with a strategy that others have used or even one we have found successful before is undoubtedly practical. It is useful to think inside the box. But if all we do is return to patterns of the past, we may be cheating ourselves out of the opportunity to experience the fruits of creativity and the discovery of more effective means to goal achievement. Imagine if Benjamin Franklin didn't fly that kite, or Walt Disney didn't play with acetate.

Stepping out of the box can sometimes result in things previously unimaginable. Good things! Yes, operating from the tried-and-true can resolve the issue or help you reach your goal, but it may not result in the "better mousetrap." There are several strategies that can assist in this process of thinking creatively and out of the box of tradition (see Table 5.1).

TABLE 5.1 Stimulating Your Creativity—Thinking Out of the Box

1. ***Turn to the expert within.*** Ask yourself, what would I do if I were still a child? You had and have a vivid imagination. You were and are creative as all get-out (remember cutting your sibling's hair? dressing the family pet? deciding to make your breakfast? or seeing if you could fly off the roof with that superman cape? Okay, that was all me, but you get the idea).
2. ***Start over from scratch.*** They say that if the only tool you have is a hammer, everything will look like a nail. Get rid of the hammer ... and the nails. Let's clear the desk and your mind. Ask yourself, if I were starting from a perfectly clean slate, no previous experience with success or failure with this challenge, how might I approach it?
3. ***Ask, why?*** As you think about possible pathways to problem-solving or goal achievement, ask yourself ... why? Why this approach? If the best answer you can come up with is "this is the way I've always done it," it may be time to think of alternatives. Identify the benefits and costs of the approach being considered, in an attempt to reconfigure to maximize the benefits and reduce the costs.
4. ***Think out loud (to self or another).*** Try to explain what it is you are trying to accomplish and why you are selecting this pathway. It is possible that merely hearing what is going on—hearing it in simple, concrete terms—can stimulate innovative solutions and novel pathways.

Not One ... Many!

All too often, in our rush to get unstuck or achieve a goal, we lock onto one approach and cut off the possibility of identifying a more effective path to follow. If time and circumstances allow, there is value in stepping back rather than jumping in with the first strategy or pathway to step back and consider other possibilities. In the process of pathfinding, it is vital to keep your options open. There are many paths to follow, and even though some may be unfamiliar, they may be worth considering.

One process for developing a large pool of possible paths to the outcome we seek—generating approaches that may be previously untried and quite creative—is "brainstorming." You are probably familiar with this process and have either formally or informally employed it on various occasions.

The process originated in the late 1930s in the field of advertising. Alex Osborne was frustrated with his employees' inability to generate creative new ideas and developed group-thinking sessions. He believed that it would be easier to tone down wild ideas than generate new, creative ones. With that as his mantra, he developed an approach that freed up his employees to think out of the box. His "brainstorming" method led to a significant boost in the quality and quantity of new ideas.

Osborne understood that it is very unlikely to think up the perfect solution on the first attempt. His recommendation was to get every idea, no matter how crazy or impractical it may seem, with the commitment to go back to examine them afterward. He believed that it was possible that an idea that upon initial consideration seemed absurd may be entirely plausible once slightly modified.

As I write this, I find myself drawn back to my teen years, driving around in the family car with all of us repeating, "What do you want to do?" and collectively responding, "I don't know. What do you want to do?" If only I had known about brainstorming in those early days, perhaps we would have identified an answer to the question, which, in turn, would have resulted in doing something other than filling time and wasting gas.

The actual approach has evolved and varies depending on the context and purpose. But for brainstorming to release its potential, a couple of "rules" should be followed. These apply even when there is only one brain that is doing the storming—yours.

1. *Target quantity, not quality.*

The goal of brainstorming is to develop as many ideas as possible. All opinions should be expressed without regard for quality. The quality of each will be assessed at a later time. The idea is that quantity will eventually breed quality as ideas are refined, merged, and developed further.

Often, an idea that might appear to have minimal value serves as a stimulus for creating another idea, which proves quite productive.

2. *Suspend judgment.*

The purpose of brainstorming is to be creative. You need to free yourself (and others if others are participating) to introduce all ideas that come to mind. Some of the ideas may seem a bit off the main track. That's okay; list them.

It is essential that you suspend judgment—quiet that inner critic. It is important not to evaluate or find fault with any of the suggestions.

Evaluation of the usefulness of the ideas will take place in a later stage of our pathfinding.

Suspending judgment when engaged in brainstorming by yourself can be difficult. It often seems that the inner critic is difficult to shut up. Just remind yourself there will be plenty of opportunities to be critical at a later point. For now, let the ideas flow!

3. *Welcome the crazy ideas.*

Push yourself (or each other if more than one person is involved) to think out of the box and introduce "pie in the sky" ideas. For now, the task is to be creative, even ludicrous. The more out of the box, the more creative the ideas, the better! Sometimes it is the craziest ideas that open the door to new and innovative techniques, which then become your ticket for success. Fantastic ideas are not always crazy; they can be creative and effective ways toward goal attainment.

Think about the crazy ideas that we now value. In the 1540s, Copernicus was certainly way out of the box with his belief that the earth revolved around the sun and was NOT the center of the universe. Or consider those wacky Wright Brothers, thinking that they could fly, or even Bill Gates, with his belief that those large, whirring boxes of computers could somehow be miniaturized and personalized.

It should be noted that the most creative ideas come when you feel as if you have run out of ideas and are about to quit. After you exhaust the ideas that readily come to mind, force yourself to review the list and generate at least three more ("off the wall"?) suggestions before you call it a day. You may be surprised. These might be the best ones yet.

4. *Build on previous ideas.*

It is useful to combine ideas previously identified or expand on ideas previously noted. Review the ideas listed and let them stimulate additional ways to go.

Before you end the process, take a moment. Review each idea listed and push yourself to see if that idea can be stretched. Ask yourself, what would your eccentric relative do with this idea? How might you as a playful, imaginative child massage this idea? Remember, the more ideas, the better!

Exercise 5.3 invites you to employ these principles in the process of brainstorming.

Exercise 5.3. Brainstorm!

Directions: In Chapter 4, you developed a concrete, realistic, achievable goal. Your task is to revisit that goal and create several pathways or strategies that would lead you toward goal achievement. You may find this process more productive (and enjoyable) if you do it with a friend.

1. Describe your goal (remember, make it SMART).
2. Remember the rules for brainstorming (and describe them to your partner, if you are engaging a friend). The rules focus on quantity, not quality; no criticism or judgments; and trying to build on other suggestions.
3. Now, set a timer for 10 minutes. If you feel like you are running out of time and have time left, get crazy. Throw out wild ideas; they may stimulate others.
4. Now ... list as many ideas for achieving your goal as you can within the time limit.

Strategies (use additional paper, write fast!)

Evaluating Your Options

Now, given the nonjudgmental nature of your brainstorming, it is likely you created quite an interesting list. And by interesting, I mean a list with some pretty creative, if not wacky, ideas. That was the goal, after all.

Not all of the pathways you identified are of equal value. If you allowed yourself to get creative, some of these pathways might seem a bit out there. That's great! Because even those that may appear ridiculous may have served as thought-provokers and may even at this stage result in a creative yet highly successful path. So let's not dismiss anything at the moment.

While not dismissing any one idea, we need to begin a process of assessing and prioritizing based on feasibility and anticipated effectiveness. Perhaps you are a person who makes decisions based merely on what feels right at the moment. You may be quite comfortable and successful using such an intuitive approach to problem-solving. There is nothing wrong with that. In contrast, you may be a person who approaches decisions with an intense and methodical, almost scientific, analysis of the data. Again, there is nothing wrong with that, assuming it has served you well. Perhaps a consideration of some hybrid of these approaches may produce the best of all worlds?

Daniel Kahneman, who won a Nobel Prize in economics for his work on human judgment and decision-making, has proposed that we have two different thought systems: System 1 is fast and intuitive; System 2 is slower and relies on reasoning.[3]

The fast system, he holds, is more prone to error. It has its place: it may increase the chance of survival by enabling us to anticipate serious threats and recognize promising opportunities. But the slower thought system, which engages critical thinking and analysis, is less susceptible to producing bad decisions.

Your gut or intuitive decision-making certainly has value. It appears that this fast, intuitive system may be perfect for those times of danger, especially when the luxury of extensive data collection and analysis is not at hand. In the absence of full data analysis, engaging the fast system may result in unexpected consequences and errors.

A little side note. Have you ever watched a horror movie where the main character is in the woods being chased by a psychopathic killer? It does seem that the engagement of the fast system, at least initially, makes sense. But it never fails—without processing the data (the slower system), the character typically ends up tripping over fallen branches, running into a tree, sliding down a ravine, or passing multiple places that could serve as hideaways.

The fast system does have its limitations.

Hopefully, you are free of psychopathic killers. But the limitations of the fast system, the intuitive approach to decision-making, need to be considered when addressing the issues you are confronting. It is not unexpected for you to jump to a definition of a problem without really collecting the data needed to understand the complexities of the issue or formulate solutions again without considering data and the alternatives. Your fast system is there as a survival tool, and often our first response to adversity is to feel the need to survive and rid ourselves of the challenge ASAP.

While an intuitive approach to problem-solving can work,[4] engaging your expert in the slow, rational, and data-driven approach to decision-making may ultimately prove more productive in guiding you to the selection of the best path to follow.

Rational Decision-Making

It may not always seem like it, but your expert within is a rational decision-making master. You may not be aware of the number of times you engage in rational decision-making throughout your day, but you do, and now is a time to tap that resource. The process, in its ideal form, is careful and methodical. It is a process that moves from an identified problem, which in this case would be selecting a useful pathway to your goal, and ends in the selection of the best alternative.

You have your goal. You have generated several options. You appreciate that not all options are of equal value. So now you must review each potential path forward in terms of its merits and challenges. Which pathway is more desirable? Which pathway is most likely feasible? Which pathway will most likely prove successful? Which pathway promises the best payoff-to-cost ratio?

Selection of a path to follow will be influenced by several factors: (a) the nature of your goal, (b) the resources required and those which you possess, and (c) the degree to which you can embrace the pathway as something that you value and that feels "right," something that feels as if it fits with you.

The following are useful, practical criteria to use in assessing your options. Exercise 5.4 invites you to review your creative solutions and measure each against the following.

1. *Goal-related?*

As you reflect on the creative solution, ask yourself, does it appear that this path will logically lead to your desired end state? Even if the answer is yes, that it at least on paper seems to be a path toward the goal, then ask yourself, does it appear to have a high degree of likelihood of leading to that desired goal? The higher the feasibility or probability that any path will result in goal attainment, the more desirable that approach is. This assumes that it also meets the next criteria.

2. *Resources?*

What types of resources are required to implement each solution? Do you have the required resources? Do you have the knowledge and skills needed?

Will you need first to acquire new skills or more information and understanding before you will be able to engage in the path? This need to develop additional personal resources should not be a reason to dismiss a particular pathway to your goal. Still, it certainly should be considered in terms of the cost of time and effort.

3. *Is it you?*

In looking at these various potential pathways, do they "speak" to you? Do they seem to resonate with you and your general style and approach?

Since resolving a problem or achieving a goal will take time and effort, the process you are using must be one with which you are excited to engage, and you must have confidence in your ability to maintain your engagement.

4. *Cost-payoff ratio*

Each of these solutions "promises" to result in goal achievement. There may even be one that leaps off the page as ideal. Before selecting a particular path to follow, think about each in terms of the likelihood or probability that it will be successful. Think about other possible payoffs that may come about (besides your goal attainment) as a result of using each pathway.

Consider the costs (physical, psychological, social, emotional, financial, etc.) to be incurred by engaging in any of these strategies. Look at the cost-to-payoff ratio for each possible approach.

Does one strategy or pathway offer the best cost-to-payoff ratio?

Chapter Five Pathfinding | 77

Exercise 5.4. Assessing Possible Pathways

Directions: After identifying your SMART goal, list each of the pathways you created during the brainstorming process. Review each strategy, considering the degree to which each logically leads to your goal, is something for which you possess the resources needed, is a strategy that fits with who you are, and provides the best cost-to-payoff ratio.

Goal: _____

STRATEGY	LOGICALLY LEADS TO THE GOAL?	SOMETHING YOU CAN EMBRACE?	SOMETHING FOR WHICH YOU HAVE THE NEEDED KNOWLEDGE, SKILLS, RESOURCES?	PAYOFF GREATER THAN COSTS?

From Planning to Action

Good job so far. You have allowed yourself to dream and then turn your dream into a SMART goal. You may have stepped out of the box, blending your intuitive and rational decision-making to devise a strategy, a plan, that will serve your needs.

Planning is valuable, if not essential to navigating adversity and achieving our goals. Planning, however, is not in and of itself sufficient. As President Eisenhower has been quoted as saying, "Good planning without good working is nothing."[5] Or, if you prefer, the oil tycoon T. Boone Pickens was quick to note, "A plan without action isn't a plan, it's a speech."[6] So let's stop "speaking," and let's get some action!

chapter six

From Plan to Action

> *Action is the foundational key to all success.*
>
> —Pablo Picasso[1]

Jack Canfield, a well-known motivational speaker and coauthor of *Chicken Soup for the Soul*, tells a story of an exercise he often does when opening one of his seminars. As he describes it, he stands in front of those in attendance and holds out a $100 bill. He asks if anyone would like it. He waits.

While the waiting may expand a couple of minutes, someone finally gets it and rushes the stage to grab the money. Sadly, most of us have been in situations where we would like something, yet we sit and look while others act.

As highlighted in the previous chapter, planning is an essential yet insufficient part of a goal achievement process. If you are like me, then a quick review of your years of making New Year's resolutions can prove this point.

New Year's resolutions? Wow, can I make them?

I can analyze the challenges, plan the goals, even organize the strategies. But too often I forget to put my engine into gear and, as a result, fail to act. It is as if the goal is placed before my eyes, and yet I sit in my chair, waiting and waiting for what? Perhaps magic?

Planning is vital if we are to make changes in our lives. However, there is often an expansive gap between planning to do things and our actual carrying through on those plans. There can be many reasons (not excuses) that inaction takes center stage. Understanding these challenges and the steps needed to remove them—freeing you up for action—is the focus of this chapter.

The Value of Doing

Sometimes the obvious can escape us. It is worthwhile to simply stop and ask the question, "What is the value of action?"

Taking action goes beyond assisting us in achieving our goals. Taking action can help us learn and grow. Engaging with your action plans can inspire, increase your motivation, and open you up to other possibilities. This is all true, even when your actions are less than totally successful.

Action and Goal Achievement

The most immediate response to the question of "Why take action?" is that action has the potential of providing goal achievement. To achieve your goals, you can wait for them to come to you, or you can get up and go get them. You can figure out which is more likely to lead to success.

While you have identified SMART goals and developed a brilliantly creative plan for achieving them, without action, without consistent, goal-directed action, these goals remain but wishes. Successful people are willing to take consistent action toward realizing their dreams and achieving their goals. People who successfully get Jack Canfield's $100 bill get off their duffs and run to the stage.

Taking Action Can Be Risky

Taking action can be risky, and that can be a good thing. Yes, when you take action, you may fail. You may fall short of your goal. With apologies to Robert Frost and his poem "To a Mouse," the truth is that the best-laid plans of mice and men (and you and me) *can* go awry. I am sure you have experienced this.

I am sure there has been a time when you have given considerable thought to how you wanted to approach something, only to find that this pathway did not lead you where you wished to go. Failure is not just possible but inevitable. Even with failure, a value can be found in our effort and our actions.

Even when the action results in less-than-desired outcomes, the action itself can be of value. There are lessons to be learned from failure. The knowledge gained about what didn't work can undoubtedly be of value as you engage "plan B."

Babe Ruth, the king of the home run, also struck out over 1,300 times. That didn't stop him from swinging the bat, and that swinging resulted in over 700 career home runs. Similarly, after one of their attempts to fly failed, the Wright brothers would go back to their workshop and make a small, quick tweak and test the plane again.

Don't be afraid of failure; see it as an invitation to growth. Yes, it may be hard to see the possibility of success following an experience of failure. Still, often it is only after several failures that we have a chance at success.

Perhaps that all sounds like psychobabble or Hallmark-speak?

Take a moment and test it out. Whether it was making an adjustment to your car's distributor (so that it stopped backfiring) or tasting and then adding salt to a dish, think about the times, big and small, where the initial outcome of your plan was less than desired. At these times, didn't you process the failure in a way that led to an adjustment, an improvement, to your plan?

Taking Action Can Be Motivating

When we engage with our action plan, even with the initial small steps, we can begin to see progress toward our goal. The experience of progress can excite and keep you working hard at your plan. People are more inclined to increase their efforts when their goal is in close proximity.

Perhaps you have had the experience where a special event, such as an anniversary, Christmas, or the date of starting your vacation, was right around the corner. While you may have been excited about planning for a vacation, if the goal is somewhat far away (in terms of time), you may have lost your enthusiasm. However, as the date gets closer and you begin to engage in your action plan, you will find that your enthusiasm may have returned. You look for your passport, wash the clothes you will be taking, and even go shopping for sunblock. The more effort you put into your action plan, the closer the goal becomes and the more motivated and excited you become. In psychology-land, this is known as the "goal-gradient effect."[2]

Simply put, the goal-gradient effect suggests that the closer you get to your goal, the more motivated you become and the more effort you will expend. As Hull, the originator of this theory, observed, rats in a maze run faster as they near the cheese than they did at the beginning of the maze.[3] Researchers[4] have found the same is true for us humans (though not necessarily for the cheese).

Actions that bring us closer to our goal result in a greater desire to continue in these actions of working toward our goal. The research on goal-gradient behavior and the positive impact on motivation can be useful as you engage in your action plan (see Table 6.1).

TABLE 6.1 Increasing Motivation via Goal-Gradient Behavior

1. ***Visualize Progress.*** Developing a method to help you visualize your progress toward your goal (for example, a chart or graph) increases your goal-gradient behavior (i.e., excitement and increased motivation resulting from coming closer to your goal).
2. ***Track Effort.*** While visualizing movement toward your goal will increase motivation, so too will tracking your effort or your engagement in your action plan. If you are one of those individuals who wear a monitor that records the number of steps you take each day, you most likely have experienced the added motivation of tracking your efforts. "Only another 800 steps, and I'll be at 10,000 for the day!" Sound familiar?
3. ***Make Action Fun.*** Moving toward a goal can be hard work, and in fact, we know it should be challenging and somewhat hard. However, research on goal-gradient theory has found that "gamification" techniques such as providing little rewards for engaging in the action plan increase a person's desire to continue that task. As crazy as it may seem, this theory is the foundation for a lot of business apps. Being able to track your pizza order, especially when you are very hungry, increases the likelihood of enjoying the process and motivating you to return (or continue with such service). This is something Domino's Pizza understands. When taking action increases your "thrill of the hunt," your motivation also increases.

It is also important to point out that the motivational benefit of working toward a goal can be experienced even when you are falling short of your goal.

Steven Spielberg was rejected three times from the University of Southern California School of Theatre, Film, and Television. Steve Jobs, a college dropout and a tech executive, was fired from the very company he formed. In a speech he gave in 2005 to the graduating class of Stanford University, Jobs reflected, "I didn't see it then, but it turned out that getting fired from Apple was the best thing that could have ever happened to me. The heaviness of being successful was replaced by the lightness of being a beginner again, less sure about everything. It freed me to enter one of the most creative periods of my life."

Action Can Foster Growth

Friedrich Nietzsche, the German 19th-century philosopher, is quoted as having mused, "That which does not kill us, makes us stronger."[5] (Of course, he said it in German.) The concept is that if you can survive setbacks, you can increase your resiliency and perseverance when taking action.

Consider the story regarding J. K. Rowling, the author of the Harry Potter stories. She is said to have submitted her first Harry Potter book to 12 publishing houses, all of whom rejected her work. I wonder where those acquisitions editors are today?

These rejections appear to have lit a fire under her. One year later, she found a publisher; and the rest, as the saying goes, is history ... a very lucrative history.

All three of these individuals—Spielberg, Jobs, and Rowling—responded to a failed action plan by increasing their motivation to persist, to grow in resiliency, and to find another plan to employ for their goal achievement. That's growth! That's what our expert within directs us to do.

Action Opens Other Possibilities

With the goal of getting to California, my plans were made and adjusted multiple times due to road construction and various other challenges encountered on the way. While the path that I initially outlined was not precisely the path taken, the action and the different adjustments to my plan opened other possibilities.

A detour on Route 70, while delaying my progress toward the coast, allowed me to experience Cawker City, Kansas, and the largest ball of twine in the United States. Come on now . . . have you experienced the largest ball of twine? Awesome.

Like me, you may encounter the need for detours in your action plan. Whether your path is ultimately successful or not, it is very likely to open doors that were unexpected and opportunities previously not considered.

"Just Do It" Sounds Easy, But ...

In 1988, Nike began the long-running *"Just Do It"* strapline. This now-iconic advertisement slogan has been employed by many as a simple directive: just do it!

The problem, however, is that "doing it" and engaging in an action plan requires motivation. The idea of motivation is certainly not new to you. What might be surprising is that you are *always* motivated. Perhaps as you sit on the couch, looking at the treadmill, this statement doesn't feel so true.

Well, as a human, you are always moved to do something. That something may not be the action listed as number one on your "to-do list." Unless sitting on the couch is number one?

To transform your plan into action requires that you are motivated to engage in that action plan's specifics. Understanding the elements that contribute to your achievement motivation positions you to manipulate those elements to support your goal achievement motivation.

Value and Expectancy

Time-out for another "brain experiment."

I would like you to identify a time when you pushed yourself to achieve some goal. Without knowing the specifics of the goal or action, I think I can accurately predict a couple of things about the situation.

First, I bet you found some value, some attraction, to either the actual action you were taking or the eventual outcomes expected or both. Second, I would predict that, even before engaging in your quest, you had a pretty good sense, or belief, that the activity you were to engage in was something that you could do successfully.

Am I right?

If so, I wish I could take the credit. The credit needs to go to Jacquelynne Eccles and her colleagues and their value-expectancy theory of motivation.[6]

The theory posits that the effort a person is willing to expend on a task is the product of two factors interacting with each other. The first factor is the degree to which you value the anticipated outcome or payoff to be gained if successful. The second element refers to the degree to which you believe you can successfully perform the task and achieve the desired outcome. The theory places these two elements into the following formula: ***Motivation = Value x Expectancy.***

A point that should be highlighted is that this formula is multiplicative and not summative.

This means that if one element is low, the outcome, motivation, will be low. If one of the components is zero or absent, as would be the case where you see no value or hold no expectation of success, your motivation to engage will be zero.

So—mind experiment number two.

How motivated would you be if I asked you to write out the alphabet 500 times? This is something you can do; this would bode well for one part of the equation, "expectancy." But what value do you assign to that task? Assuming that you find no value in such an exercise, we could predict that your motivation to act would be zero, based on the formula.

Now let's consider the other factor in this equation, "value."

How motivated would you be if I offered, as a goal, $100,000? The value seems enticing, but remember, there are two factors involved: this valuing and the expectancy of success. To estimate your expectancy of success, you would have to know what you have to do to achieve that goal of getting $100,000. In this case, the task is for you to leap a tall building with a single bound (like Superman).

Unless you have a superpower that no one knows about, you will reject the offer. You would reject the offer even if the payoff was one million dollars. In this case, it is not the value; it is the expectancy that is controlling the motivation. Zero expectancy times gigantic value still equates to zero motivation.

As you move from planning to acting, understanding these elements of motivation can prove quite useful. Learning how to increase the value of both the action you are about to engage in and the value of the goal you seek will kick-start your transition from planning to acting and help to sustain you through the entire plan of action. Similarly, taking the time to structure your strategy so that it increases your expectation of being able to engage in the process and that the process will prove successful will serve as the added booster for your action-taking.

Increasing Value

When you began this journey to goal attainment, you started with a need and a vision. Before engaging in the work that needs to be done to achieve the goals, it is useful to remember why this journey was undertaken. What are the needs that are going to be met by your actions? What is the payoff as a result of all your efforts?

Given that we are often people who demand and expect immediate gratification, the fact that your goal may take work to achieve and that the payoff may be delayed for some time can undermine the value of all your work and reduce your motivation. It is vital to identify those payoffs that you anticipate and that you value. Jot down the reasons you believe your action is essential. Create as many reasons as you can and post them. Remembering these can help you get through some of the struggles encountered on your way to goal achievement.

Another challenge to maintaining your awareness of the value of what you are doing is that the effort it takes and the costs you experience begin to outweigh the anticipated positive outcome. The steps you may need to take as you move toward a goal will be physically, psychologically, and socially costly. The costs experienced at any one moment along your path may be greater than the payoff accrued in that moment.

When your plan requires a lot of work, it helps to break the plan down into smaller, less costly steps. Engaging with less demanding, less costly steps in your action plan, while having clear evidence of the progress being made, will help increase each step's immediate value and help maintain your motivation to persist.

Increasing Expectancy via Self-Efficacy

In Chapter 3, you were introduced to the concept of self-efficacy. Self-efficacy refers to your belief in your ability to succeed in a particular situation.[7,8] Those who study self-efficacy have noted that people who have a strong sense of self-efficacy generally (a) develop a deep interest in the activities in which they are engaged, (b) are strongly committed to their actions, (c) see challenging problems as tasks to be conquered, and (d) recover quickly from a setback. What a set of valuable characteristics to have as you prepare for action.

First introduced by Albert Bandura in 1977, the concept of self-efficacy has been extensively researched.[9] This research has helped define the nature of self-efficacy and its value to motivation and productivity and has identified factors that contribute to the development of self-efficacy.

Reflecting on Your Mastery and Successes

Experiencing success is a primary contributor to a person's sense of efficacy. Therefore, review your action steps and break them down into "doable" segments. Arrange the action steps in a way that ensures early and continued success. Each step, when successful, will foster the efficacy needed for the next.

Stretching

When looking at your goals, it is vital to make sure that they are within your reach—but require some stretching.

Self-efficacious people reach for goals that make the most of their abilities and require effort. The stretching to successfully achieve a goal increases your belief in your ability to take on challenging tasks.

Benefiting from Others

Observing and vicariously experiencing others' efficacy and success is another way that your self-efficacy can be increased. Seeing others putting in effort and succeeding contributes to your "can do" attitude.

If possible, develop an action plan that places you in the context of others doing the same. There are financial and convenience benefits to be accrued when engaging in an exercise program at home, vis à vis joining a gym. However, participating in a group exercise or in the context of others doing the same that may be experienced in a gym can contribute to the modeling effect on your self-efficacy.

Several companies have tapped the value of social modeling and the convenience of home when it comes to home exercise. For example, companies such as NordicTrack, ProForm, and Echelon now provide a smart-connect exercise bike that, while used at home (i.e., convenient), is also connected to live trainers and group lessons (i.e., social modeling).

Being Affirmed

Receiving positive feedback from others can contribute to your growing sense of self-efficacy. Obviously, this observation would also direct you away from the "naysayers."

Share your actions (not just your plan) with those who can and will provide positive social feedback.

Stopping the Inner Critic

Just like a friend who is negative can erode your sense of self-efficacy, be on guard of your inner critic. Be aware of negative thoughts, and replace this negativity with positive self-talk. Not just "Yes, I can," but "Yes, I am!"

Exercise 6.1. Boosting Self-Efficacy

Directions: Each of the following strategies can help you boost your self-efficacy beliefs. Consider them as you prepare for action.

Reflecting on your mastery and successes. Review the elements of your plan and select specific parts with which you have had previous success.

Stretching. Remember the Goldilocks principle. Make sure that your action steps are not too hard nor too easy. They should require effort but be within your grasp.

Benefiting from others. As you review your action plan and the steps you will be taking to achieve your goal, is there a role for or a place to include others? Especially others who have a history of successfully doing what you are trying to achieve?

Being affirmed. Don't look for empty praise, but find those who can understand and appreciate all you are doing and provide you with deserved encouragement. Self-affirmation is also a valuable contributor to your developing self-efficacy, so be sure to give yourself a pat on the back when earned.

Stopping the inner critic. Tune into your thoughts about the plan and your engagement in the process. Identify those "can't-do thoughts" and argue; don't let that nonsense deter you.

Engaging in the actions needed to achieve your goals will take effort and will require the maintenance of your motivation. As you prepare to engage with your action plan, you may want to consider all of the elements that can contribute to the development and maintenance of your motivation and take steps to maximize each (see Exercise 6.2).

> **Exercise 6.2. Increasing Value and Expectancy**
>
> **Directions:** In the previous chapters, you were asked to develop a vision or dream, translate that vision into a SMART goal, and then develop a reasonable strategy or path to achieving that goal. The following steps will help you increase your motivation by increasing your task and goal value and your expectancy of success.
>
> Step 1: Write down the goal (the SMART goal) that you created in Chapter 5.
>
> Step 2: Write down the strategy or action you identified as the path to follow in Chapter 6.
>
> Step 3: Using your expert skills at brainstorming and a 10-minute timer, list all of the possible positive outcomes of engaging in the strategy that you developed.
>
> Step 4: Continue your brainstorming process, but this time use the 10-minute timer to list all of the possible benefits/outcomes of achieving your goal.
>
> Step 5: Review the two lists you created in steps 3 and 4, and from each list, select two of the positives to be experienced and write those on a separate piece of paper. Posting this reminder will help you maintain your motivation to engage in the action plan.
>
> Step 6: Return to Exercise 5.3, where you identified a strategy and a path to follow. Review the plan of action. Given the realities you currently face and the competing demands on your time, energy, and other resources, adjust this strategy in a series of small, achievable steps. The goal of your reformulation is to increase your belief in the "doability" of this plan. Suppose the plan as initially developed appears very doable. In that case, nothing more needs to be done, except to remind yourself, "Yes, I can!"

Preparation Then Action

Eager to jump in and start your plan? Great! But there are a few additional preparatory activities that you may want to consider before jumping totally into action.

Before you venture forth, it is helpful to consider the possible obstacles that could stand in your way and develop strategies to remove these before they disrupt your progress. It is better to plan for all contingencies before beginning the journey than to attempt to adjust on the fly.

A strategy that may help structure for success is one that was created by social psychologist Kurt Lewin. The idea behind his technique, *the force-field analysis*, is that, when attempting to achieve a goal, it is crucial to identify all of the forces that are pushing you toward your goal, as well as those that are forces of resistance and thus standing in your way of goal achievement. The model suggests that moving forward is dependent on the "driving forces" being stronger than the "resisting forces" (see Figure 6.1).

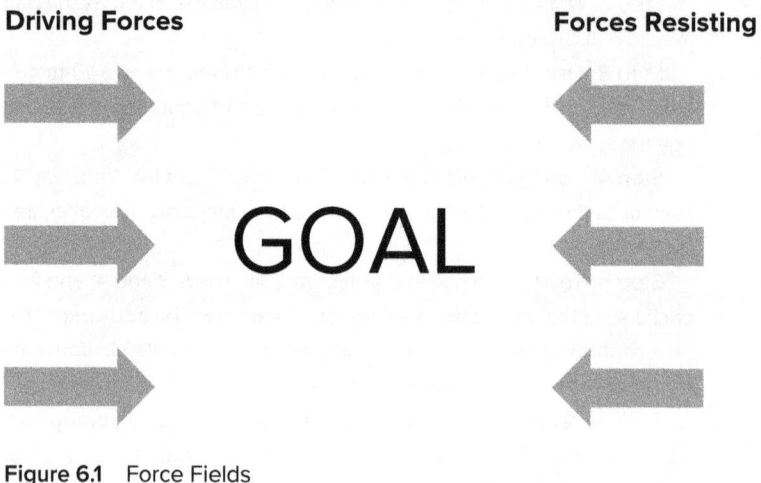

Figure 6.1 Force Fields

As depicted in Figure 6.1, the forces driving and those that are resisting are of equal strength, and thus there is no change, no movement. In this situation, goal achievement will require you to either increase the number and strength of the driving forces and/or reduce the resisting forces' number and power.

Now here is something to consider. Kurt Lewin was a very thoughtful human being. His concept of force-field analysis is used in various contexts and situations, and it is handy. But then again, you knew that. Your inner expert has most likely been using this model for a long time.

Have you ever tried to open a glass jar and found the lid was difficult to turn? The forces holding the top (or those resisting movement) were stronger than the forces (maybe your grip strength) employed to move the lid in the desired direction. Now, you may have decided that the best strategy to achieve the goal of getting that pickle was to increase your grip strength by using a towel or resting the jar against your stomach. You may have also decided that a good strategy would be to reduce the forces resisting your attempt to open the jar. Without knowing the physics behind the process, you may have turned the jar upside down and given it a good smack. This activity moved the pickles up to the lid. It disturbed the vacuum inside, thus reducing the vacuum as a force of resistance.

I am sure there are many other similar times and circumstances in your life. When confronted with an obstacle to a goal, you simply found more resources (forces) to push forward or found ways to reduce those forces that were standing in your way. Voila! Force-field analysis at work.

Exercise 6.3 provides an example and invites you to apply this force-field analysis to your action plan.

Exercise 6.3. Applying Force-Field Analysis

Directions: Before jumping into engaging with your strategy, take a little more time to anticipate the good and the bad. Use the example provided to assess your force field and identify steps that you can take to make it supportive of your goal achievement.

Example:

Goal: To lose 20 pounds

Strategy: Go to the gym five days a week—every other for weights, each day for cardio.

Driving Forces:

   a.   blood sugar is high, want to reduce
   b.   cholesterol is high, need to reduce and get off medication
   c.   knees hurt as a result of the excess weight
   d.   clothes too tight ... uncomfortable

Resisting Forces:

   a.   gym costs $50.00 a month
   b.   gym is a 20-minute drive from my house

c. need to purchase gym clothes, sneakers, sweatpants
d. feel sore after working out, especially in the beginning

Plan to increase the number/strength of driving forces

a. post latest blood work—highlight cholesterol and blood sugar levels
b. pick out some new clothes (from favorite retailer) and post pictures
c. see if my wife will join me

Plan to reduce the number/ strength of resisting forces

a. as a first step, consider using exercise video at home to minimize drive time and monthly costs
b. write out an exercise plan, starting with only 5-minute aerobic exercise and five-pound weights
c. do only low-impact, yoga-type exercises to reduce strain on knees

Task Management—The Final Step to Action

Another valuable part of pre-action planning is establishing a method to monitor and direct your time—energy—and action steps. At a minimum, it is helpful to specify a starting point and the detailing of a measurable endpoint, your goal, and identify the actions that need to be taken as you move from what is to what is desired.

Perhaps you have already engaged in some rather lengthy action plans, such as planning a wedding, building a house, or even arranging for a family Thanksgiving dinner. Suppose you have employed a multistep action plan in your past, one requiring sequencing of actions. In that case, you already can appreciate the value of "task management."

A good management plan will outline a chain of actions where each link reflects a subgoal or mini action, along with time requirements for completing that action. Using such an approach may be over the top if your action plan is rudimentary and doesn't demand many mini actions or an extended period. However, when your action plan is somewhat complicated, having many subparts, and extends over a lengthy period of time, a more detailed management approach may be of value.

A good task management plan will help break down all that needs to be done in discrete, interconnected parts arranged in a logical sequence. Knowing what step A is and that it leads to step B and so on provides the structure needed for helping you to stay on task and make progress.

One approach to developing a task management plan would be to work backward in time, from the date targeted for goal accomplishment back to the starting date. As you move back, you can identify the subtasks that need to be completed at specific points along your timeline.

For example, in planning your wedding, you might specify the moment of saying "I do" as the endpoint, one that you anticipate achieving on June 14 at 2:00 p.m. With that as the endpoint, what of significance needs to be done before that occurrence?

Time needs to be assigned to each subtask leading up to that moment. Subtasks might include transporting the wedding party from the hotel to the church, having the rehearsal and pre-rehearsal dinners. As you continue to consider the tasks further back toward the beginning of the timeline, you may list things such as finalizing the numbers attending the reception or finding and purchasing a gown. As you continue to work back, you may find that the starting point was the moment of saying "I will!"

This may seem to be exhausting, and it can be. But placing the time and energy into creating a management plan increases your chances of success. Indeed, it will reduce the unneeded stress of not knowing where you are or what comes next. Let's give it a try (see Exercise 6.4).

Exercise 6.4. Chaining and Task Management

Directions: Identify the action plan that you are about to begin. Create a timeline (see below) and identify your starting and finishing points (dates). Now, working backward from your ending point of goal achievement, label the significant subtasks or mini actions that need to be accomplished, chaining them back to the beginning of your plan. Review the linked events and identify any unique resources you may need as you move from starting, through subgoals, to your desired endpoint.

(Continued)

```
o___x___x___x___x___x___x___ ☺
Start  subtask 1  subtask 2  subtask 3  subtask 4  subtask 5  subtask 6  goal achieved
```

Resources needed (if any one subtask requires additional resources to complete):

subtask _____

subtask _____

subtask _____

subtask _____

subtask _____

subtask _____

What Next?

You are set and ready to go. What's next?

Get going!

There is progress to be made, tasks to be conquered. Table 6.2 provides you with a few reminders to take along on your goal-directed journey.

TABLE 6.2 Reminders for Your Journey

1. **Eyes on the prize.** Remind yourself of why you are doing this and what you will achieve. Keep the value of this process in your vision at all times.
2. **Baby steps.** Break the plan down into tiny tasks. It is not the size of the step, just the repetition of steps, that will get you where you want to go. Focus on doing consistently—doing something.
3. **Effort counts.** Progress slowly—remember, effort counts! Pat yourself on the back for giving it the good old college try (or high school or neighborhood try). Hush the critic and think positively about any effort in the right direction.
4. **Give it time.** Don't *let* your plan happen; *make* it happen by blocking off your calendar—your time—to give it time. Don't think in terms of massive blocks of time, just enough to make a dent, to complete a micro task.
5. **Ticklers.** When ending a part of your plan, set up a trigger, or tickler, to get you started on the next part of the plan (maybe leave your gym membership card, or the meditation tape, out on the vanity).

6.	***Step away.*** Sometimes it is helpful to take a break, to step away from the plan. They say muscles grow in the rest period between workouts. The same may be true for motivation and a positive attitude.
7.	***Reduce the noise.*** Try to eliminate distractions and cut out the noise (silence the phone, turn off the emails). Focus on the plan.
8.	***Blow your own horn.*** Once engaged in your action plan, share with others; be open to their suggestions and encouragement.

Oh, and yeah—one other thing.

There is a good chance that you will experience a few stumbles and setbacks along the way. So let's prep your resiliency; it may be needed.

chapter seven

Resiliency—Essential for Success

Do not judge me by my success, judge me by how many times I fell down and got back up again.

—Nelson Mandela[1]

Life might be so much easier, and our journey toward our goals more rewarding, if failure or setbacks didn't exist. But failure does exist; it is part of life and our journey. After all of your hard work, experiencing a setback can be more than disappointing. Depending on the nature of the goal and the setback experienced, it can feel devastating.

In the moment of failure's darkness, it may be hard to appreciate that failure can be a stepping stone toward success. Suggesting that failure can make you stronger and wiser may be a little too "Hallmark-card-like" and thus very easy to dismiss. But many others, besides Nelson Mandela, give evidence of the truth of the value of failure (see Table 7.1).

TABLE 7.1. Responding to Adversity with Resilience

Albert Einstein	Failed his entrance exam to the Swiss Federal Institute of Technology, located in Zurich, at 16 years old. After eventually graduating from college, Einstein worked as an insurance salesman but quit after some time because he failed at that as well.
Charlie Chaplin	Grew up in sheer poverty in the UK. His father abandoned his mother when he was just 2 years old, and he was forced to live in a workhouse at the age of 7 years old. When he was 9 years old, his mother was permanently committed to an insane asylum.
Theodor Geisel (Dr. Seuss)	Intended to earn his PhD in literature at Lincoln College, Oxford, but failed and subsequently dropped out of school. After he wrote his first book, *And to Think That I Saw It on Mulberry Street*, it was rejected 28 separate times.
Henry Ford	His first company went bankrupt. His second company also went south when, after a dispute with partners, he was forced to walk away with only the rights to his name.
Jim Carrey	Grew up extremely poor as a child; didn't have his fame handed to him. At the age of 15, Carrey worked as a janitor to help his family pay the bills. During his first performance at Yuk Yuk's, a comedy club in Toronto, he was booed off the stage.
Oprah Winfrey	Born to a single mother living on welfare; her upbringing was wrought with pain and anguish. She was physically, mentally, and sexually abused during her childhood. She ran away at 13 years old and got pregnant at 14 years old.
Thomas Edison	One of the most successful innovators in American history; reported to have failed over 10,000 times.

Sometimes the rich, the famous, or those we hold up as models of success were successful because of their ability to respond to failure positively. In his memoir, *A Promised Land*, President Barack Obama describes a moment in his early political life when he experienced a series of painful losses: "I was almost forty, broke, coming off a humiliating defeat and with my marriage strained."[2] This was also a time when he lost his mother to uterine cancer. It was a dark time for Barack Hussein Obama, and yet he found the strength, the will, the resiliency to come back. You know the rest of that story.

As you read this, you might be thinking, "Sure, this can happen to famous people, special people, but not us normal folk." If you can pause for a moment and listen to your expert within, you know that resiliency has been part of your journey and that of most other "normal folk."

Chapter Seven Resiliency—Essential for Success

The child who falls from the two-wheeled bike only to resaddle, the skateboarder who lands on his bottom rather than his feet and board, the person who gets up and goes back to work after a previous rough day, and indeed, the response of those directly impacted by the events of September 11, 2001—these are all evidence of the gift of human resilience, the resiliency of "normal folk." How about you?

Exercise 7.1 invites you to take stock of your own experience with resilience. We will return to this exercise as we proceed through the chapter, so keep your responses handy.

Exercise 7.1. Personal Experience with Resilience

Directions: Let me go out on a limb and make two assumptions about you and your life. First, I assume that you have, at different points in your life, experienced failure. This may have been something very significant and something that had a lasting negative effect. Or your experience with failure may have been less life-altering—a minor setback. In either case, you have not only experienced failure, but (and again, it is my assumption) you have rebounded from that setback, that failure.

This exercise invites you to identify two failure events, one of minor significance and one more impactful on your life. Describe each situation, each experience, with as much detail as you can remember. This information will be useful in later exercises.

Event 1 (a minor setback or failure).

   a. Describe the event:
   b. Describe the impact of the failure on you, on others:
   c. Describe how you responded in the moment:
   d. Describe how you eventually "bounced back" (what helped you with your resilience?):

Event 2 (a significant experience with failure).

   a. Describe the event:
   b. Describe the impact of the failure on you, on others:
   c. Describe how you responded in the moment:
   d. Describe how you eventually "bounced back" (what helped you with your resilience?):

Completing Exercise 7.1 should have helped you to see that your expert within is and can be resilient. Understanding the nature and value of resiliency and the elements contributing to resiliency development can go a long way toward increasing that expertise and serving you as you navigate life's challenges.

Resiliency

Resilience is the ability to get up, dust yourself off, and try again. It reflects your ability to effectively cope and adapt, even when faced with adversity. Resiliency is that which sees us through difficult times.

You are probably familiar with the story of Christopher Reeve, "Superman." At the age of 42, he had a horseback-riding accident that changed his life. His fall from the horse caused significant spinal cord damage, and this once "man of steel," who could (at least on film) leap tall buildings with a single bound, found himself unable to walk.

The injury placed him in the hospital for 5 weeks, during which time he fought for his life. He left the hospital with 90% of his body absent of sensation and the need to be on a ventilator for his breathing. At the age of 42, his life was changed, and his dreams and goals certainly challenged, if not destroyed.

How do you "bounce back" from such a life-altering and very likely dream-ending experience like this?

Reeve died in 2004, at the age of 52. However, in the years of his life post-accident, Christopher Reeve gave voice and form to human resilience. He set new goals—challenging goals, but achievable goals. As a result of his resilience, his ability to reframe life and life goals and get back into the fight, he reclaimed movement in his fingers and toes. He began to feel sensations and was able to tell the difference between hot and cold temperatures. He refused to see himself as a victim, and yet, being realistic, he accepted that much of what he had wished to accomplish was no longer possible. Still, this setback was an invitation to opportunity.

No longer focusing on his acting career, he worked tirelessly to promote spinal cord injury research, raising tens of millions of dollars for the Christopher and Dana Reeve Paralysis Resource Center. His story is a story of resiliency. His story highlights the factors that contribute to our resiliency, including the need for and value of embracing reality, holding on to hope, and revising goals in a way that gives life meaning and direction.

While his is a story of celebrity, it is a story played out by so many others who have faced significant setbacks and called forth their resiliency. Take a moment to simply reflect on those who you know—family members, coworkers, neighbors, school friends. It is a safe bet that you will be able to identify a person who showed the strength of resiliency in addressing significant adversity in their life. In fact, that person is very likely you.

Given that resiliency is a contributor to our well-being,[3] as well as a significant "buffer" protecting us from adverse life conditions,[4] cultivating and building on your resilience is something to consider.

Factors Contributing to Resiliency

Some individuals seem to "bounce back" from adverse events quite effectively, whereas others are caught in a rut, seemingly unable to get out of their negative streak. We might assume that what distinguishes these individuals, like Christopher Reeve or Barack Obama, has to do with a personality trait, even genetics. From this perspective, it would be easy to throw our hands up when experiencing adversity, believing that it is lucky for those who have resiliency, and shame on us who don't.

While resiliency does reflect specific characteristics of an individual, it is something we all have and something that can be nurtured and developed. To a large extent, our resiliency reflects our perspective on ourselves, our life, and life's challenges.

As noted in Table 7.1, Thomas Edison has been reported to have failed over 10,000 times in his experiments. An often-repeated anecdote, one attributed to his longtime associate Walter S. Mallory, states that when Mallory expressed sympathy about Edison's failure to get the desired results while working on the creation of the nickel-iron battery, Edison responded, "Results! Why, man, I have gotten a lot of results! I know several thousand things that won't work."[5]

Now, that is a useful psychological frame of mind! One that would undoubtedly position Edison to be resilient and to continue his quest.

The way we interpret our failures can and will undermine our resiliency if it focuses on roadblocks more than goals, on setbacks more than progress. Being turned down at a job interview can be upsetting, but it also can be a motivation to review not only the type of job to which one applies but the approach taken. Failing at one job interview is, as Edison would suggest, a way of eliminating things that will not work on your way to finding that which will work. Embracing such a philosophy invites resiliency.

Research reports that individuals with high resiliency have proactively worked to develop the characteristics that contribute to resiliency. Those with high resiliency use rational planning to lower the levels of risk. They engage in activities that foster a sense of self-efficacy, and they cultivate positive emotionality through humor and optimistic thinking.

So how are you at fostering your sense of resilience? Exercise 7.2 has been taken from the work of Al Siebert, the founder of the Resilience Center in Portland, and will help you answer the question, "How resilient are you?"

Exercise 7.2. How Resilient Are You?

Directions: Rate the following statements from 1 to 5 (1 = strongly disagree; 5 = strongly agree):

- I'm usually optimistic. I see difficulties as temporary and expect to overcome them.
- Feelings of anger, loss, and discouragement don't last long.
- I can tolerate high levels of ambiguity and uncertainty about situations.
- I adapt quickly to new developments. I'm curious. I ask questions.
- I'm playful. I find the humor in rough situations and can laugh at myself.
- I learn valuable lessons from my experiences and the experiences of others.
- I'm good at solving problems. I'm good at making things work well.
- I'm strong and durable. I hold up well during tough times.
- I've converted misfortune into good luck and found benefits in bad experiences.

Interpretation

Less than 20: Low Resilience—You may have trouble handling pressure or setbacks and may feel deeply hurt by any criticism. When things don't go well, you may feel helpless and without hope. It is suggested that you connect with others who share your developmental goals or perhaps reach out to an external expert who can help you in this developmental process.

20–30: Some Resilience—You have some valuable pro-resiliency skills but also plenty of room for improvement. Strive to strengthen the characteristics you already have and to cultivate the characteristics you lack. You may also wish to seek some outside coaching or support.

30–35: Adequate Resilience—You are a self-motivated learner who recovers well from most challenges. Learning more about resilience and consciously building your resiliency skills will empower you to find more joy in life, even in the face of adversity.

35–45: Highly Resilient—You bounce back well from life's setbacks and can thrive even under pressure. You could be of service to others who are trying to cope better with adversity.

Adapted from Chapter 2 in The Resiliency Advantage *(Berrett-Koehler) by Al Siebert, PhD*

Strengthening Resilience

We know that measures taken to support a healthy lifestyle, such as regular exercise, a healthy diet, and sufficient sleep, contribute not only to a healthy body but also to a healthy, resilient psyche. In addition to these general habits of well-being, resilience can be strengthened by fostering a growth mindset and positivity.

Growth Mindset

So you've been knocked down, dealt a bad hand—get up, dust yourself off, learn to maximize the play of the hand you were dealt. Sorry! That sounds, at best, like a Pollyanna platitude and, at worst, like a very insensitive dismissal of real suffering.

But actually, the directive reflects what we (in psychology) know about the power of our belief systems, especially as they frame our view of our abilities and our prediction of future success. Carol Dweck (see her book *Mindset, the New Psychology of Success*[6]) has spent much of her professional life researching the power of our beliefs, our mindsets, and the impact they have on life choices and responses, including that of resiliency.

Some people take setbacks and failures and attribute these to some unchangeable personal characteristic or trait. Such a "fixed mindset" sets an individual to believe that character, intelligence, creative ability, and resiliency are static givens that we can't change in any meaningful way. You have them, or you don't.

With this as a mindset, a person will view their setback as a terminal experience, announcing the death of their goal. They will feel as if they are a victim. Such a perspective not only stops progress but undermines resiliency.

The alternative perspective, supported by the research, is a "growth mindset."

A growth mindset is based on the belief that your basic qualities are things you can cultivate through your efforts. With this as a perspective, failure is not evidence of being doomed due to the nonpossession of essential traits or attributes, but rather a recognition of the areas of our life where the possibility for growth and for stretching our abilities exists. A growth mindset fuels a person's experience with resiliency. Failure or setbacks do not mean the end, a terminal point, but rather a marker on your developmental journey.

Take a moment and return to your responses in Exercise 7.1. The exercise invited you to remember times of your own resilience. As you review these experiences, ask yourself, did you experience some level or form of growth as a result of working through those setbacks?

If so, remember that.

Look for a similar opportunity to grow the next time you experience a block to your goal achievement. The growth mindset invites you to search for what you can learn or how you can grow from this setback.

Strengthening your growth mindset takes effort. But you are not starting from zero. Your inner expert has exhibited your resiliency on numerous occasions, some big (like dealing with a personal loss), and many less earth-shaking (e.g., getting back on that two-wheeled bike). It is not about creating but strengthening this growth-mindset perspective.

It is a process that starts by really listening to how you are interpreting a challenge or a setback. Are you telling yourself, "That's it, I can't do this," or are you thinking, "What the hell am I going to do? Let me think about what just happened. I can do this!"

Maybe the reality is that you lack the personal knowledge or skills necessary to achieve the goal. So? With a growth mindset, you will hear yourself say, "I can get better at this," rather than merely concluding, "I'm no good at this."

A growth mindset means you accept that anything and everything you do can be improved. With this attitude, failure is simply an opportunity to learn and grow. The same is true for those times when you experience success.

Individuals who are resilient and operate from a growth mindset do not settle for success. They turn their focus on ways to improve. It is this mindset of accepting the possibility of growth in both good and bad situations that nurtures resiliency.

> **Exercise 7.3. Developing a Growth Mindset**
>
> **Directions:** The goal of this exercise is to practice employing a growth mindset to life's challenges.
>
> Identify a goal that you are currently having difficulty achieving. If none is current, identify a goal that you may have given up on because of having difficulty achieving it. Review your experience and respond to the following two questions.
>
> 1. What did you learn from that experience that will be helpful to you?
> 2. While falling short or failing in this particular situation, did your experience open other opportunities that you had not previously envisioned?

Optimism and Positivity

Another factor that contributes to resilience is the experience of harnessing positive emotions. The research is abundant in supporting the physical and mental health benefits of being a positive thinker.[7] Positivity isn't magical. It doesn't automatically result in goal achievement or the avoidance of hardship. It does, however, support resiliency by promoting hope and reframing challenges as something manageable.

A positive perspective can be strengthened by practicing gratitude and focusing on the good things in your life. There is value in looking for the silver lining in life's challenge, even when the treasure, the gift, is that you've survived! Yes, looking for the silver lining is a cliché, but it is one that is true.

Practicing finding that which is good, as opposed to dwelling only on that which is problematic, increases resiliency.

This is not to suggest you should ignore the real challenges of life or the real adversity you face. These are things that need to be addressed and resolved. But responding to adversity is best done when your focus is also on the positive, the optimistic, the hopeful.

Problem-solving requires you to identify the elements of the problem you are confronting. However, it is valuable to identify the opportunity presented, even at a time of challenge. There is value in determining that which can be learned and the opportunities that can be claimed by addressing this adversity. This is a positive perspective.

Engagement with such a positive perspective is not something that you should employ only in times of adversity. A positive outlook on life needs to be fostered, developed, and used—not as a tool, but as a lifestyle.

The development of this perspective can be aided by strategies such as finding humor in life situations and laughing, as well as spending time with others who are positive. It is very easy to immerse yourself in the world's problems and the negativity of many of the "talking heads" on television. While it is essential to know the challenges we are facing, this awareness of the problems and the negativity of life must be balanced with understanding the gifts encountered each day.

Start each day on a positive note. Find something uplifting—a mediation, a song, a reminder of a pleasant experience—as a way of buffering yourself from what may indeed be a day of challenges.

Consider practicing gratitude and the use of a gratitude journal. This is not new to your expert. I would venture to say that you engage in gratitude practice on special occasions, such as Thanksgiving. But given the positive effects that the practice of mindful gratitude has on body and soul, consistently engaging in this practice can result in significant returns on your investment.

Research in positive psychology and cognitive theory points to the benefit of practicing gratitude to reduce stress, improve self-esteem, and foster resilience. Merely thinking about individuals or experiences that have brought or bring you comfort or meaning and then expressing gratitude for these in your life is a valuable strategy for increasing positivity, optimism, and resiliency (see Exercise 7.4).

> ### Exercise 7.4. Gratitude Journal
>
> **Directions:** With all that you have to do each day, taking time to reflect on the many gifts and joys of your life may not be at the top of your to-do list. However, given the research pointing to the positive physical and psychological benefits of experiencing gratitude, the practice of a gratitude journal may be something that should be high on your to-do list.
>
> It is not complicated, nor do you need to buy a fancy diary or journal. Simply get in the habit of entering a daily journal entry using the following template.
>
> "I am grateful for _____ because _____."
>
> The goal isn't to list everything, merely to practice the habit of identifying that which life presents and for which you are grateful. This will increase your positivity mindset and, as a result, your resiliency.

The importance of resiliency is highlighted by the fact that the American Psychological Association developed a list of 10 techniques that serve that purpose.[8] In reviewing their suggestions (see Table 7.2), you may find that your inner expert is way ahead of them. Similarly, you might find several new strategies that you can employ.

TABLE 7.2 Ten Ways to Build Resilience

Make connections.	Good relationships with close family members, friends, or others are essential. Accepting help and support from those who care about you and will listen to you strengthens resilience. Some people find that being active in civic groups, faith-based organizations, or other local groups provides social support and can help reclaim hope. Assisting others in their time of need also can benefit the helper.
Avoid seeing crises as insurmountable problems.	You can't change the fact that highly stressful events happen, but you can change how you interpret and respond to these events. Try looking beyond the present to how future circumstances may be a little better. Note any subtle ways in which you might already feel somewhat better as you deal with difficult situations.

(Continued)

TABLE 7.2 *(Continued)*

Accept that change is a part of living.	Specific goals may no longer be attainable as a result of adverse situations. Accepting circumstances that cannot be changed can help you focus on circumstances that you can alter.
Move toward your goals.	Develop some realistic goals. Do something regularly, even if it seems like a small accomplishment, that enables you to move toward your goals. Instead of focusing on tasks that seem unachievable, ask yourself, "What's one thing I know I can accomplish today that helps me move in the direction I want to go?"
Take decisive actions.	Act on adverse situations as much as you can. Take decisive actions rather than detaching completely from problems and stresses and wishing they would just go away.
Look for opportunities for self-discovery.	People often learn something about themselves and may find that they have grown in respect to their struggle with loss. Many people who have experienced tragedies and hardship have reported better relationships, a greater sense of strength even while feeling vulnerable, increased self-worth, a more developed spirituality, and heightened appreciation for life.
Nurture a positive view of yourself.	Developing confidence in your ability to solve problems and trusting your instincts help build resilience.
Keep things in perspective.	Even when facing a very painful event, consider the stressful situation in a broader context and keep a long-term perspective. Avoid blowing the event out of proportion.
Maintain a hopeful outlook.	An optimistic outlook enables you to expect that good things will happen in your life. Try visualizing what you want rather than worrying about what you fear.
Take care of yourself.	Pay attention to your own needs and feelings. Engage in activities that you enjoy and find relaxing. Exercise regularly. Taking care of yourself helps keep your mind and body primed to deal with situations requiring resilience.
Additional ways of strengthening resilience may be helpful.	Many have reported that activities such as writing about their deepest thoughts and feelings related to trauma or other stressful events in their life, meditating, or engaging in spiritual practices helps build connections and restore hope.

Adapted from "Building Your Resilience" (APA, 2012), https://www.apa.org/topics/resilience

For Your Expert

Imagine you are stuck in the airport. Your flight has been delayed. Getting to your destination is essential, and it is something for which you have made extensive preparation. Does this mean your goal of getting to that destination is over? Or is this a delay, a temporary setback? Any setback can be a disappointment and will have consequences. What do you do? Whine? Feel like a victim? Convince yourself that this is totally unfair and, as a result, become furious? Or do you attempt to problem-solve, looking for available alternative flights? When another flight or alternative means to get to your destination is not available, do you shift your focus to that which you can control (e.g., calling those waiting for you or beginning to work on that novel)? Do you sit and obsess about this problem, or do you find a place for a meal or reflection or walk the concourse for exercise?

Your choices at these times will not only contribute to your experience in the moment but can foster (or interfere) with your ability to bounce back—to be resilient. Factors that contribute to your resilience include a perspective that recognizes the "real" impact of the setback, the fact that the setback is temporary, and the fact that even in disappointment, there are things you can control and experience as an opportunity for growth.

As we end this chapter, you may find it useful to return to your previous experience with resilience (see Exercise 7.1). Exercise 7.5 invites you to consider the factors that contributed to your resilience and contrast those to the suggestions offered throughout this chapter. Were these factors in play?

Your expert is pretty amazing—but may still have room to grow.

Exercise 7.5. The Factors Contributing to My Resiliency

Directions: Review your experience with resiliency (see Exercise 7.1) and identify which, if any, of the following factors were in play in support of your resiliency. Factors that contributed to your resiliency should be something to remember, and those that were not present might be considered with future adversity.

1. I approached the failure as temporary.
2. I maintained a realistic view of the challenge and did not over- or underexaggerate the impact or the level of difficulty.
3. I was able to see the opportunity for growth, even within this setback.
4. I kept my focus on that over which I had some control.
5. I approached the situation with a "can do" positive mindset.

chapter eight

More Than Surviving ... Thriving and Flourishing

*My mission in life is not merely to survive,
but to thrive;
and to do so with some passion,
some compassion,
some humor, and some style.*

—Maya Angelou[1]

A mission in life is something that moves us beyond problem-solving, navigating challenges, coping with adversity, and merely surviving. Having a mission, a calling, invites us to strive. Having a mission in life is not only for the few and the famous, like Maya Angelou.

We are all called to a personal mission. We are all wired to flourish and thrive. We have the inner drive to become the "best me" possible. Attempting to give form to that drive and respond to our mission, our calling, is not easy, but it is something achievable and most certainly something worth pursuing.

Called to Be Me

A mission is more than surviving; it is a call to fulfillment, thriving, and flourishing. This is what your inner expert has been directing you toward all of your life. Sadly, life's daily challenges and adversity can stand in the way of our "hearing" and responding to this call. Setting goals and resolving issues are a part of life, but they should not be the only driving force in your life.

My professional field (psychology) has fostered our greater understanding of how to survive and endure under conditions of adversity. The theories and research of psychology that help us meet our life challenges have been weaved throughout the previous chapters. The principles discussed in these chapters are elaborations of those that your expert knows and has employed. The material in the book is simply a reminder.

Your expert is not merely a problem-solver, passively waiting for adversity to emerge and then engaging in directing you out of these times of trial. Your expert, your inner self, is wired not just to survive but to thrive. Our inner expert invites us to make decisions that give form to our "best" self.

The reference to "best" is not meant to be a moral or value statement. "Best" in this case is referring to the most authentic you. The you that can and "should" be. I am referring to the idea that you would make a not-so-good me, but you (and I) can genuinely be the best reflection of what you are wired or called to be. We have an inner directedness, one that is inviting us to thrive.

The challenge, of course, is that there are external conditions imposed on your journey. There is adversity that demands resolution. There are so many requirements to be met simply to survive that it is easy to become unaware of the inner directedness to thrive.

With apologies if the following analogy appears a bit hokey, I hope it helps make the point. When I think of a flower, say, for example, a marigold, and take time to reflect on its formation, a couple of things strike me. First, a marigold is not now, nor ever will be, a zinnia. How's that for some grand insight? A marigold doesn't have to be taught to be a marigold; those instructions are wired into the seed. Finally, under supportive conditions, the instructions found within the marigold's seed put into operation a series of events that transforms the seed into the eventual creation that we can enjoy.

Chapter Eight More Than Surviving ... Thriving and Flourishing | **113**

Hopefully, my less than sophisticated analogy helps to clarify the concept of personal mission and inner directedness. As I suggested, you would make a not-so-good me, and I, a not-so-good you (you can decide which of us is the marigold or zinnia!). You do have a calling—a unique unfolding, a wired-in directive—to "become." Getting in tune with the directive and nurturing the conditions (the soil, if you will) that foster the development of the directive is what thriving and flourishing require.

Becoming

In the early 1950s, a "school" of psychology emerged, with proponents such as Abraham Maslow and Carl Rogers. This humanistic school of psychology emphasized the positive nature of the human condition. It highlighted concepts such as free will, self-efficacy, and the natural pull to self-actualization.

Those embracing this perspective are concerned with the fullest growth of the individual in the areas of love, fulfillment, self-worth, autonomy, and self-actualization. Rather than concentrating on dysfunction, humanistic psychology focused on helping individuals fulfill their potential and maximize their well-being. The movement of this positive approach to the human condition took form in many books, videos, workshops, and conferences, all offering the magic of developing your unique potential. The approach had an intuitive appeal; after all, who doesn't prefer our better angel to an adversity-laden life?

However, research supporting the concepts and approach was limited. It was limited until the emergence in 2000 of positive psychology, with Martin Seligman and Mihaly Csikszentmihalyi's scientific work.

Positive Psychology

Positive psychology has turned the scientific lens onto the question of *eudaimonia*, the Greek term for the "good life."

As employed within positive psychology research, the "good life" is not defined by the amount in your bank account, the acquisitions accumulated, or even the power and status achieved. The "good life" is that which you experience in those moments when you are genuinely content, optimistic, in the flow, and flourishing.

This is not a static state, one that is achieved and everlasting. However, it is an experience that you have encountered. It is an experience that can be developed with a better understanding of the "conditions" that nurture its development. Positive psychology has been scientifically researching this issue to identify "... what makes life worth living."[2] Their findings are beneficial and applicable to your life journey.

Money Doesn't Buy Flourishing

You have probably heard the phrase "Money can't buy happiness." American author Gertrude Stein had a response to this and stated, "Who said money can't buy happiness simply didn't know where to go shopping."[3]

If material things make you smile, make you feel happy, that's wonderful. But this type of happiness tends to be fleeting. For instance, the fine meal or glass of wine that you have had is quite the sensory experience. It is enjoyable. However, we are programmed for more than just fleeting happiness. Our inner expert seeks and knows how to find deep satisfaction and experiences that move beyond a momentary pleasure to those that help us flourish.

Flourishing

Flourishing is one of the most significant concepts in positive psychology. We flourish when we not only achieve our goals, the more traditional objects that we set out to accomplish, but when we experience a real sense of fulfillment in life.[4] Flourishing is the experience of cultivating our talents and strengths, developing deep and meaningful relationships, feeling pleasure and enjoyment, and making a meaningful contribution to the world. Positive psychologist Dr. Lynn Soots described flourishing as "the product of the pursuit and engagement of an authentic life that brings inner joy and happiness through meeting goals, being connected with life passions, and relishing in accomplishments through the peaks and valleys of life."[5]

When you experience positive emotions, positive social and psychological functioning, you are operating within your optimal range of functioning. That is thriving; that is flourishing. Individuals who flourish are happy people. They are people who do for themselves and others with balance. They find meaning in the positive relationships

Chapter Eight More Than Surviving ... Thriving and Flourishing | **115**

they experience. They are optimistic in their approach to life, setting and accomplishing realistic goals. They view life as worth living and even setbacks as opportunities to grow.

It is fair to assume that many of those individuals we hold up as unique, exceptional individuals who have made significant contributions to others' lives are those who we see as having flourished. You know the names. Individuals such as Thomas Jefferson, Albert Einstein, Maya Angelou, and so many other renowned individuals have experienced flourishing.

As you read this, you may conclude, "That's not me."

It is easy to dismiss the possibility of flourishing if we restrict our application to the famous. But flourishing can be seen in Christopher the young man living down the street; Lydia, who works at the local store; Malcolm, the schoolteacher; and others you know.

Flourishing is not something you have or don't. It is not something with which some people are gifted and others are not. Flourishing is the result of choices and actions, which can be made by each of us. You can flourish, and your inner expert is directing you to do just that—flourish.

Elements of Flourishing

According to the research in positive psychology,[6] flourishing requires the experience of (a) positive emotions, (b) engagement in that which is interesting, and (c) the experience of finding meaning and purpose in life.

Remember Malcolm? Our schoolteacher. Follow him any one day and watch the number of times he projects not just a smile but inner joyfulness (i.e., positive emotions). Watch as he gets lost in his lesson, excited to see the children's reaction and amazed at his discoveries (i.e., engaging in that which is of interest). Listen to his story at the end of the day, a story that highlights the fact that he was able to get Raul to volunteer to come to the board, something that he has been working on for the past two weeks (i.e., experiencing meaningfulness). This is a man, with his positive emotions, engaging in that which is interesting and finding purpose in his life. This is a man who is flourishing.

The elements that contribute to our thriving, our flourishing, are not absolute, fixed, or the same for each of us. That which instills positive emotional experience, engages us with interest, and is seen, by us, as meaningful is defined by each of us individually. No one thing is "interesting" to all; there is no one way to define "meaningful." Even the element of happiness is experienced and expressed uniquely. Some individuals are demonstrative, bubbly, whereas others experience happiness in a more quiet, reflective way. Similarly, what holds your interest, and that which stimulates meaning for you, need not be the same for me. Solving a math problem might be a chore for one person and a gift to another.

Exercise 8.1 invites you to reflect on what you find interesting, that which brings you happiness and provides the experience of meaning and purpose in your life. Identifying these factors will lead you to recognize what it feels like to move beyond surviving—to thriving and flourishing.

Exercise 8.1. Elements of Flourishing

Directions: Take time to consider and respond to each of the following. Looking for common threads may help you understand the "inner directedness" your expert is attempting to share.

Interests:

While you may have many interests, take a moment, perhaps listing them on paper, with the intent of identifying those that, if you had the freedom to pursue, you would engage in almost 100% of the time. As you reflect on these core interests—what, if anything, do they hold in common? What is the element of value that makes these points of interest? Write it down.

Happiness:

Perhaps you are a real "belly laugher," or maybe you experience happiness more privately. Whichever way you experience happiness, identify a couple of recent times in which that happiness filled you, even if it was for a brief moment. Again, what, if anything, seems to connect these experiences? Write it down.

Purpose and Meaning:

You are busy. You are engaged. There are many things that you do and others that you wish you could do. Take a moment to reflect on the following "miracle question":

Chapter Eight More Than Surviving ... Thriving and Flourishing

> *If you awoke tomorrow morning and found that your life and the choices you could make were no longer constrained by pressing needs or limited resources, how would you spend your day(s)?*
>
> Review your response to this "miracle" question in light of the themes you may have found running through your experiences of interest and happiness. Can you see a trend? Can you see a pathway—one moving from surviving to thriving? If so, write it down. It won't happen tomorrow, but knowing that it is an inner direction may help you better navigate today on your way to the "good life."

Flowing: Moments of Thriving

Those who study positive psychology would suggest that a thriving person experiences flow in their life.

I once had a client who was a downhill skier and tried out for the Olympics. On one occasion, he was sharing his experience with a recent competition. He described one of his runs down the slope. He described his body's rhythmic movement; the rapid progression of markers and snow-covered trees; the shifting pressure points on his ankles, his thighs, as his ski's shifted from one edge to another; and the experience of "flying" down the mountain. As he explained the complexity of this process, I became aware of the intricacy of the coordination of mind and body required for this activity. I asked him, "How do you this? It is all happening so quickly—how do you keep it all straight?" His response: "I don't. It just happens!"

Well, we both realized that it doesn't just happen but is the result of his hard work and training. In the moment, however, it is happening without his self-awareness. It is happening because he is wholly in the moment. He is in the flow.

His description of the experience and his sense of "mindlessly" engaging in the process, all the while feeling exhilarated—enlivened—or as I saw, flourishing, reminded me of another individual I know, who is a classically trained guitarist. Talking to him following a recital, in addition to sharing my appreciation for his talent, I noted that there were times when he appeared as if he were almost surprised, almost startled, by the applause at the end of the song. While I was interpreting that as his believing that it did not go so well, he quickly corrected my assumption. He said there are some pieces that he plays where he feels that he, the guitar, and the music all merge and that nothing else exists. He noted that he is sometimes startled by the applause because up to that point, he was not conscious of others in the room.

That is flow.

As I write this, I am reminded of one more individual who gave clear evidence of being in the flow. The person? My surgeon. As mentioned previously, I underwent robotic surgery several years ago. The surgery took over 6 hours. I was amazed by the process. Here I was on the operating table. The surgeon who was operating was 20 feet away from me. Before they knocked me out, I was able to see him sit down at what appeared to be a flight simulator. There was a screen, many buttons, and two joysticks. Behind the screen, and somehow attached, was a mechanical creature. Okay, not quite a beast, but certainly an unusual cluster of wires, tubes, and metal tentacles extending from his seat in front of the video console to me and the operating table. I was a bit too drowsy to suggest that perhaps we stop and reconsider this.

He stayed in that "gaming position," manipulating the surgical knives via robotics, for the entire 6 hours. After the operation, I asked him how he could do that. How could he sit and concentrate so intently on a video screen and perform the very delicate movement of this massive cutting monster (sorry—not a monster, a wonder) for over 6 hours. His response? "I get into a zone, and I'm not even aware of how much time has passed. I just really get absorbed." He then smiled and added, "It is really cool, isn't it?"

I had to agree it was really cool. However, the "it" that I'm referring to was not just this DaVinci surgical system; it was seeing the value and impact of being in the flow.

Often, the stories, the recounting of the experiences of flow, reflect the experiences of individuals with unique talents who are engaged in times and circumstances that are unique and dramatic. Flow isn't limited to those with unique talents or to situations that are dramatic. Flow is the experience of a grandmother spending hours coloring with her grandchild. Flow is the experience of a teenager engaged in learning a new song on the guitar. Flow can be experienced by the person who loses all sense of self while comforting a friend in need. There are many illustrations of individuals, regardless of gender, age, country, or culture, who have experienced flow. As Csikszentmihalyi noted, "Flow is reported in essentially the same words by men and women, by young people and old, by teenagers from Japan, by adults from

Chapter Eight More Than Surviving ... Thriving and Flourishing | **119**

India and Thailand, by old women from Korea, by Navajo shepherds, by farmers in Italy, and by workers on the assembly line in Chicago."[7]

You don't have to be anything other than who you are to experience flow. According to the research in positive psychology, it is the full involvement of flow that makes for excellence in life.[8] It is the full involvement of flow that moves us beyond surviving to thriving.

Your Flow Experience

I have been in the flow. Nothing so dramatic as performing delicate surgery, or as skillful as downhill skiing, but flow has accompanied me at times in some of my woodworking projects, or in my experience on a Christmas morning building Legos with my children, or even sometimes when writing a chapter.

I know the experience of flow. I know that it is precious and something I seek to create. I know you have had experiences with flow; perhaps they went unnoticed at the time.

Think about an activity that you were doing that was challenging. An activity that stretched your abilities and yet one in which you could see progress, success. When engaged with that task, that activity, were you bored? I would doubt it. Were you feeling overwhelmed? I bet not. At these times, when you are really into what you are doing, and when that which you are doing is challenging, stimulating, engaging—whether you are conscious of it or not—you are flourishing. It is this type of experience that engages you in the flow.

When you are deep in the flow, you can lose track of time for hours at a time. The experience is so life-giving that you may have forgotten to eat lunch, drink your coffee, or even go to the bathroom. When you are in the flow, you will find that your focus is so intense on your purpose that what you are doing feels effortless and, while perhaps physically exhausting, as in the case of our skier, the experience does not drain but energizes.

Understanding the experience of flow is a good step in preparing to engage flow. Take a moment to think about a time when you were completely immersed in what you were doing. A time when you were so focused that many of the things going on around you went unnoticed. You need not search for a big event or dramatic circumstance. Flow can happen in the context of your daily activities. Your focus should not be on the "what" you were doing, but rather "how" you were experiencing that which you were doing.

The experience you are searching for is one in which you were so involved that the rest of the world seemed to disappear. Your mind wasn't wandering; you were totally focused and concentrated on that activity. Your engagement was to such an extent that you were not even aware of yourself. This is the measuring stick for identifying flow.

So, what have you found? Have you experienced flow when listening to music? Perhaps a flow experience occurred as you lost yourself in a novel, where what started as a brief read turned into hours, with pages of the book seemingly turning themselves? Maybe the experience of flow that sticks out in your reflection is when you sat by the side of a friend who needed someone to hold her hand and hear her story. Whatever the conditions or circumstances surrounding your flow experience, these were times when you were so absorbed in the moment that you were not thinking about what happened, nor were you pondering what would come next after that task was accomplished. You were lost in the moment, taken up in the flow.

When we are in the flow, we have a personal sense of control and find a deep level of satisfaction in what we are doing. Our rewards at these times are intrinsic to what we are doing. We are not looking for a paycheck or an external reward. We are not even goal-focused or striving for achievement. The goal is likely to be achieved, but that is not our point of focus. It is the experience of the moment that is all worthwhile and all-consuming. This is how flow feels.

Creating Flow

Flow often occurs when you are engaged in one of your favorite activities. Research suggests that flow seems to happen more often when you are active rather than passively engaged with a leisure activity, such as watching television. If you are a gardener, that process may invite a flow experience. If you love to cook or work on crafts, these are opportunities for flow. Flow can even be experienced in times of engaging the mundane, or even at work!

The retail salesperson who is paying attention to the customer in an attempt to best match product to the person, or the teacher providing a little individual instruction to a student struggling with the problem, or the writer who is seeking clarity in her writing—all of these can experience flow. They are engaged in perhaps what might be seen as routine activities. Yet they engage with a focus on making a difference. By focusing on what we are doing and pondering ways

Chapter Eight More Than Surviving ... Thriving and Flourishing | 121

to improve, or attempting to make even the dullest job something of value, we can move into the flow.

In researching the experience of flow, Csikszentmihalyi interviewed thousands of people from many different walks of life—sports figures, mountain climbers, ballet dancers, surgeons, etc.[9] He concluded that flow is an experience available to all of us, regardless of what we are doing, as long as the experience has the following characteristics.

- *Clear goals, and immediate feedback on progress.*

Competing in an athletic event where it is clear who is winning or losing is conducive to flow. Setting the table for a grand Thanksgiving dinner with arrivals expected at 4:00 p.m. can invite flow.

- *Complete concentration.*

Focus demands the exclusion of other thoughts or considerations. Thus, listening for the starter's pistol marking the beginning of the race or carefully attending to the gravy's roux mixture requires concentration and invites flow.

- *Actions and awareness merged.*

The situation is one in which the activity feels automatic. The fingers of the pianist and the music produced become one.

- *Time transformed.*

While in flow, one is unaware of time or duration. The experience can be one in which time passed faster (or sometimes slower) than expected. Waiting for the moment of hearing a response to the question *"Will you marry me?"* may seem like an eternity, with all time standing still.

- *Loss of self-awareness.*

Sense of self, awareness of the thinking/doing process, seems to fade at the moment of flow. The inner voice that is assessing what you are doing at any moment, directing the next moment, introducing irrelevant distractions—that "you"—is quieted.

- *Sense of control.*

When in flow, there are no worries or concerns about failure; the focus is on doing. Yes, our sprinter has all intentions of winning, but in the process of the race, the actions take precedent, not reflections on the goal.

- *Experiencing intrinsic reward.*

The activities with which one is engaged at the time of flow serve as their own rewards. It is not the achievement of a goal that is the payoff; it is the experience of doing. As my surgeon so brilliantly proclaimed, when you are in the flow, what you are doing is "really cool!"

Moving from Surviving to Thriving

Being able to describe and even recognize the state of flourishing and the experience of flow is super. More super would be figuring out how we can gain these experiences more frequently on our way to thriving.

Martin Seligman, one of the founders of positive psychology, has identified five core elements that support the quest for a life of fulfillment, happiness, and meaning.[10] The elements, when employed, move one from merely surviving to thriving.

The five elements are positive emotions, engagement, relationships, meaning, and accomplishments (PERMA).

Positive Emotions (P)

The concept of positive emotions refers to your ability to remain optimistic, without ignoring the lows of your life. Experiencing positive emotions can be stimulated by remembering experiences that are joyful and resulted in a sense of real satisfaction.

As previously noted, positive emotions about past events and experiences can be cultivated by the practice of gratitude. Positive emotions in the present can be maximized by learning to be mindful of the experience we are encountering and savoring the pleasures experienced.

There is real value to slowing down—smell the roses, or at least savor the meal.

Engagement (E)
The idea of engagement refers to something more than mere "doing." Tasks or activities that require you to call up your skills in a way that allows you to stretch your capabilities and provides evidence of success is the type of engagement that produces the experience of flow. When you are involved in a genuinely absorbing activity, experiencing "flow," you will be flooding your body with positive neurotransmitters and hormones that elevate your sense of well-being.

Positive Relationships (R)
We are social beings, and deep, meaningful relationships are nurturing and contribute to our flourishing. In the context of positive relationships, we often experience laughter, great joy, a feeling of belonging, and purpose. The connections that serve us are authentic and positively valuing. These are relationships that promote love and call forth acts of kindness.

Meaning (M)
You exist. That's a fact! Now, given this fact, this fact of your existence, what will you do? Of course, you will and have done quite a bit to survive. However, unless we find meaning and value in that which we do, we will only survive, not thrive.

Dedicating yourself to a cause, something bigger than yourself, can help you experience a sense of meaning. Finding meaning in what you do is genuinely life-giving, not life-draining.

Accomplishments (A)
We all thrive when we are succeeding, achieving our goals, and bettering ourselves. Without a drive to accomplish and achieve, we miss one of the puzzle pieces of authentic well-being.[11] Having accomplishments in life is important to push ourselves to thrive and flourish. Remember, the goals—that which we seek to achieve—will serve us well when they stretch abilities and are in some way in service of our thriving.

Get Going

You, like Maya Angelou, are called to move beyond surviving. Your mission is to thrive.

The research in the area of positive psychology is providing us with valuable information on how we can move from merely surviving to thriving and, in the process, truly experience the "good life."

Seligman's PERMA model provides a valuable framework for improving your well-being and moving toward flourishing. The message is clear. Moving beyond surviving to thriving is well within your abilities and clearly within the directives found in research and the message coming from your inner expert. Exercise 8.2 invites you to respond to that research and that inner direction and "Thrive."

Exercise 8.2. Thriving

Directions: There are steps to be taken that can facilitate your experience of thriving. Review the following with an intent to make the choices necessary to move from surviving to thriving.

1. *Enjoy*

It is essential to experience happiness. Make plans, as a daily activity, to engage in something that brings joy and positive emotions. Don't let it be happenstance. Write it down, schedule it, make it happen.

2. *Engage—experience flow*

Yes, you are busy—but even with the demands you navigate, it is vital to identify the activities (e.g., hobbies) that stimulate your passion and place you in flow experiences. Again—it won't just happen; you need to plan and do.

3. *The gift of others*

Life energy can be shared. Improve the quality of your relationships. Find and nurture those relationships that are positive, supportive, and life-giving.

4. *Something more significant than the moment*

You may not have the time or the energy to make a significant commitment to volunteer for a world cause. Still, even if that is the case, you need to seek out meaning in your life. Perhaps the work you do brings that meaning. If so, remind yourself of the value of what you do, and remind yourself daily. If work is not the meaning you seek, then take time to revisit the "miracle question." Ask yourself, if there were no constraints or real-life demands and a miracle freed you to be able to respond to your life calling, what would that be? It may not be possible to jump into this calling at this point in your life, but allow your response to serve as a jumping-off point for identifying how you could begin to experience some level of involvement with that in which you find meaning.

5. *Succeed*

In the early chapters, we discussed dreaming, developing SMART goals, and creating pathways to achievement. Use your knowledge and skills to stretch and accomplish those goals that reflect your dream.

Epilogue

Who Needs 120 Million Experts When You Have You?

We started this journey together by noting that there is an abundance of self-help resources to guide us through life and life's challenges. As is true for this book, many of these resources have their foundation in behavioral science and research. The information provided by these resources undoubtedly has value. Should you be interested in reading more about the research and findings that guide our understanding of goal setting, pathfinding, maintaining perspective, and experiencing flow and flourishing, additional resources are provided at the end of the book.

As with many of the other self-help texts, this book attempts to present the research and findings in a way that will help provide you with direction for navigating a life that flourishes. But perhaps unique to this book is the underlying goal of awakening your awareness of the degree to which your expert within has already guided you in the application of many of these researched-based concepts and techniques. It is also hoped that while increasing your awareness and valuing of the expert within, you have identified those areas in which personal growth is possible and desirable.

Your competency, your ability to thrive, is truly amazing. Perhaps most striking is that you need not stop in your thriving. Hopefully, this book, *Connecting with the Expert Within*, has served to reawaken you to your strengths and your competence and stimulated your desire to thrive.

Endnotes

Chapter 1

1. Georg Wilhelm Friedrich Hegel quotes. (n.d.). BrainyQuote.com. Retrieved January 1, 2021, from https://www.brainyquote.com/quotes/georg_wilhelm_friedrich_h_400845
2. Eurich, T. (2018). What self-awareness reality is (and how to cultivate it). *Harvard Business Review.* https://hbr.org/2018/01/what-self-awareness-really-is-and-how-to-cultivate-it%20 (p.3)
3. Sutton, A. (2016). Measuring the effects of self-awareness: Construction of the Self-Awareness Outcomes Questionnaire. *Europe's Journal of Psychology, 12*(4), 645–658.
4. Silvia, P. J., & O'Brien, M. E. (2004). Self-awareness and constructive functioning: Revisiting "the human dilemma." *Journal of Social and Clinical Psychology, 23*(4), 475–489.
5. Ridley, D. S., Schutz, P. A., Glanz, R. S., & Weinstein, C. E. (1992). Self-regulated learning: The interactive influence of metacognitive awareness and goal-setting. *The Journal of Experimental Education, 60*(4), 293–306.

Chapter 2

1. Jennifer Lopez quotes. (n.d.). Pininterest.com. Retrieved January 1, 2021 from https://www.pinterest.com/pin/503488433326185581/

Chapter 3

1. Piper, W. (1976). Goodreads.com. Retrieved January 6, 2021 from https://www.goodreads.com/quotes/741131-little-engine-that-could---i-think-i-can-i

2 Piper, W. (1976). *The little engine that could.* Penguin Random House LLC.

3 Parsons, R. D. (2020). *Defeating your crazies.* Outskirts Press.

Chapter 4

1 George Lucas quotes. (n.d.). Pinterest.com. Retrieved Jan 4, 2021 from https://www.pinterest.ca/pin/389350330271082743/

2 E.g., Seijts, G. H., Latham, G. P., Tasa, K., & Latham, B.W. (2004). Goal setting and goal orientation: An integration of two different yet related literatures. *Academy of Management Journal, 47*(2), 227–239.

3 Michelangelo quotes. (n.d.). BrainyQuote.com. Retrieved January 4, 2021 from https://www.brainyquote.com/quotes/michelangelo_108779

4 de Shazer, S. (1988). *Clues: Investigating Solutions in Brief Therapy.* New York: Norton & Co.

5 E.g., Locke, E. A., & Latham, G. P. (2002). Building a practically useful theory of goal setting and task motivation: A 35-year odyssey. *American Psychologist, 57*(9), 705–717.

Chapter 5

1 Leavitt, C. (2011). All Roads Lead to Rome: New acquisitions relating to the Eternal City. Retrieved from https://italianstudies.nd.edu/news-events/news/all-roads-lead-to-rome-new-acquisitions-relating-to-the-eternal-city/

2 de Jong, P., & Kim Berg, I. (2002). *Interviewing for solutions* (2nd ed). Wadsworth.

3 Kahneman, D. (2011). *Thinking Fast and Slow* (7th ed.) Farrar, Strauss, & Giroux.

4 See Park, J., & Song, J. (2020). How is intuitive thinking shared and elaborated during small-group problem-solving activities on thermal phenomena? *Research in Science Education, 50,* 2363–2390. https://doi.org/10.1007/s11165-018-9784-x

5 Dwight D. Eisenhower quotes. (n.d.) Pinterest.com. Retrieved January 6, 2021 from https://www.pinterest.co.uk/pin/829717931322605516/

6 Pickens, T. B. (n.d.). Myfrugalbuisness.com Retrieved January 6, 2021 from https://www.myfrugalbusiness.com/2018/12/t-boone-pickens-quotes.html

Chapter 6

1 Pablo Picasso quotes. (n.d.). BrainyQuote.com. Retrieved January 6, 2021, from https://www.brainyquote.com/quotes/pablo_picasso_120309
2 Hull, C. L. (1932). The goal-gradient hypothesis and maze learning. *Psychological Review, 39*(1), 25–43.
3 Hull, C. L. (1932). The goal-gradient hypothesis and maze learning, *Psychological Review, 39*(1), 25–43.
4 E.g., Kivetz, R., Urminsky, O., & Zheng, Y. (2006). The goal-gradient hypothesis resurrected: Purchase acceleration, illusionary goal progress, and customer retention. *Journal of Marketing Research, 43*(1), 39–58.
5 Friedrich Nietzsche Quotes. (n.d.). Goodreads. Retrieved April 3, 2021, from https://www.goodreads.com/author/quotes/1938.Friedrich_Nietzsche
6 Eccles, J. S., & Wigfield, A. (2002). Motivational beliefs, values, and goals. *Annual Review of Psychology, 53,* 109–132. https://doi.org/10.1146/annurev.psych.53.100901.135153
7 Bandura, A. (1997). *Self-efficacy: The exercise of control.* W. H. Freeman.
8 Bandura, A. (2005). Evolution of social cognitive theory. In K.G. Smith & M. A. Hitt (Eds.) *Great minds in management* (pp. 9–35). Oxford University Press.
9 Bandura, A. (1977). Self-efficacy: Toward a unifying theory of behavioral change. *Psychological Review, 84*(2), 191. https://doi.org/10.1037/0033-295X.84.2.191.

Chapter 7

1 Nelson Mandela quotes. (n.d.). Pinterest.com. Retrieved Jan 4, 2021 from https://za.pinterest.com/pin/314759461439230507/
2 Obama, B. (2020). *A Promised Land.* Crown. See p. 38.

3   Grant, L., & Kinman, G. (2012). Enhancing well-being in social work students: Building resilience for the next generation. *Social Work Education, 31*(5), 605–621.
4   Jackson, D., Firtko, A., & Edenborough, M. (2007). Personal resilience as a strategy for surviving and thriving in the face of workplace adversity: A literature review. *Journal of Advanced Nursing, 60*(1), 1–9.
5   Quote Investigator. (n.d.) I have gotten a lot of results! I know several thousand things that won't work. Retieved from https://quoteinvestigator.com/2012/07/31/edison-lot-results/
6   Dweck, C. (2016). *Mindset: The new psychology of success.* Ballantine.
7   E.g., Conversano, C., Rotondo, A., Lensi, E., Della Vista, O., Arpone, F., & Reda, M. A. (2010). Optimism and its impact on mental and physical well-being. *Clinical Practice and Epidemiology in Mental Health, 6*(1), 25–29. https://doi.org/10.2174/1745017901006010025
8   American Psychological Association. (2014). The road to resilience. Retrieved from https://studentsuccess.unc.edu/files/2015/08/The-Road-to-Resiliency.pdf

Chapter 8

1   Maya Angelou quotes. (n.d.). BrainyQuote.com. Retrieved December 29, 2020, from https://www.brainyquote.com/quotes/maya_angelou_634520
2   Peterson, C. (2008). What is positive psychology, and what is it not? *Psychology Today.* Retrieved from https://www.psychologytoday.com/us/blog/the-good-life/200805/what-is-positive-psychology-and-what-is-it-not
3   Gertrude Stein quotes. (n.d.). BrainyQuote.com. Retrieved December 29, 2020, from https://www.brainyquote.com/quotes/gertrude_stein_163501
4   Seligman, M. E. P. (2011). *Flourish: A visionary new understanding of happiness and well-being.* Atria Books.
5   Soots, L. (2015). Flourishing. *The Positive Psychology People.* Retrieved from http://www.thepositivepsychologypeople.com/flourishing/
6   E.g., Huppert, F. A., & So, T. T. C. (2011). Flourishing across Europe: Application of a new conceptual framework for defining well-being. *Social Indicators Research, 110*(3), 837–861. https://doi.org/10.1007/s11205-0119966-7.

7 Csikszentmihalyi M. (1990). *Flow: The psychology of optimal experience*. Harper & Row. See p. 4.
8 Csikszentmihalyi M. (1997). *Finding flow: The psychology of engagement with everyday life*. Basic Books.
9 Csikszentmihalyi M., & Csikszentmihalyi, I. (Eds). (1988). *Optimal experience*. Cambridge University Press.
10 Seligman, M. E. P. (2018). PERMA and the building blocks of well-being, *The Journal of Positive Psychology, 13*(4), 333–335. Retrieved from https://ppc.sas.upenn.edu/sites/default/files/permawellbeing.pdf
11 Seligman, M. E. P. (2011). *Flourish: A visionary new understanding of happiness and well-being*. Atria Books.

www.ingramcontent.com/pod-product-compliance
Lightning Source LLC
Chambersburg PA
CBHW032300150426
43195CB00008BA/526